Hot & Spicy
Caribbean

Also by Dave DeWitt, Mary Jane Wilan, and Melissa T. Stock

Hot & Spicy Southeast Asian Dishes

Hot & Spicy & Meatless

Hot & Spicy Latin Dishes

Hot & Spicy Chili

Hot & Spicy Caribbean

Dave DeWitt

Mary Jane Wilan

Melissa T. Stock

Illustrations by Lois Bergthold

Prima Publishing

PRIMA PUBLISHING and its colophon are trademarks of Prima Publishing, a division of Prima Communications, Inc.

Portions of this book first appeared in *Chile Pepper* magazine. Used by permission.

Illustrations by Lois Bergthold

Library of Congress Cataloging-in-Publication Data

DeWitt, Dave.
    Hot and spicy Caribbean : 150 of the best and most flavorful island recipes / Dave DeWitt, Mary Jane Wilan & Melissa T. Stock.
      p.   cm.
    Includes index.
    ISBN 0-7615-0126-6
    1. Cookery, Caribbean.   2. Cookery (Hot peppers)   I. Wilan, Mary Jane.
II. Stock, Melissa T.   III. Title.
TX716.A1D48   1995
641.59729—dc20   95-21228
                                               CIP

95 96 97 98 99 AA 10 9 8 7 6 5 4 3 2 1

Printed in the United States of America

How to Order:
Single copies of this book may be ordered from Prima Publishing, P.O. Box 1260, Rocklin, CA 95677; telephone (916) 632-4400. Quantity discounts are also available. On your letterhead, include information concerning the intended use of the books and the number of books you wish to purchase.

Acknowledgments

Thanks to the following lovers of hot & spicy Caribbean cuisine for their assistance in this project:

Michael Baim, Peggy Barnes, Robert and Mary Jane Barnes, Chel Beeson, David Brown, Thomas Brown, Michael Coelho, Jeanette DeAnda, Cathy Decker, Rodolfo de Garay, Nancy Gerlach, Kat Hardy, Kellye Hunter, Shirley Jordan, Jay McCarthy, Vernon Montrichard, Jim O'Malley, André Niederhauser, Marie Permenter, Jack Shapansky, Norma Shirley, Denice Skrepcinski, Robert Spiegel, and Robb Walsh.

Contents

Introduction

We love the Caribbean islands and just cannot stay away. During the past twenty-five years, the three of us have explored the West Indies by jets, prop planes, cruise ships, yachts, busses, cars, and even on foot in some cases. Of course, we have not visited every single island and country, but we've sampled enough of them to provide a comprehensive survey of the hot and spicy foods of a vast region.

Some of our favorite hot and spicy culinary memories include:

- Finding a twelve-foot-tall kitchen pepper plant at the Good Hope Great House in Jamaica.
- Carefully trying a Scotch bonnet-infused conch salad in a small restaurant in Nassau, The Bahamas.
- Catching, grilling, and devouring mangrove snapper with coconut and Melinda's hot sauce on the tiny island of Ambergris Caye, Belize.
- Shopping for Congo peppers in the markets of Trinidad and Tobago.
- Getting burned out on flying fish with incredibly hot piri-piri sauce on the *Jolly Roger* in Barbados.
- Tasting the spiced-up beach food at Magen's Bay on St. Thomas.
- Sampling jerk pork right off the grill at the Double V Jerk Center in Ocho Rios, Jamaica.

There are certain countries that border the Caribbean that are not included here. We've covered Central America in *Hot & Spicy Latin Dishes,* and we're saving dishes from the Yucatán Peninsula for the next book in this series, *Hot & Spicy Mexican Dishes.*

The West Indies are noted for the unusual names of some of their ingredients and dishes, from Shadow Bennie to Solomon Gundy; to clarify unfamiliar terms we have included a rather extensive Glossary (p. 299). Some of the ingredients in the recipes may seem exotic, but they're becoming more available all the time. Many hot sauces, spices, and dried herbs can be ordered from the Mail-Order Sources (p. 293). Other ingredients, such as tubers, banana leaves, fruits, and miscellaneous items can be found at Caribbean markets and Latin markets in North American cities. Cooks should be advised that many Asian markets carry Caribbean foodstuffs, both fresh and packaged.

We continue to use the same heat scale that we devised for *Chile Pepper* magazine and the other books in the Hot & Spicy series: Mild, Medium, Hot, and Extremely Hot. Each rating takes into consideration the type of chiles in the dish, the number of chiles used in the recipe, and the degree of dilution. The relative heat of each recipe can be easily adjusted. Cooks will discover that the extreme heat of Scotch bonnet and habanero chiles is tempered greatly by the other ingredients used in Caribbean cooking. Substitutes—such as they are—for the Caribbean chiles are found at the end of Chapter 1.

We hope that you enjoy our cruise around the West Indies. For more coverage of hot and spicy Caribbean dishes—and other spicy world cuisines—subscribe to *Chile Pepper* magazine, P. O. Box 80780, Albuquerque, NM 87198, (800) 359-1483.

Hot & Spicy
Caribbean

A West Indies
Heat Wave

When measured from the west end of Cuba to the island of Trinidad, the Caribbean Sea stretches more than 1,700 miles and encompasses hundreds of islands, dozens of countries, and many different cultures and languages. The cuisines of the countries are mostly an amalgamation of New World ingredients with Old World cooking styles, with a heavy African influence. Tying together many disparate elements is the source of the heat of many island dishes: chile peppers.

Hot Peppers of the Caribbean

The first peppers to inhabit the islands of this sea were the bird peppers, the small, spherical pods the Mexicans call *chiltepíns* and many people around the world call bird peppers. These are of the species *Capsicum annuum*, but they are the progenitors from which such varieties as jalapeños and anchos evolved, with human assistance. They were, indeed, spread by birds throughout the tropical and semitropical regions of the Americas. The birds were attracted to the bright red fruits, which provided valuable vitamin A for their brilliant plumage.

We observed these bird peppers growing along the highway in the Northern Range in Trinidad and have collected them in Jamaica as well. They are sometimes raised in backyards as perennial providers of tiny-podded peppers to add to soups and stews, and they are the pepper of choice for flavored vinegars and sherries.

The other popular peppers of the Caribbean basin belong to the species *Capsicum chinense*; the most famous pepper of the species is the habanero of the Yucatán Peninsula. Introduced from the Amazon basin, where the species originated, the seeds were carried and cultivated by Native Americans and the *chinense* species hopped, skipped, and jumped around the West Indies, forming—seemingly on each island—specifically adapted pod types that are called land races of the species. These land races were given local names in the various islands and countries, although the terms *Scotch bonnet, goat pepper,* and *habanero* are also used generically throughout the region.

In the eastern Caribbean, habanero relatives are called Congo peppers in Trinidad and booney or bonney peppers in Barbados. In the French Caribbean islands of Martinique and Guadeloupe, *le derrière de Madame Jacques* describes the hot peppers, and in Haiti *piment bouc* translates as goat pepper. In the western Caribbean are the familiar Jamaican Scotch bonnets,

Puerto Rican rocotillos, and the Cuban *cachucha* (cap) peppers. Incidentally, the habanero variety, which is thought to have originated in Cuba, was transferred to the Yucatán Peninsula, where it was given the name, which means "from Havana." These land races with the colorful names became the dominant spicy element in the food of the Caribbean.

The pods of the *chinense* species vary enormously in size and shape, ranging from chiltepín-sized berries one-quarter inch in diameter to wrinkled and elongated pods up to five inches long. The familar habaneros are pendant, lantern-shaped, and some are pointed at the end. Caribbean varieties of *Capsicum chinense* are often flattened at the end and resemble a tam, or bonnet. Often the blossom ends of these pods are inverted. The pods are green at immaturity and usually mature to red, orange, yellow, or white. Purple and brown mature pods have also been described. *Chinense* pods are characterized by a distinctive, fruity aroma that is often described as "apricot-like." Interestingly enough, that aroma is present regardless of the variety, heat level, or the size of the pod.

The heat level of the *chinense* species has been the subject of much discussion. Phrases like "hottest pepper in the world" and "a thousand times hotter than a jalapeño" have been bandied about for years, but they don't really tell the story. In actuality, the species does have nonpungent varieties, just like the bell peppers of the *annuum* species. Thus the heat scale ranges from zero to 577,000 Scoville units, the hottest *chinense* ever measured. In terms of the average number of Scoville units, a habanero, for example, is about fifty times hotter than a jalapeño—as measured by machines, not the human mouth. Because humans have varying numbers of taste buds, reaction can vary enormously from person to person.

Another member of the *chinense* species that is commonly used, especially in the eastern Caribbean, is the seasoning pepper. It is a medium-hot, elongated pepper that is used in quantity for seasoning pastes in Trinidad, Barbados, Saint Lucia, and other islands.

One of the most common uses for hot peppers in the Caribbean is in hot sauces. The Carib and Arawak Indians used pepper juice for seasoning and, according to *Chile Pepper* magazine's Shirley Jordan, "the Caribs were accomplished pepper-sauce makers. Not knowing how to extract salt from the sea, they flavored their food with *coui*, a sauce of hot peppers and cassava juice. The tradition has persisted. Almost all West Indians like hot peppers in their food, and when a dish is not spicy enough they reach for the ever-present bottle of hot sauce. This is made in many homes by steeping diced hot peppers in vinegar, rum or sherry."

After the "discovery" of chile peppers by Europeans, slave-ship captains combined pepper juice with palm oil, flour, and water to make a "slabber sauce" that was served over ground beans to the slaves aboard ship. The most basic hot sauces on the islands were made by soaking chopped Scotch bonnets in vinegar (making pepper pickles) and then sprinkling the fiery vinegar on foods. Over the centuries, each island developed its own style of hot sauce by combining the crushed chiles with other ingredients such as mustard, fruits, or tomatoes.

Homemade hot sauces are still common on the islands of the Caribbean (see Chapter 2), and there are numerous commercial sauces available in North America (see Mail-Order Sources, p. 293).

Congos, Bonnies, and Seasoning Peppers: The Eastern Caribbean

While on assignment to write a book on the multifaceted cuisines of Trinidad and Tobago (T&T), Dave and Mary Jane had the opportunity to experience Congo pepper fever on those two islands. In Trinidad, *Congo* means anything large and powerful, and this type of *chinense* lived up to its name. We found some as large as lemons, and they had thicker walls than most of the habanero relatives we were familiar with.

Our hosts and guides were Marie Permenter and Vernon and Irene Montrichard, who own thirteen Royal Castle fried chicken restaurants on Trinidad. What makes their chicken different from Kentucky Fried Chicken, the competition, is that the Royal Castle chicken is marinated in a sauce made from Congo peppers and a number of fresh herbs (Spanish and French thyme, mostly) that are grown in the hills of Paramin. The hot sauce base is exported to Jacksonville Beach, Florida, where it is manufactured into Trinidad Habanero Sauce.

Marie and Vernon took us on a tour to their pepper fields, where the Congo peppers are grown for the Royal Castle hot sauce. The well-established planting was several acres in size and was surrounded by thick vegetation. We were introduced to the growers, who lived in a nearby shack. We learned that the Congo pepper plants grow about three feet high in a single year and are picked twice. Then they are plowed off and the site is replanted. The growers told us that the plants would live for decades, but would produce smaller fruits each year.

We also met up with Congo peppers in Tobago. Scarborough, the capital, has a chile-filled Botanic Station that is nicely landscaped. There we met with Reginald Phillips, the technical officer in charge. He told us that one of the station's main projects was the raising of Congo pepper seedlings to supply small farms. Evidence of his efforts was widespread at the market downtown, where vendors sold the brightly colored pods in plastic bags.

Nobody seemed to know exactly how many acres were in pepper production in T&T, but after talking to a few knowledgeable people close to growers, like Vernon Montrichard, the figure of 2,000 acres seemed to be the best estimate. Much of this crop is exported. Total exports to Canada, the United States, and the United Kingdom amounted to TT$ 1.6 million in 1991, with about 131 tons alone exported to the United States.

The rest of the crop is sold in markets and is used to make hot sauces. Every family in T&T seemingly has its own recipe, but the plethora of home-made sauces has not prevented a large hot sauce industry from springing up. There are perhaps five major manufacturers of hot sauce in T&T and about ten minor ones. The best known T&T hot sauces in the United States are the Matouks' hot sauces, which are used extensively to flavor the eastern Caribbean curries.

Although curries in some form appear in the cuisines of most of the Caribbean, they are particularly prevalent in the countries where the East Indian population is the greatest: Trinidad and Tobago, Martinique, and Jamaica.

In 1838, four years after slavery was abolished in the British Caribbean islands, the food history of the Caribbean islands began to change profoundly. That year, the mandatory, four-year postslavery apprenticeship ended and some 20,000 slaves who worked the enormous sugar cane plantations left the estates and became squatters—resulting in an enormous labor shortage that was filled by freed slaves from other islands, plus a huge influx of indentured laborers from India. Beginning in 1845, a mass migration of workers from India over the next seventy-two years increased the population of Trinidad by 145,000. By the 1940s, the East Indian influence was so prevalent that travel writer Patrick Leigh Fermor wrote: "Wide tracts of Trinidad are now, for all visual purposes, Bengal."

Unlike the Africans before them, the East Indian immigrants were allowed to keep their language, clothing, and culture. Two animals that immigrated with them were the water buffalo—useful for heavy labor—and the white, humped cattle that provided the milk for the beloved yogurt and butter, which was made into ghee.

Many East Indian foods and cooking techniques were introduced into the Caribbean, notably curries and rice (rice is still grown on Trinidad today). Curries have become enormously popular in Trinidad, as noted by calypso writer Daisann McLane. "Without access to their curry," she wrote, "Trinidadian cooks would be as lost as Sicilians without fresh garlic."

A typical commercial mixture usually contains varying amounts of coriander, cumin, turmeric, fenugreek, celery seed, fennel, and may or may not contain chile powder. The curry powder capitol of Trinidad is Tunapuna, a town about halfway between Port of Spain and Arima. Daisann McLane vividly described it in 1991: "Clouds of roasted cumin and turmeric, garlic, coriander, and those acidly hot Caribbean peppers . . . simply by breathing, one was exposed to hazardous levels of piquant longing."

Most of the curry powders made today are much milder than those of India because the early cooks lacked powdered hot peppers. However, hot pepper sauces are often added to curried dishes at the table. Some cooks still use old-fashioned curry pastes, which usually have Congo peppers (a Habanero relative) added to them, and our recipe for Trinidadian Curry Paste (p. 22) is a typical example.

Every imaginable foodstuff is curried in Trinidad and Tobago, including mangoes, pumpkins, eggplants, potatoes, green tomatoes, okra, chicken, fish, shellfish, beef, pork, goat, and lamb. These curries are commonly served in *roti* shops, which dot the two islands. The curried mixture is placed on the flat, thin *roti* bread, and then is wrapped up into an easy-to-eat package of curry.

Dave and Mary Jane toured Trinidad and Tobago in 1992 and dined on nine different curried fillings for the *roti* bread at the Patraj Roti Shop in San Juan: fish, beef, chicken, goat, conch, shrimp, liver, duck, and potato. The fillings were wrapped in the bread or were served in bowls accompanied by torn-up bread called Buss-Up-Shut, which is slang for "burst up shirt," because the bread resembles torn-up cloth. The curry itself was not spicy, but the Congo pepper hot sauce served in squeeze bottles solved that problem.

Sophisticated citizens of Trinidad, who have traveled outside the country, realize that there is more to curry than just the Trinidadian style, but any changes are unlikely. One restaurant owner told us she was quite disappointed when Gaylord's, a restaurant on Independence Square that served authentic East Indian curries, failed because the locals said: "This isn't curry." Noted food writer Julie Sahni believes that "curry is such an integral part of Trinidadian cuisine that its Indian origin is actually being lost." She was amazed when a Trinidadian saleswoman in a curry factory asked her: "Are you from India? Do they have curry powder in India?"

Other islands in the eastern Caribbean have their own hot and spicy traditions. Barbados is famous for its mustard-based hot sauces, of which there are dozens and dozens of commercial brands in addition to the restaurant-made sauces. They are made with the booney or bonney peppers—the Bajan equivalent of the Congo peppers of Trinidad—that also appear in the herb seasonings that parallel those of Trinidad. One particular specialty is flying fish; journalist Shirley Slater noted in an article on the island: "Always served are flying fish, the famous delicacy of Barbados, sometimes lightly battered and crisply fried, sometimes braised in a fiery tomato, onion, and pepper creole sauce."

In nearby Grenada, "Today's mix of races and cultures has produced a society proud of its heritage and passionate about its food, but it is the pepper, dating from the earliest settlers, that serves as the common bond," wrote Shirley Jordan in *Chile Pepper* magazine. "Indeed, the Caribs were using *Capsicum* peppers in their cooking when the French arrived. The plant grows profusely on the islands, and its fruit comes in every imaginable shape, size, color, and degree of pungency. Innumerable pepper sauces are created by the islanders."

And remember the bird peppers? Shirley witnessed a very traditional use for them during her visit to Grenada. "We discovered a delightfully piquant pepper sauce at the table of Betty Mascoll, one of the island of Grenada's most revered hostesses," she wrote. "Bushes near her back door burst with red, pea-sized *wiri-wiri* berries from Guyana. Betty drops these into dry cocktail sherry, and in two or three days the fiery mixture awaits its enthusiastic fans."

The French Caribbean has a well-deserved reputation for fiery foods. "Martinique is an island where, in the finest French tradition, people love to talk about food even more than they love to talk about politics," notes food writer Bob Payne. "And if there is one thing they agree on, it is that to eat food the way it was meant to be eaten means that you can't forget the pepper—by which they mean the hot pepper."

"If a native of Guadeloupe warns you that a dish may be hot, take heed," warn Caribbean food experts Jinx and Jefferson Morgan. "Our notes on *le crabe farci de Grand Terre* say: 'Scotch bonnets marinated in gasoline.'" They also mentioned that at La Créole Chez Violetta in the town of Le Gosier, "a huge Mason jar of her homemade hot sauce stood in the middle of the table. Rumor has it that the recipe is a state secret known only to the French space agency."

Curried dishes are also popular in the French islands, where the word for curry is *colombo*, named for the capital of Sri Lanka. A typical *colombo*, such as the Christmas specialty with pork from Martinique, begins with a *colombo* paste that contains, in addition to some standard curry spices, crushed fresh garlic, ginger, and those *le derrière de Madame Jacques* chiles.

Scotch Bonnets, Country Peppers, and Rocotillos: The Western Caribbean

In the western Caribbean, some islands are hot and some are not. The Spanish islands such as Puerto Rico, Cuba, and the Dominican Republic are not hotbeds of chile peppers, although as we will see, Cuba does have some spicy dishes. The spicy haven of the area is Jamaica, and its fiery cuisine is as varied as that of Trinidad—but the pepper nomenclature leaves a lot to be desired.

During several visits to Jamaica we had futilely endeavored to differentiate between Scotch bonnets and country peppers, two terms that seemed to be interchangeable. According to vendor Bernice Campbell in the Ocho Rios market, country peppers were more elongated than Scotch bonnets, were milder, and had more flavor. With a typical pepper contrariness, cook Betty Wilson of Port Antonio had disagreed. She claimed country peppers were hotter than Scotch bonnets but were more "flavored." Our room attendant at Ciboney Resort in Ocho Rios, Carol Burrell, insisted that no, country peppers were milder than Scotch bonnets. To add to the confusion, habanero grower Graham Jacks had written to us that: "One of these country peppers is a deep brownish purple when ripe, and is truly ferociously hot; much hotter than the Scotch bonnet."

Other mysterious Jamaican peppers had cropped up in various books. A variety called "Jamaican Hot" was described by author and chef Mark Miller in his guide, *The Great Chile Book*, as "smaller than the habanero but similar in shape." It is possible that this variety is the same as the "West Indian Hot" mentioned by Jean Andrews in *Peppers: The Domesticated Capsicums*, but pepper importer Joe Litwin had told us that the "hots" are generic terms used in the United States but not in Jamaica. A search of the 1994 edition of *Seed Savers Yearbook* revealed common names of cultivated varieties to be "Jamaica Large Red," "Jamaica Orange," "Jamaica Small Red," and the appellation "Scotch bonnet" with the descriptors "orange," "yellow," and "red" added. The nomenclature had become increasingly murky.

During our most recent trip to Jamaica, we were on our way to tour the Good Hope Great House when Dave asked our guide, David Brown, if they had a garden there. David replied yes, and that there would probably be some peppers in the garden.

"Do you know much about peppers?" we asked him.

"A lot," he replied, grinning.

"Tell us about Jamaican peppers," Dave begged.

"We have many peppers that are hot," he replied while driving us through St. Ann's parish. "Scotch bonnets stand out because of their incomparable flavor. From our East Indian ancestors came the long, thin cayenne that is very hot and coolie peppers, those long green ones like the ones you grow in New Mexico. Old lady peppers are also called grandmother's pepper, and we have kitchen peppers that grow outside of kitchen windows, and bird peppers that grow wild and are extremely hot. The bird peppers were not commonly used until people started jerking pork. They are less expensive than Scotch bonnets and are often used when Scotch bonnets are not abundant."

"But what about country peppers," we asked, explaining our country pepper predicament.

He laughed. "Yes, it would be confusing to ask Jamaicans to compare country peppers to Scotch bonnets."

"Why?"

"Because Scotch bonnets are country peppers but not all country peppers are Scotch bonnets," he replied mysteriously.

While we attempted to sort that one out, David continued. "Country pepper is just a general term for garden peppers. Any cultivated pepper is a country pepper. Say a man goes into a restaurant and sees hot sauce and black pepper on the table. Those are two kinds of pepper but he wants another. He says to the waitress, 'Do you have any pepper?' The waitress would say, 'Country pepper?' The man would say, 'Yes, what kind you have?' The waitress might say, 'Scotch bonnet and kitchen pepper' and then the man might order some freshly chopped Scotch bonnnets. Country peppers could even be sweet peppers, what you call bell peppers."

The country pepper mystery was finally solved, but we still had no idea what old lady peppers and kitchen peppers were. That would have to wait for a while, but we did learn more about the uses of Scotch bonnets in Jamaican cooking. In addition to their use in hot pepper sauces, Scotch bonnets are also pickled whole and in crushed form. In cooking, yellow Scotch bonnets are used with escovitch fish, which are fillets cooked with pepper slices in vinegar, lime juice, and Jamaican pimento (allspice). The whole pods are often floated in stews or stewed dishes such as oxtail soup, curry goat, fricasseed chicken, and stew peas and rice, and are removed just before serving. Cooks take care not to let the pods burst or the meal may be too hot to eat!

You'll also find Jamaican peppers in jerk sauces, which are a combination of spices and Scotch bonnet chiles used as a marinade and baste for grilled meats. The word "jerk" is thought to have originated from the word *ch?arki* (the phonetic symbol [?] is part of the word), a Quechua word from Peru. The Spanish converted the term to *charqu*, which meant jerked or dried meat, which in turn became known as "jerk" and "jerky" in English.

The technique of jerking originated with the Maroons, Jamaican slaves who escaped from the British during the invasion of 1655 and hid in the maze of jungles and limestone sinkholes known as the Cockpit Country. The Maroons seasoned the pork and cooked it until it was dry and would preserve well in the humidity of the tropics. During the twentieth century, the technique gained enormous popularity in Jamaica and today "jerk pork shacks" are commonly found all over Jamaica. The method has evolved, however, and the pork is no longer overcooked.

The East Indian population of Jamaica is considerably smaller than that of Trinidad, but their curries are also esteemed. The first East Indians arrived in Falmouth aboard the *Athenium* in 1843, and within fifty years curries had risen to prominence on the island. *The Jamaica Cookery Book*, published in 1893, offered several curry recipes, including a simple but ingenious tropical curry sauce: coconut jelly (the immature center of a green coconut) boiled in coconut water with cinnamon and curry powder.

The most popular curry dish in Jamaica is curry goat (not "curried goat"). In fact, according to Helen Willinsky, author of *Jerk: Barbecue from Jamaica*, it is "one of our national dishes." She wrote: "We always serve it for our special occasions, and it seems to be one of the best-remembered dishes by tourists."

The first time Dave tasted curry goat in Jamaica, in a restaurant frequented by locals in Ocho Rios in 1984, he had to be careful not to swallow numerous sharp slivers of bone. In a truly authentic recipe, the goat meat is chopped up—bones and all—because Jamaican cooks believe that the marrow in the bones helps to flavor the dish. The goat was cooked in a large, cast-iron kettle over a wood fire in the backyard of the restaurant.

The second time Dave tasted curry goat in Jamaica, in 1993, the venue was a bit fancier, but the taste was the same. That time, the goat was prepared by the chef of the Ciboney Resort (also in Ocho Rios) and was served at a rather elegant buffet at a beach party.

In the early days, curry goat was considered to be a masculine dish, and there was a certain ritual involved with its serving. Zora Neale Hurston, an American anthropologist who traveled extensively in Jamaica in the 1930s, was fortunate enough to be invited to an all-male curry goat party where only ram goat was served. In our recipe for Jamaican Curry Goat (p. 121), rams are not so critical—either gender of goat is permissible.

In nearby Cuba, several questions have sprung up regarding chiles and hot and spicy foods. Do habaneros—supposedly from Havana—still grow in Cuba? And is any Cuban food hot and spicy? The answer to the first question was easy, because we have grown Cuban habaneros from seed passed on to us from immigrants. Some writers insist that only rocotillos—the mild *chinense* variety—grow in Cuba, but we have discovered that there are several varieties of Cuban habaneros.

Is any Cuban food hot and spicy? We asked Rodolfo de Garay and Thomas Brown, who wrote on the subject for *Chile Pepper* Magazine. "Ask any Cuban–American about the spicy heat of Cuban food and you'll get a leery look," they replied. " '*La cocina Cubana no es picante,*' they'll say: Cuban food isn't hot. And truly the Cuban dishes known to North Americans are rarely spicy. *Ropa vieja, picadillo, boliche,* and *escabeche* all depend on peppers for flavor, but nearly always the mild and sweet kinds: Cubanelles, bells, and pimientos.

"But then remind that incredulous Cuban of recipes such as shrimp *enchilado*, baby goat *chilindrón*, chicken with Habanero glaze, *rabo encendido*, or tamales *pican* or *no pican*—that bite or don't bite. Somewhat confused, they will retort that the only way you can make these recipes is by using something hot. You could also remind them of the *guaguao* (or piquin) peppers pickled in vinegar, the light heat of the *cachuchas* (or rocotillo) that add crunch and perfume to black beans and are sold as a staple produce in

Miami supermarkets. Most Cuban homes, whether in Cuba or Miami—where an estimated 600,000 Cuban–Americans reside—have one or two chile plants growing in their yard. They are usually piquin, which is known simply as *aji picante*, or hot pepper. The home cook uses the peppers with discretion according to family tastes."

So ends the myth that Cuban foods cannot be hot and spicy. We complete our introduction to the hot and spicy Caribbean with a note on chile substitutions, then conclude with basic recipes for Coconut Milk and Tamarind Sauce, which are used in many of the dishes in this book.

Substitutions for Chiles in These Recipes

The *chinense* species is renowned not only for the extreme heat of its pods, but also for its aroma and flavor. Many recipes in other books suggest jalapeños or serranos as adequate substitutes, but they are not. Their flavor is completely different from the characteristic fruitiness of the habanero relatives. The truth is that the only fresh chile that remotely substitutes is the rocoto, called *canario* in Mexico. This chile, a variety of the *Capsicum pubescens* species, is even rarer than the habanero in the United States, so it is hardly an adequate substitute. It is easier to substitute the dried forms of habaneros—see the next section.

Habaneros are available in some form in most parts of North America, either in stores or by mail order. Here are some basic substitutes.

For fresh habaneros, Scotch bonnets, and so on, substitute:
Commercial habanero hot sauce, about 1 to 2 tablespoons per pod
Rehydrated dried habanero pods
Pickled habanero pods
Habanero powder, about 2 teaspoons per pod

For dried Habanero pods, substitute:
¼ ancho pod plus 5 piquins or chiltepíns

For Habanero powder, substitute:
Three times the amount of cayenne powder plus a few drops of lime juice

Tamarind Sauce

Tamarind is available commercially in many forms. When you find pods, as we easily can at our local supermarket, this is the way to make a simple sauce for use in other recipes.

6   tamarind pods

3   cups water

2   teaspoons sugar (or more or less, depending on taste)

Shell the tamarind pods and remove the seeds from the pulp. Bring the water to a boil in a saucepan, add the pulp, and simmer until the liquid is reduced to about 1 cup. Add the sugar and simmer for an additional 5 minutes. Strain the sauce through a piece of muslin and squeeze as much liquid as possible from the pulp.

Yield: 1 cup

Coconut Milk and Cream

Both coconut milk and cream are extracts from coconut and it is important
to differentiate them from the highly sweetened, canned coconut cream
(or syrup) that is used to make drinks called piña coladas. The sweetened,
canned cream is not a substitute and should not be used in any recipe in
this book. Coconut milk is used extensively in Caribbean dishes and it is
best when made from freshly grated coconut meat. But if that is not available, use desiccated, unsweetened coconut flakes and substitute cow's milk
for the water. Coconut milk powder, now available in some specialty markets, mixes well with water to make coconut milk. Canned coconut milk is
also commonly available, but cooks should check the label to make certain
that sugar has not been added. New, low-fat canned coconut milk is now on
the market.

Coconuts are widely available in Latin and Asian markets and large
supermarkets across America. Look for a coconut without cracks or any
sign of mold. The fresher the coconut, the more liquid it has. To break a
coconut open, heat the oven to 350 degrees. Puncture a hold through one
of the "eyes" and drain the liquid. This coconut water makes an excellent
drink and can be consumed straight or mixed with rum or scotch. Place the
coconut in the oven for 20 minutes, then remove it and allow it to cool.
Break it open with a hammer, and the meat should fall away from the shell.
If some meat still clings to the shell, carve it out using a small knife. Use a
vegetable peeler to remove the thin brown skin from the meat, and then
grate the meat on a metal grater, or carefully chop it in a food processor
using the "pulse" mode.

4   cups grated coconut
2¼   cups boiling water or hot milk

In a bowl, cover the grated coconut with the boiling water (or milk for a
thicker coconut "cream") and let it steep for 15 minutes. Using a strainer,
drain the coconut and reserve the "milk." The coconut meat may be
squeezed through muslin cloth or a double layer of cheesecloth to collect
the rest of the "milk."

Store the "milk" in the refrigerator (it has about the same shelf life as whole milk), and the "cream" will rise to the top.

Variation: For a thicker milk, approaching cream, instead of steeping the grated coconut in hot water, purée it in a blender with the water and then strain it through cloth.

Yield: 2 cups

Coconut Milk Substitutes

One cup of coconut milk contains—depending on its thickness—about 45 to 60 grams of fat—quite a bit in today's world of low-fat diets. Fortunately, a low-fat coconut milk is now available that reduces the fat level to about 12.5 grams. To lower the level even further, we suggest using a coconut flavoring. Several companies manufacture coconut flavoring, or extract, which concentrates the flavor while removing nearly all of the fat. Two brands of coconut extract on the market are Nielsen–Massey Coconut Extract and Wagner's Coconut Flavor—they are available at gourmet shops and by mail order. By combining such extracts with whole milk, the amount of fat is decreased to 8 grams; when combined with low-fat milk, that figure is further reduced to 5 grams. These substitutes may not be perfect, but they are a lot healthier. Since the consistency of coconut-flavored milk is thinner than that of canned coconut milk, cooks may need to add more of the substitute to a recipe and cook it a bit longer to achieve good results. Yogurt can also be combined with coconut extract; the consistency will be thicker, the taste will be different and interesting, but the fat count will be even lower, about 3 grams.

1   cup milk (whole or low fat)
½   teaspoon coconut extract

Combine the ingredients in a bowl and stir.

Yield: 1 cup

Moko Jumbie: Spirited Seasonings, Sauces, and Condiments

Named for the Carnival spirits that inspire some of the hottest sauces, this chapter features the essential flavorings of many a Caribbean meal. These are the elemental concoctions that enhance, marinate, or garnish many of the recipes in this book.

We begin with the curry-related seasonings that are found wherever immigrants from India form a large part of the population—particularly Jamaica, Trinidad, and the French islands. West Indian Massala (p. 20) forms the basis of many curry powders and pastes, or is simply added to curry dishes as is. Cooks should remember that a curry is a method of stewing meats with spices rather than just a yellow powder. Colombo Curry Paste (p. 21) and Trinidadian Curry Paste (p. 22) are hot and handy seasonings that quickly convert meats or poultry to a curried state.

It is difficult to duplicate the flavors of most jerk dishes because they are traditionally smoke-grilled over pimento wood and leaves, as Jack Shapansky, chef at the Ciboney Ocho Rios, demonstrated for us on a poolside grill at the Jamaican resort. However, by grilling over hardwoods after first marinating the meat with North Coast Jerk Marinade (p. 23), a rather close rendition of classic Jamaican jerk can be made.

In the eastern Caribbean there is a tradition of marinating meats in pastes of the same consistency—but a completely different flavor—than jerk marinades. Trinidad Herb Seasoning Paste (p. 24) depends on fresh herbs, and although the French and Spanish thyme we found growing on the hills of Paramin won't be available, we have suggested substitutions that will approximate their consistency and flavor. Over in Barbados, cooks use Bonney Bajan Seasoning (p. 26), and one of their favorite tricks is to insert the paste between the skin and flesh of a chicken, allow it to marinate for a few hours, and then roast the bird.

The next four recipes reflect the most basic island sauces: those that involve steeping peppers in various liquids, including another kind of spirit. With Trinidadian Bird Pepper Sherry (p. 27), the liquid is alcoholic and this technique is identical to one in Bermuda, which is far away but culturally related because of the British Navy of many years ago. Vinegar is the liquid for Pique de Vinagre y Ajíes Bravos (Bird Pepper Vinegar *Pique*, p. 28), a Puerto Rican sauce that proves that some people there like hot and spicy food, despite rumors to the contrary. Another sauce that proves this contention is Puerto Rican Sofrito (p. 29), to which many cooks add rocotillo chiles. Vegetable oil is a natural for hot sauces, as evidenced by Piri Piri Oil (p. 31) and

Creole Congo Pepper Sauce (p. 32). We tasted the latter at the Tiki Village at the Kapok Hotel in Port of Spain and at first were surprised at the full flavor of such a basic sauce. But then we remembered the powerful flavor of the Congo peppers; a single one sliced open had driven Mary Jane out of the hotel room!

Only slightly more sophisticated is Moko Jumbie Papaya Pepper Sauce (p. 33), so named because of the "spirit on stilts" that appears at Carnival celebrations on various islands. Saba Scotch Bonnet Sauce (p. 34) proves that the Dutch islands are not immune from the fiery influence of the *chinense* species.

Perhaps because sauces were a convenient way to package vitamin C to prevent scurvy, there are a number of lime-based Caribbean hot sauces. The Virgin Islands (both U.S. and British) have a concoction known as Asher Sauce (p. 36), which is a corruption of "Limes Ashore." It combines limes with bird peppers, cloves, allspice, salt, vinegar, and garlic. Sauce Chien (p. 37) from Martinique and Guadeloupe means "dog sauce" and seems to indicate the aroma of the habaneros because a Mayan sauce, *xnipec*, also refers to dogs. Sauce Ti-Malice (p. 38), a mean sauce from Haiti, is similar.

Although tomato-based sauces are more common in Mexico and the southwestern United States, they occasionally make their appearance in the Caribbean. Ciboney Tomato Rundown Sauce (p. 39) is chef Jack Shapansky's version of a classic Jamaican sauce that is particularly tasty over vegetables, while Bajan Hot Seafood Sauce (p. 40), is a bonney pepper-infused sauce that is perfect with shrimp cocktails or fried clams in addition to the traditional flying fish.

Hot sauces from the Spanish Caribbean are few and far between, but we have found three with some pungency. Ajilimojili (Pepper–Pepper Sauce, p. 42) alludes in its name to the combination of bell and habanero peppers. It is a Puerto Rican sauce served with pork. Salsa Roja para Frijoles Negros (Red Hot Sauce for Black Beans, p. 43) is precisely that, while Puerto Rican Sofrito (p. 29) is served with bland meat dishes and spooned into soups and stews.

And what to serve with all the curries in Chapter 5, you ask? Two classic condiments—both made with green mangoes—are Jamaican Green Mango Chutney (p. 44) from the western Caribbean, and Mango Kucheela (p. 45) from the eastern Caribbean.

May the spirits inspire your sauces as you prepare for primal heat!

West Indian Massala

This spice blend is superior to commercial massalas because the freshly ground seeds have not oxidized and lost their flavor. Generally speaking, when turmeric is added to massala, it becomes curry powder. By adding habanero powder—only now commonly available—it becomes hot massala.

6	tablespoons coriander seed	1½	teaspoons cumin seed
1	teaspoon fenugreek seed	2	teaspoons turmeric (optional)
2	teaspoons fennel seed	½	teaspoon habanero powder (optional)
1	teaspoon mustard seed		

Toast all the seeds in a dry skillet, stirring well, until they begin popping. Lower the heat and cook for an additional 5 minutes, taking care not to burn the seeds. Cool the seeds and grind them all together finely in a spice mill or with a mortar and pestle. Add the turmeric and mix well if you wish to make a curry powder. Add the habanero powder for a hotter massala.

Yield: About ½ cup

Heat Scale: Medium with habanero powder

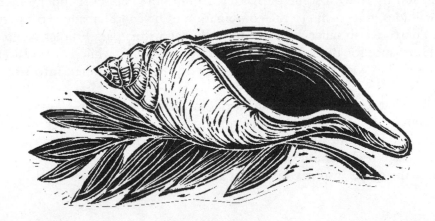

Colombo Curry Paste

This fiery hot curry blend from Martinique and Guadeloupe is named after Colombo, the capital of Sri Lanka, which is appropriate considering the heat levels of the curries from that island. The pepper of choice, shaped like the behind of Mrs. Jacques, is recommended because of its unique, fruity aroma. Habaneros are the perfect substitute.

1½	tablespoons turmeric	1	1-inch piece of fresh ginger, peeled and grated
1½	tablespoons coriander seed		
1½	tablespoons mustard seed	2	*le derrière de Madame Jacques* peppers (or habaneros), seeds and stems removed, minced
1½	tablespoons black peppercorns		
1½	tablespoons cumin seed		Water
3	cloves garlic, crushed		

In a spice mill, combine the turmeric, coriander seed, mustard seed, black peppercorns, and cumin seed. Grind the mixture into a coarse powder. Add this powder to the garlic, ginger, and peppers, and mix well, adding water to achieve the desired consistency of a medium paste. Allow the mixture to sit for at least an hour to blend the flavors.

Yield: ½ cup

Heat Scale: Hot

Trinidadian Curry Paste

Most curry powders from Trinidad lack chile peppers, which are added to the meal in the form of hot sauces. However, this paste, found in an early Trinidadian cookbook, calls for hot peppers. The paste can be used in any recipe calling for massala or curry powder. Compare this to Colombo Curry Paste from Martinique and Guadeloupe (p. 21).

6	tablespoons coriander seed	1	teaspoon turmeric
1	teaspoon anise seed	2	cloves garlic, chopped
1	teaspoon cloves	1	large onion, chopped
1	teaspoon cumin seed	½	Congo pepper (or habanero), seeds and stem removed, chopped
1	teaspoon fenugreek seed		
1	teaspoon black peppercorns		Water
1	teaspoon toasted mustard seed		

Toast the spices in a dry skillet over medium heat until they release their aromas, about 3 minutes, taking care not to burn them. Transfer to a food processor, add the turmeric and remaining ingredients, and process into a paste, adding water as needed. This paste will keep for about a week in the refrigerator.

Yield: 1½ to 2 cups
Heat Scale: Medium

North Coast Jerk Marinade

Variations on Jamaican jerk sauces and marinades range from the early, simple pastes of three or four ingredients to the more modern and rather complicated concoctions with as many as twenty-one spices, herbs, and vegetables. By varying the amounts of vegetable oil and lime juice added, the cook can change the consistency from that of a paste to a sauce. Traditionally, it is used with pork, chicken, or fish.

¼ cup whole Jamaican pimento berries (or ⅛ cup ground allspice)	⅓ cup fresh thyme
	1 teaspoon freshly ground nutmeg
3 Scotch bonnet chiles (or habaneros), seeds and stems removed, chopped	1 teaspoon freshly ground cinnamon
10 scallions (green onions), chopped	1 teaspoon salt (or more, to taste)
½ cup chopped onion	1 tablespoon freshly ground black pepper
4 cloves garlic, chopped	¼ cup vegetable oil
4 bay leaves, crushed	¼ cup lime juice
1 3-inch piece ginger, peeled and chopped	Water

Roast the pimento berries in a dry skillet until they are aromatic, about 2 minutes. Remove and crush them to a powder in a mortar or spice mill.

   Add the pimento powder and the remaining ingredients to a food processor and blend with enough water to make a paste or sauce. Remove and store in a jar in the refrigerator; it will keep for a month or more.

Yield: 2 to 3 cups

Heat Scale: Hot

Trinidad Herb Seasoning Paste

This seasoning paste and marinade enlivens otherwise bland grilled lamb, pork chops, or chicken. Try it as a basting sauce for grilled vegetables, too—such as eggplant and zucchini. When using this sauce to marinate meat, combine 3 tablespoons of this seasoning mixture with ½ teaspoon soy sauce, ground black pepper, ½ cup chopped tomatoes, and 1 teaspoon Worcestershire sauce. Add it to 1½ pounds of meat and marinate, preferably overnight or at least for 2 to 3 hours. Some of the measurements are authentically vague, so get your bunches together.

½	Congo pepper (or habanero), seeds and stems removed, chopped	1	leaf Spanish thyme or substitute 2 teaspoons fresh thyme and ½ teaspoon fresh Greek oregano
3	bunches chives or green onions, coarsely chopped	½	cup vinegar
1	bunch parsley, coarsely chopped	1	tablespoon salt (or less to taste)
½	bunch celery leaves, coarsely chopped	1	tablespoon ground ginger
1	cup garlic cloves, peeled	1	tablespoon fresh or dried thyme Water

Combine all ingredients in a food processor and blend thoroughly, adding water as necessary to make a medium paste.

Yield: 2 to 3 cups

Heat Scale: Medium

A Scotch Bonnet Fable

A West Indian folktale tells of a Creole woman who loved the fragrant island pods so much that she decided to make a soup out of them. She reasoned that since the Scotch bonnets were so good in other foods, a soup made just of them would be heavenly. But after her children tasted the broth, it was so blisteringly hot that they ran to the river to cool their mouths. Unfortunately, they drank so much water that they drowned— heavenly, indeed! The moral of the story is to be careful with Scotch bonnets and their relatives, which is why many sauce companies combine them with vegetables or fruits to dilute the heat. And water, of course, is hardly the best cool-down; dairy products are.

Bonney Bajan Seasoning

There are an astounding number of variations on Bajan seasoning, which is similar to seasoning pastes found in Trinidad. All contain herbs and chiles, and a myriad of other ingredients. They are added to soups and stews and used as a marinade and basting sauce for grilled meats.

1   bunch green onions, coarsely chopped (about 1½ cups)

3   tablespoons fresh lime juice

¼   cup coarsely chopped fresh parsley

1   tablespoon fresh thyme

1   tablespoon fresh marjoram

1   tablespoon fresh chives

2   cloves garlic

1   bonney pepper (or habanero), seeds and stem removed, halved

1   teaspoon paprika

¼   teaspoon ground cloves

⅛   teaspoon salt

Water

Combine all of the ingredients except the water in a food processor and purée on pulse, adding water until the desired consistency is reached. Use immediately or store in the refrigerator for up to a week.

Yield: ¾ cup

Heat Scale: Hot

Trinidadian Bird Pepper Sherry

This recipe, which we found in a 1940s Trinidad cookbook, is probably one of the earliest methods of preserving peppers in the tropics. It is also called "pepper wine." The sherry, which gradually picks up heat from the bird peppers, is sprinkled into soups and stews and makes them quite exotic. The peppers can be either fresh or dried.

20 "bird peppers" (or chiltepíns
      or piquins), stems removed
1   cup dry sherry

Add the peppers to the sherry and allow to steep for several days. Keep in a jar in the refrigerator.

Yield: 1 cup

Heat Scale: Hot

Note: This recipe requires advance preparation.

Pepper Wine

"Eight yellow and eight red peppers cut into small pieces, or sliced, and put into a glass bottle or jar. Pour a half a pint of sherry on this, and put in the sun for twelve hours. It is then fit for use. If you can get cherry peppers, the green and red mixed look very pretty together; some people prefer the tiny bird peppers which are commonly to be had. A little pepper wine is a very great addition to soups or made dishes."

John Kenneth McKenzie Pringle, 1893

Pique de Vinagre y Ajíes Bravos (Bird Pepper Vinegar *Pique*)

Here is a classic pique recipe from Puerto Rico. As usual, the longer the chiles steep, the hotter the sauce will be. It should be stored in a bottle with a sprinkler cap so that the amount of sauce can be controlled as it is sprinkled over grilled fish, poultry, or even into salads.

1 cup cider vinegar	10 whole peppercorns
10 to 20 "bird peppers" (chiltepíns), or any small, hot chile, fresh or dry	⅛ teaspoon salt
	1 sprig fresh oregano, cilantro, or mint (optional)
4 cloves garlic, halved	

Combine all ingredients in a glass jar and allow to steep in the refrigerator for at least 24 hours to blend the flavors.

Yield: 1 cup

Heat Scale: Hot

Note: This recipe requires advance preparation.

Puerto Rican Sofrito

Here is an unusual sauce that is almost a stew. In Puerto Rico, some cooks depend on only the bell peppers for *Capsicum* flavor; others add some rocotillo chiles, as we do if we can find them. Otherwise, we use habaneros (one-quarter the amount). Serve this sauce over a rice or black bean dish from Chapter 8.

½	pound salt pork, diced	½	pound ham, diced
2	tablespoons annatto (*achiote*) seed	3	large tomatoes, peeled and chopped (about 2 cups)
4	onions, finely chopped	1	tablespoon minced cilantro
2	cloves garlic, chopped	1	tablespoon fresh oregano leaves
2	green bell peppers, seeds removed, chopped		Salt to taste
4	rocotillo chiles, seeds and stems removed, chopped, or substitute 1 habanero		Freshly ground black pepper to taste

In a large skillet, fry the salt pork over medium heat, stirring occasionally, until the pieces have no fat and are crisp and brown. Remove the pork and reserve, leaving the fat in the pan. Add the annatto seed to the pan and cook, stirring occasionally, over medium heat for 5 minutes. Remove the skillet from the heat, strain the mixture, discard the seeds, and return the fat to the skillet.

Add the onions, garlic, bell peppers, and rocotillo chiles and sauté until the onion is tender soft, about 5 minutes. Add the remaining ingredients and simmer over low heat, uncovered, for 30 minutes, stirring from time to time.

This sauce may be canned in sterilized jars or kept in the refrigerator for about 5 days.

Yield: About 2 cups

Heat Scale: Medium

Pukka Chileheads

"Thomas, my Bookkeeper, accosted me after breakfast and insisted I accompany him to his Place. When we arrived it was to find his usual gaggle of some of the prettier estate girls (one of these days that lad will get himself into deep trouble) engaged in some sort of Food Preparation. There were mortars and pestles all around and the air was sharp with a Pungent yet delightful Smell. It seems that he had been doing a little experimentation of his own and had produced a Hades hot pepper sauce. He gave me a little. T'was as fiery as all Hell and would have done for the Devil himself. It was made by pulverising good quality Scotch bonnets with a little vinegar. Since it was indeed the real thing, we decided there and then to call it Pukka Sauce. A fitting name we also thought for those pukka people who like their food and other things hot and spicy."

Busha Browne's Diary, November 15, 1837

Piri Piri Oil

This interesting sauce is the Caribbean oil-based variation on the African sauce from Angola, which was transferred to the region by Portuguese immigrants working the cacao plantations in Trinidad and Guyana. Use it to spice up soups and fried fish. Pimento leaves are traditionally used in this recipe, but they are hard to find.

3	cups extra virgin olive oil	1	teaspoon lemon zest
2	Congo peppers (or substitute habaneros), cut in half	2	bay leaves

Combine all ingredients in a jar and seal tightly. Place in the refrigerator and let steep for 2 weeks. Remove the top and stir every 2 days. The longer it steeps, the hotter the sauce will become.

Yield: 3 cups

Heat Scale: Hot

Note: This recipe requires advance preparation.

Creole Congo Pepper Sauce

At a lunch at the Tiki Village in Trinidad's Kapok Hotel, Dave and Mary Jane met Ramesh Ghany (a chef of East Indian descent cooking at a Chinese restaurant) who told us how he makes his simple Creole congo pepper sauce. Ramesh told us that he uses 300 Congo peppers to make a gallon of sauce, so we've scaled the recipe down to more modest dimensions. This was the hottest sauce we encountered in the Caribbean, but it was very flavorful.

1½ cups vegetable oil
20 large Congo peppers (or habaneros), seeds and stems removed, minced extremely fine or puréed in a food processor

Bring the oil to a boil, add the minced Congo peppers, and turn off the heat. Allow to sit for at least a half hour.

Yield: 1½ cups
Heat Scale: Extremely hot

Moko Jumbie Papaya Pepper Sauce

Named after the zombie-like stilt character that prowls around during Carnival celebrations, this sauce features two ingredients common to Trinidadian commercial sauces: papaya and mustard. The sauce can be used as a condiment or as a marinade for meat, poultry, and fish.

1	small, green papaya	2	tablespoons salt (or less to taste)
2	quarts water		
5	Congo peppers (or habaneros), seeds and stems removed, chopped	3	cups vinegar (or 1½ cups vinegar mixed with 1½ cups water)
1	large onion, chopped fine	½	teaspoon ground turmeric
2	cloves garlic, minced	1	teaspoon Trinidadian Curry Paste (see recipe, p. 22)
4	tablespoons dried mustard		

Boil the papaya in its skin for 10 minutes, then remove and cool. Peel the papaya, remove the seeds, and chop it into 1-inch cubes.

Combine the papaya with the remaining ingredients in a saucepan. Bring to a boil, reduce heat, and simmer for 20 minutes.

Remove from the heat, cool the mixture, purée it in a food processor, and bottle it. The sauce will last for weeks in the refrigerator.

Yield: 3 to 4 cups

Heat Scale: Hot

Saba Scotch Bonnet Sauce

From the Netherlands Antilles island of Saba comes this simple, steeped hot sauce that graces seafood dishes or simple rice. Malt vinegar, made from malted barley, is the secret taste ingredient. Because of the vinegar, this sauce can be kept for a month or so in the refrigerator.

1 Scotch bonnet chile (or habanero), seeds and stem removed, minced	½ cup malt vinegar
	½ cup water
	½ teaspoon salt
¼ cup finely chopped onion	¼ cup olive oil
1 clove garlic, minced	

Place the chile, onion, and garlic in a small bowl and mix well. Combine the vinegar, water, and salt in a saucepan and bring to a strong boil. Pour the boiling mixture over the chile mixture, stirring constantly. Add the oil and stir well.

Yield: About 2 cups

Heat Scale: Hot

Yes, We Have Some of Those Yellow Fruits

"Bananas and plantains, first planted in the Caribbean in 1516, then carried to the mainland in the 1520s, outproduced even the tubers. Within a generation, they had spread through much of tropical America, emerging as a staple for the poorer classes, who used them in combination with tubers and grains. Bananas enjoyed such popularity because they consistently outproduced traditional staples, required little work, only some weeding now and then, and produced throughout the year. Nutritionally, bananas supplied abundant carbohydrates, vitamins, and minerals. Humboldt was astounded at the productivity of bananas, calculating that they produced one hundred thirty-three times more food by weight than wheat and forty-four more than potatoes. In calories produced per unit of land, bananas led all of the common staples of the sixteenth century. Then came manioc and potatoes, followed by maize, wheat, barley, and rice. Translated into the practical necessities of life, this meant that five days of work produced enough bananas for one year."

John C. Super

Asher Sauce

Island legend holds that the name of this sauce is a corruption of "Limes Ashore!," the phrase called out by British sailors who found limes growing on the Virgin Islands. The limes, originally planted by the Spanish, would save them from scurvy. We presume that the bird peppers would save them from bland food. Add this sauce to seafood chowders.

15	limes, Key limes preferred	2	cardamom pods
1	cup salt	1	tablespoon whole cloves
3	cups water	5	allspice berries
10	whole bird peppers such as piquins or chiltepins or 2 habaneros, halved	¼	teaspoon freshly ground black pepper
½	cup vinegar	4	cloves garlic, sliced
½	cup sugar	1	bunch green onions, white part only, chopped

Quarter the limes but do not cut all the way through. Open up each lime and rub them with salt. Place the limes on cutting boards, cover them with cheesecloth, and set them in the sun for about a week. Protect them from rain.

    The limes will shrink and their skins will turn brown. Rinse the limes to remove as much salt as possible. Place the limes in a large pan, cover with water, and add the remaining ingredients. Bring to a boil, reduce the heat, and simmer uncovered for 1 hour. Cool and strain the sauce. It will keep for several weeks in the refrigerator.

Yield: 2½ cups

Heat Scale: Hot

Note: This recipes requires advance preparation.

Sauce Chien

From Martinique and Guadeloupe in the French Caribbean comes a "dog sauce," which seems to refer to the habanero's aroma. Some variations on this sauce add vegetable oil, cinnamon, various herbs, spices, and capers. Sauce Chien is often served over fried fish.

½   habanero or Scotch bonnet
      chile, thinly sliced
      Juice of 1 lime or lemon
3   green onions, minced
1   teaspoon fresh thyme leaves

1   onion, minced
1   clove garlic, crushed
      Salt and pepper to taste
2   cups boiling water

In a jar, combine all ingredients and allow to steep for at least 1 hour.

Yield: 2¼ cups

Heat Scale: Medium

Sauce Ti-Malice

From Haiti comes a "bad" lime-based sauce to accompany meats such as roasted pork. This sauce keeps for several weeks if refrigerated.

2	cups onion, finely chopped	2½	teaspoons minced Scotch bonnet or habanero chiles
1	cup fresh lime juice, strained		
3	tablespoons butter	1½	teaspoons minced garlic

In a bowl, marinate the onions in the lime juice at room temperature for 30 minutes. Drain the onions in a sieve and reserve the marinade.

In a heavy skillet, melt the butter over medium heat. When the foam begins to subside, add the onions. Stir frequently and cook for about 5 minutes or until the onions are transparent. Stir in the chile and garlic, reduce the heat, and cover the skillet. Continue cooking for 10 minutes or until the chiles are tender. Turn off the heat and add the reserved marinade. Cool to room temperature before serving.

Yield: 1½ cups

Heat Scale: Medium

Ciboney Tomato Rundown Sauce

Here is one of Jack Shapansky's innovative creations that combines the best of Jamaica with his own gourmet touches. In Jamaica, this sauce is served over a wide variety of fish and even lobster. It is such a tasty sauce that it is wonderful when served over pasta. The term "rundown" ("oildown" in Barbados and Trinidad) refers to cooking vegetables in coconut milk until most of the milk is absorbed, leaving a light oil.

	Meat from 2 coconuts, grated (about 4 cups)	2	sprigs fresh thyme
4	cups warm water	1	Scotch bonnet chile, left whole (or more to taste), or substitute habanero
1	small onion, chopped		
¼	cup chopped bell pepper	⅛	cup tomato paste
¼	cup chopped scallions		Salt and pepper to taste
1	clove garlic, minced		

In a blender or food processor, combine the grated coconut meat and the water and purée as smooth as possible. Remove and strain, reserving the milk and using the "trash" for candy or pies.

Place the milk in a large pot and bring to a boil to reduce it. Boil for about 30 minutes, or until the oil begins to separate. Add the onion, bell pepper, scallions, garlic, thyme, and Scotch bonnet. Reduce the heat and cook over medium for about 20 minutes.

Add the tomato paste and salt and pepper and cook for 5 minutes longer. Remove the Scotch bonnet. Place the sauce in a blender or food processor and purée until smooth. The sauce should be creamy, with a heavy consistency and a light pink color.

Yield: 2 to 3 cups

Heat Scale: Mild

Bajan Hot Seafood Sauce

When in Barbados, what sauce should be served with fried flying fish? Why this one, of course. Yes, it depends on ketchup, but the bonney pepper—or use habanero—makes this sauce sing. It is also served with shrimp cocktail, raw oysters (if you dare eat them these days!), and crab cakes.

1	bonney chile (or habanero), seeds and stem removed, minced	1	tablespoon sugar (or less to taste)
1½	cups ketchup	2	tablespoons minced chives
½	cup water		Salt and freshly ground black pepper to taste
¼	cup Worcestershire sauce or to taste		

Combine all ingredients in a bowl and mix well. Use that day; it keeps only a little while in the refrigerator.

Yield: About 2 cups
Heat Scale: Hot

The Birth of Outerbridge's Sherry Peppers

"When we were growing up, the crystal decanter filled with amber-coloured sherry and loaded with its sunken treasure of hot peppers, sat on the mahogany sideboard in our dining room. At mealtime it was moved to the dinner table and its contents reverently and sparingly added to our steaming soup bowls. I don't remember when the decanter disappeared from our home, but it was probably soon after Uncle Yeaton, his wife Betsey and cousin Robbie cooked up the original secret Outerbridge's recipe for sherry peppers sauce."

Alexis Outerbridge

Ajilimojili (Pepper–Pepper Sauce)

Just try to say this word fast three times in a row: *ah-hee-lee-mo-hee-lee*"!
This sauce is a Puerto Rican classic that is served with roasted suckling pig.

3	habanero chiles, seeds and stems removed, chopped	4	cloves garlic, peeled
3	red bell peppers, seeds and stems removed, chopped	1	teaspoons salt
4	peppercorns, crushed	½	cup lime juice
		½	cup vegetable oil

Combine the chiles, bell peppers, peppercorns, and garlic in a mortar or
food processor and crush into a coarse paste. Add the salt and stir. Transfer
this mixture to a bowl and beat in the lime juice and oil.

Yield: About 3 cups
Heat Scale: Hot

Salsa Roja para Frijoles Negros (Red Hot Sauce for Black Beans)

This Cuban recipe has its origins in Africa, where it was originally served over pigeon peas. It works just as well over black beans that have been cooked with bacon until tender. Serve with any of the (already hot) bean dishes from Chapter 8.

1	cup olive oil	1	teaspoon finely chopped basil
1½	cups diced tomatoes	2	teaspoons dried oregano
3	to 4 cloves garlic, diced		Freshly ground black pepper
1	teaspoon sugar	½	cup vinegar
1	teaspoon habanero powder		

In a skillet, heat the oil and sauté the tomatoes for 5 to 10 minutes or until soft. Stir in the remaining ingredients, except the vinegar. Simmer on low heat, stirring occasionally for 20 to 30 minutes or until the sauce has thickened. Remove the skillet from the heat and let it stand for 3 to 5 minutes, and stir in the vinegar.

Yield: 2 cups
Heat Scale: Hot

Jamaican Green Mango Chutney

Here is how they make chutney in Kingston. Note that this style is far less sweet than other chutneys around the world. Serve it with Jamaican Curry Goat (p. 121). It keeps for a couple of weeks in the refrigerator.

6	medium-sized green mangoes, peeled, pits removed, chopped fine	1	teaspoon garlic, finely chopped
		2	teaspoons minced Scotch bonnet chile (or habanero)
2	cups malt vinegar	1	teaspoon ground allspice
½	cup sugar	½	cup Tamarind Sauce (see recipe, p. 13)
¼	cup seedless raisins		
¼	cup finely chopped ginger root		

Place the mangoes and vinegar into a large saucepan. Bring to a boil over high heat and cook briskly for 10 minutes, stirring occasionally. Stir in the sugar, raisins, ginger, garlic, Scotch bonnet, allspice, tamarind sauce, and salt, reduce the heat to low, and simmer uncovered for about 45 minutes or until the mango is tender, stirring occasionally.

Remove the pan from the heat. It is the cook's option to serve the chutney as is or to purée it into a smooth sauce.

Yield: About 4 cups

Heat Scale: Medium

Mango Kucheela

This chutney-like Trinidadian relish is commonly served with the street food called *doubles* and curried dishes of all types, as well as with Pelau (p. 171). Ripe mangoes are never used in *kucheela*.

2   cups grated meat of green mangoes

4   cloves garlic, minced

2   Congo peppers (or habaneros), seeds and stems removed, minced

2   teaspoons mild curry powder

½   cup mustard oil (or substitute vegetable oil), or more for texture

Squeeze as much juice as possible out of the grated mango meat, then spread it on a cookie sheet and place in the oven at 250 degrees. Cook for 2 hours, or until the meat has dried out. Combine the dried mango with all of the other ingredients and mix well. Store in sterilized jars in the refrigerator.

Yield: 2 cups

Heat Scale: Hot

And You Thought It a Mere Spice

" 'Anyone who has tasted this spice no longer desires others,'
wrote the French gastronome Curnonsky about nutmeg.
Hyperbole, perhaps, but it does serve to point out the high
esteem in which this musk-scented nut has been held since
the Middle Ages. The Portuguese—the first Europeans to
market the spice—published erroneous navigational charts to
keep secret the location of the Molucca Islands, where nutmeg grew. When the Dutch seized the islands in 1602, they
imposed the death penalty on anyone caught smuggling the
seeds of the precious nutmeg tree. Someone succeeded in
secreting the nutmeg to Grenada, which today is the world's
second-largest producer of this perfumed nut, after Indonesia.
Nutmeg is the kernel of an apricotlike fruit that grows on a tall
tree. Each nut is covered with a lacy red membrane, which
when dried becomes another spice in its own right: mace. For
the best results, buy whole nutmegs and grate them as you
need them in soups, stews, desserts, and atop rum punches,
Grenada style."

Steven Raichlen

Of Doubles and Souse:
Appetizers and Salads

"All mixed up and born in the islands," is an excellent way to describe the appetizers and salads of the Caribbean. Our search for the tastiest tidbits and best-seasoned salads led us from Trinidad to Jamaica and almost every island in between. One of the characteristics we looked for in the recipes we included in this chapter was the use of sizzling seasonings. Nutmeg, ginger, allspice, and our obvious favorite, the chile pepper, play a heavy role in our adventurous agenda. So rev up your tastebuds and save your appetite, we've got the appetizers you'll taste with great delight!

You'll go back for seconds after you taste our first recipe, Doubles (p. 50). This appetizer is found only in Trinidad, and features garlic, curry, and habaneros. Our other Trinidadian dish is Aloo Pie (p. 52). The best versions of it are often sold by street vendors. For the most authentic taste of this island, use fresh thyme.

The early European settlers on the islands obviously were not concerned with their sodium intake! In fact, the food-preserving techniques of the old days have remained popular through classic Jamaican dishes such as Salt Fish and Ackee (p. 51), as well as A & S Pie (p. 54). Salt fish is the local name for salted imported cod, which was originally brought to the islands because local fish spoiled too quickly. Peggy Barnes highly recommends the next recipe, Jamaican Patties (p. 56). According to Peggy, she had one of the best lunches in her life feasting on this spicy appetizer; add a few cold beers and you will too!

If you enjoy experimenting in the kitchen, Solomon Gundy (p. 57) is the dish for you. It is very salty, but very good. We suggest the addition of mango or pineapple for an interesting change. The last of our salt-of-the-earth dishes is Salmau na Pekel (Pickled Salmon, p. 58), which offers a taste of Spain in Curaçao. Olive oil, capers, and pimiento-stuffed olives blend together with the salmon to produce a recipe that has held its popularity even after Spain lost control of the island to the Dutch, following a century of rule.

Our next destination is Martinique, where Melissa toured a rum distillery and tasted what seemed like a few hundred samples. Fortunately, she lived to tell the tale and collect the following sizzling starters. *Feroce d'Avocat* (Savage Avocado Appetizer, p. 59) is the French name for what we have deemed ferocious finger food. The unusual mixture of crab, avocados, and habaneros works very well together. The avocado, also known as the alligator pear, is the star of our most fabulous dip, Tropical Guacamole with Fruit (p. 60). What makes this really interesting is the addition of those tropical treats coconut, papaya, and, of course, habanero.

We suggest that your guests will enjoy tasting our two heavenly fritter recipes. We invite you to try our light-as-air shrimp fritters, Shrimp Fritters on the Wild Side (p. 62). The secret to this recipe from Martinique is to fry the fritters right before you serve them. The fresher, the better! Our Fruity Fritters (p. 63) offer a taste of sweet and heat with almost every bite. Feel free to substitute your favorite tropical fruit for the pineapple.

On the island of Trinidad, you may receive a burnt mouth salad for Sunday brunch. Sound strange? Not really, if you consider that our first salad recipe, Buljol (p. 64) translates to exactly that phrase in French. We suspect the use of Congo peppers in this dish helps give it the hot, but delicious, reputation it deserves.

Our next six salad samplings offer a specific taste of the islands for everyone. Nancy Gerlach collected the Hearts of Palm Salad with Dry Jerk Seasoning (p. 65) recipe. Don't be fooled by this light-looking salad—it packs a punch with its more than eight spicy ingredients used in the jerk seasoning alone. Fresh mangoes right off the tree is one of the sweetest memories Melissa has of the Caribbean. The Mango Fandango (p. 66) salad is a tribute to her love of the mango and all tropical fruits.

If you like squash, you'll want to make our Cho-Cho Salad (p. 67). This single-seeded, pear-shaped fruit originated in Mexico and is used all over the Caribbean. Our next two recipes are guaranteed to relieve stress. Conch, the main ingredient of both the Chile–Conch Salad (p. 68) and Quick Conch Salad (p. 69), requires a thorough pounding before it is ready to be cooked. Who could ask for more; a great dinner and a workout! And have we ever got the answer to boring iceberg lettuce salads: the Curried Rice and Pigeon Pea Salad (p. 70) blends together the rich tastes of curry and cashews, red bell peppers, and pigeon peas. You'll never want to buy ranch dressing again!

Last but certainly not least, we wrap up this chapter with three equally diverse dishes. Red Stripe Sweet Potatoes (p. 71) combines yams and Red Stripe Beer. We think this Barbados-based recipe represents the great attitude the Caribbean people have concerning mixing ingredients. Just think of it as a twice-baked potato with an island attitude! Our Banana Chips (p. 72) are not only tasty, they're good for you. They are excellent eaten alone, or crunched up on salads. Trotter Souse (p. 73), so named for its use of pig's feet as a main ingredient, is our final recipe in this chapter. However, pork stew meat may be substituted if your guests have an aversion to porcine feet.

Doubles

This snack food may well be the islander's version of the empanada. Found exclusively in Trinidad, doubles are composed of two pieces of *bara* bread and a filling of *channa*, hot sauce, and *kucheela*. *Channa* is curried chick-peas, which are also known as garbanzo beans. Canned, cooked garbanzos can be used, but the taste will not be as good as the freshly cooked ones.

1	pound channa (curried chick-peas), or 1 16-ounce can drained chick-peas	1	Congo pepper (or habanero), seeds and stem removed, minced
6	to 8 cups water	1	teaspoon ground cumin
3	tablespoons West Indian Massala (see recipe, p. 20)		Salt and pepper to taste
2½	cups water		Split Pea Bara Bread (p. 230)
3	tablespoons canola or corn oil		Hot sauce from Chapter 2
5	cloves garlic, minced		Kucheela Mango (see recipe, p. 45)
1	onion, chopped		

Soak the channa in the water overnight (or gently boil it with a little massala for about 3 hours).

Mix the massala with ½ cup of water. Heat the oil in a large skillet and add the garlic, onion, and the massala mixed with water. Sauté for 2 to 3 minutes.

Drain the channa, add it to the skillet, and stir well. Add 1½ cups water, the Congo pepper, and the cumin, cover, and simmer, stirring occasionally, until the channa is very soft, about 1 hour. Add the remaining ½ cup water if the channa begins to dry out. Add salt and pepper to taste.

To assemble the doubles, take one piece of bara bread and spread the channa mixture over it. Add hot sauce and kucheela to taste, then place the second piece of bara bread over it to make a sandwich.

Yield: At least 15 doubles

Heat Scale: Medium to Hot

Salt Fish and Ackee

This interesting recipe is known as the national dish of Jamaica. Traditionally served at breakfast, ackees have a texture similar to that of scrambled eggs. If you are lucky enough to find fresh ackees, make sure you choose a ripe one, which on splitting reveals the white flesh of the fruit. Ackees, although theoretically forbidden for import into North America, occasionally can be found in Latin or Caribbean markets.

2	dozen ackees in pods	½	Scotch bonnet chile (or habanero), seeds and stem removed, minced
½	pound salt cod		
2	tablespoons butter	1	small tomato, chopped (optional)
¼	cup oil		
2	onions, sliced		Black pepper
1	sprig thyme		

Choose ackees that are completely open, with the black seeds and yellow fruit clearly visible in the scarlet pods. This is important, as unripe ackees contain a highly toxic substance.

Remove the ackees from their pods. Discard the seeds and the pink membrane found in the cleft of each fruit. Wash them and set them to boil in a large pot of water with the salt fish. As soon as the ackees are tender, pour the contents of the pot into a large sieve, discarding the water. Separate the ackees from the fish. Run some cold water over the fish so that you can remove the bones and skin comfortably, then flake the fish and set it aside.

Heat the butter and oil in a frying pan. Add the onions, thyme, and chile, and the tomato if desired. Stir for a few minutes, then add the flaked fish. Stir for a few more minutes, then add the drained ackees, carefully stirring so as not to crush them. Add a little more oil if necessary, sprinkle with plenty of freshly ground black pepper, and the dish is ready.

Roasted breadfruit or plantains make excellent accompaniments to this famous dish.

Serves: 4

Heat Scale: Medium

Aloo Pie

Aloo, which mean potato in Hindi, is most often served in Trinidad and Guyana. Many roadside stands offer these as snacks or lunch items.

Dough

2	cups flour		2	cups water
¼	teaspoon salt			Vegetable oil
1	teaspoon baking powder			

Filling

4	cups water		1	teaspoon thyme
½	teaspoon salt		¼	teaspoon West Indian Massala (see recipe, p. 20)
1	pound potatoes, peeled and quartered		1	habanero chile, stemmed, seeded, and minced
1	small onion, finely chopped			Salt and freshly ground black pepper
2	cloves garlic, crushed			
1	green onion, very finely chopped		4	cups vegetable oil for deep frying
2	teaspoons ground cumin			

To make the dough, combine the flour, salt, and baking powder in a bowl. Add enough water to form the dough, then knead it. Rub a little oil over the dough and let it rest while preparing the filling.

To make the filling, bring the water and salt to a boil in a saucepan and boil the potatoes until tender. Next, drain the water. While the potatoes are still hot, mash them with the onion, garlic, green onion, cumin, thyme, massala, habanero, and salt and pepper to taste.

Divide the dough into six parts and knead each for 1 minute to form six smooth balls. Place the balls in a nonreactive bowl and let them rest for 5 minutes.

On a floured surface, roll out one portion of dough into a circle 5 inches in diameter (a coffee can lid works well as a cutter). Spoon 1 to 2 tablespoons of filling in the middle of the dough and fold it into a semicircle. Dab a little water around the edges and pinch to seal.

Heat the oil in a deep saucepan. Deep fry the pies, a few at a time, until golden brown on all sides. Drain on paper towels and serve hot.

Serves: 6

Heat Scale: Hot

Along the Fruited Trail

"The road [in Guadeloupe, 1886] was excellent, made with broken stone covered with earth, and stretched straight away through vast fields of sugar-cane, gardens, and fruit plantations. All these fruits were tropical, children of the sun. There were mangoes, pink-and-yellow peach-shaped balls hanging by slender stems; sour and sweet sops, containing a custard-like pulp with the delicious odor of strawberries; oranges, bananas, plantains, fragrant pine-apples, sapodillas in coats of russet hue, avocado pears, star-apples, limes, lemons, tamarinds, water-lemons, citrons, guavas, and 'forbidden fruit.'"

F. A. Ober

A & S Pie

Ackee and salt fish also make a very good starter when served as ackee pie. Ackee sometimes can be found canned in Caribbean or Latin markets. We like this quiche-of-sorts with a bit of mango chutney on the side.

Dough

2	cups all-purpose flour	1	teaspoon baking powder
¼	teaspoon salt	1	cup water

Filling

8	ounces salt cod	1	onion, sliced thinly
	Water	½	habanero chile, seeds and stem removed, minced
24	ripe, fresh ackees, or 15 ounces canned ackees	1	tomato, chopped
½	teaspoon salt		Salt and pepper
¼	cup vegetable oil		

For the dough, combine the flour, salt, and baking powder in a bowl. Add the water to the mixture slowly, using only enough water to form the ingredients into a dough. Knead the dough to a smooth consistency. Next, rub a little oil over the dough, then put it in a nonreactive bowl, cover it with a dish towel, and let it rest while preparing the filling.

For the filling, soak the salt cod in a saucepan with enough water to cover for at least 2 hours. When the fish is done soaking, drain the fish, discard the water, and set aside. If you are using fresh ackees, remove the flesh and throw away the pods. Next, wash the flesh under cold water. Place the ackees in a pan and cover with water. Add the salt and cook for 10 to 15 minutes until the ackees are soft but not disintegrating. Drain the ackees and set them aside.

Place the fish back in the saucepan and cover with fresh water. Boil the fish until it easily flakes, about 11 minutes. Remove the fish from the pan. Cool the fish until it is easily handled, then remove the skin, debone, and flake the fish. In a separate saucepan, heat the oil over a medium flame. Add the onion and habanero and sauté until the onion is very soft. Add the tomato and fish and stir fry for a few minutes. Add the ackees and salt and pepper to taste. Set aside.

Roll out the dough on a floured surface, then line an 8- or 9-inch pie tin with it. Fill the pastry with ackees and salt fish and bake for 45 minutes at 400 degrees. Serve the pie warm.

Serves: 4

Heat Scale: Medium

Note: This recipe requires advance preparation.

The Island of the Bearded Figs

"The derivation of the name Barbados is obscure and there have been various suggested ways in which it received its name. The most accepted of these comes from Los Barbados, which is the bearded fig tree which grew abundantly on the island at the time of its discovery by Europeans in the 16th century. This tree is very strange in that it sends down aerial roots from its branches, thus giving the impression of being bearded."

John A. Lake

Jamaican Patties

This recipe for Jamaica's favorite fast food is from Peggy Barnes, who wrote about her island culinary adventures in *Chile Pepper* Magazine. She suggests that this recipe may be simplified by using dough from the dairy case. For more heat, split the patties in half after they are done baking, and serve habanero-based sauce to spoon inside.

½	pound ground beef	1	teaspoon seasoned salt
½	pound ground pork	1	teaspoon dried thyme
1	teaspoon ground red chile pepper	2	tablespoons soy sauce
1	teaspoon paprika	½	cup bread crumbs
¼	cup minced celery	1	tablespoon all-purpose flour
½	cup minced onion	2	cans grand-size refrigerator biscuits
¼	cup minced green onion tops	1	egg yolk beaten with 1 tablespoon milk
¼	cup diced red bell pepper		
2	cloves garlic, crushed		

In a large skillet over medium-high heat, brown the pork and beef and drain off any excess fat. Add the ground red chile pepper and paprika. Cook, stirring, for 1 minute. Add the celery, onion, green onions, bell pepper, garlic, salt, thyme, and soy sauce, and cook until the celery is tender, about 5 minutes. Add the bread crumbs and flour and combine thoroughly. Remove from heat and allow to cool.

Preheat the oven to 375 degrees. On a floured surface, roll out the biscuits to 6-inch circles and place 2 to 3 heaping tablespoons of meat in the center. Moisten the edges of each circle with water and fold the dough over to form crescents. Crimp the edges with a fork and brush the crust with the egg–milk mixture. Place the crescents on a baking sheet and bake at 375 degrees for 30 minutes, or until they are golden brown.

Yield: Ten 6-inch patties

Heat Scale: Mild

Solomon Gundy

According to Caribbean food expert Cristine Mackie, Solomon Gundy was brought to the West Indies from England in the early 1600s. An old saying associated with the dish says, "you always make Solomongundy of such things that you have according to your fancy." In the spirit of the dish, feel free to experiment with the ingredients. This dish is usually served as a salad.

1	pound salted herring	¼	cup chopped parsley
1	pound cold cooked potatoes, thinly sliced	2	large hard-boiled eggs, cold and chopped
1	mild red onion, chopped		Olive oil
2	carrots, grated		Wine vinegar
2	beet roots, peeled, cooked, and sliced		Black pepper to taste
1	Scotch bonnet chile (or habanero), seeds and stem removed, chopped fine		

Soak the herring overnight. Peel off the skin, debone, and chop. Combine it with the potatoes, onion, carrots, beets, chile, parsley, and eggs, including any leftovers of cold meat from beef, lamb, or roast chicken. Dress the salad with a vinaigrette of olive oil and wine vinegar to taste. Grind fresh black pepper over it. If salted herrings are not available, use a dozen or so anchovies. Chill before serving.

Serves: 4

Heat Scale: Hot

Note: This recipe requires advance preparation.

Salmau na Pekel (Pickled Salmon)

This recipe is from Curaçao. The cooking on this island has a prominent Spanish influence, largely because Spain held the islands for more than a century before the Dutch took over in 1634. This salad or spread takes some time to make, but it's worth it.

2½	pounds salted salmon	3	cloves garlic, crushed
3	medium onions, sliced thin	2	bay leaves, slightly bruised
	Water	10	cloves
1	cup white wine vinegar	1	tablespoon capers
3	tablespoons olive oil		Pimiento-stuffed olives to taste
1	habanero chile, seeds and stem removed, minced		

Soak the salmon in a large quantity of water for a day. Change water several times. Clean, debone, and cut the salmon into strips.

Place the onions in a bowl of hot water until they are softened.

Combine the wine vinegar and olive oil, then add the chile, garlic, bay leaves, cloves, capers, and pimiento-stuffed olives and mix well. In a serving bowl, alternate layers of the salmon, the onions, and the marinade. Let stand for 24 hours, then serve with a variety of crackers.

Serves: 10

Heat Scale: Medium

Note: This recipe requires advance preparation.

Feroce d'Avocat (Savage Avocado Appetizer)

Feroce d'Avocat is the French name of this hot crab appetizer, which is popular in Martinique. The avocado, sometimes referred to as an alligator pear, adds a rich taste to this dish.

8   ounces fresh or canned crab meat

1   tablespoon vinegar
    Juice of 1 lime

2   tablespoons vegetable oil

2   cloves garlic, finely chopped

4   shallots, finely chopped

4   green onions, chopped

1   habanero chile, seeds and stem removed, minced

4   avocados, peeled, seeded, and diced

1   cup manioc flour (tapioca or cassava meal)
    Extra lime juice for serving
    Lettuce or spinach leaves

Drain the crab, pat it dry, and place in a bowl. Add the vinegar, lime juice, oil, garlic, shallots, green onions, and chile. Mash the avocado with manioc flour, add to the crab mixture, and blend to form a thick paste. Spoon onto lettuce or spinach on individual serving dishes, or roll into balls and arrange on a plate. Sprinkle with lime juice just before serving.

Serves: 4

Heat Scale: Hot

Tropical Guacamole with Fruit

The only similarity between this French Caribbean guacamole and its Mexican cousin is the green color. This sweet, hot combination of fruit, coconut, and avocado is an unusual way to bring a bit of the Caribbean to a barbecue or luncheon.

About ½ pound Hawaiian or Portuguese sweet bread, also called Easter bread

2 tablespoons sweetened flaked dried coconut

1 small (about 1 pound) firm-ripe papaya

1 medium, ripe mango

1 large (about ¾ pound) firm-ripe avocado

2 tablespoons lime juice

1 teaspoon sugar

¼ teaspoon crushed dried habanero chile

Cut the bread into ¼-inch-thick slices, then cut them diagonally into triangles. Arrange the triangles in a single layer in a 10 by 15 inch pan. Bake them in a 300 degree oven until lightly browned, about 10 minutes, turning the slices over halfway through baking. Cool on racks. If made ahead, wrap them airtight and store at room temperature for up to a day.

In a frying pan, stir the coconut over medium-high heat until golden brown, about 3 minutes. Remove the mixture from the pan and set aside.

Cut the papaya and mango in half lengthwise. Discard the seeds and peel, leaving the halves intact. From one half, cut two lengthwise slices, about ¼ inch thick. Dice the remaining papaya and mango, and set the fruit aside.

Cut the avocado in half lengthwise. Discard the pit and peel, leaving the halves intact. From one half, cut two lengthwise slices, about ¼ inch thick. Chop the remaining avocado and mix with the lime juice, sugar, and habanero.

On a serving platter, arrange the avocado mixture and diced papaya/ mango mixture side by side in separate mounds. Fan the reserved avocado slices next to the diced papaya and mango, and the reserved papaya, mango, and avocado slices next to the avocado mixture. Sprinkle all with coconut. Guests can spread the guacamole and fruit mixture on the bread slices.

Serves: 6 to 8

Heat Scale: Medium

Roti on the Run

"One of the most delicious and popular foods to be found [in Trinidad] is the roti. A complete meal, roti consists of a delicate Indian flat bread filled with curried beef, chicken, goat, shrimp, or vegetables. Curried potatoes and chickpeas are added and the bread is folded over everything to create a portable crepe. Rotis are sold from roadside stands, bars, and restaurants, and are practically the cheapest food you can buy."

Knolly Moses

Shrimp Fritters on the Wild Side

Some people say that the best restaurant dining in the Caribbean is found on the French islands, such as Martinique. Melissa tried this tasty appetizer while she was there. Add a few more appetizers from this chapter and one of our punches from Chapter 9, and you've got the makings for a fun cocktail party.

2	cups unbleached all-purpose flour	1	teaspoon distilled white vinegar
1½	cups chopped onion	½	teaspoon baking soda
3	tablespoons chopped fresh parsley	1	cup milk
2	tablespoons chopped fresh chives or green onions	5	ounces medium uncooked shrimp, peeled, deveined, and chopped
½	teaspoon minced habanero chile		Salt and pepper
3	cloves garlic, chopped		Vegetable oil for deep frying
2	teaspoons chopped fresh thyme		Lime wedges for garnish

Combine the flour, onion, parsley, chives, chile, garlic, thyme, vinegar, and baking soda in a medium bowl. Add the milk and stir until the mixture is smooth and sticky. Next, stir in the shrimp and season generously with salt and pepper.

Heat the vegetable oil in a heavy deep saucepan to 375 degrees. Working in batches, scoop up the batter by heaping teaspoonfuls and push the batter off of the spoon into the oil. Fry the fritters until they are golden brown, about 3 minutes. Using a slotted spoon, transfer the fritters to paper towels to drain. The fritters are best when made just before you're ready to serve them. They go well with Jamaican Green Mango Chutney, (p. 44).

Serves: 8

Heat Scale: Hot

Fruity Fritters

We like this recipe because it blends the sweet and spicy tastes of the islands for a hearty and tangy treat. If you're feeling really adventurous, substitute underripe mangoes for the pineapple.

Pineapple Mixture

2	cups fresh pineapple, cut into chunks	1	onion, minced
1	habanero chile, seeds and stem removed, minced	2	cloves garlic, crushed
5	chives, minced	8	green onions, minced
		½	teaspoon ground turmeric

Batter

1¼	cups flour	2	eggs, beaten
½	cup milk (or more if needed)		Salt and pepper
½	cup vegetable oil for frying		Pineapple rings for garnish

Mix the pineapple with all the vegetables and herbs and set aside.

Combine all the batter ingredients (not the vegetable oil) and beat well with an electric mixer. Cover the mixture and refrigerate for 4 hours. When the time is up, combine the two mixtures.

Heat the vegetable oil in a deep skillet. Drop spoonfuls of the batter into the oil and fry for 5 minutes until they are golden brown. Remove the fritters with a slotted spoon and drain on paper towels. Serve cold, garnished with pineapple rings.

Serves: 6

Heat Scale: Medium

Note: This recipe requires advance preparation.

Buljol

The name of this Trinidadian salad of shredded salt fish comes from the French *brule*, meaning burnt, and *geule*, slang for mouth. Since it is served at room temperature, the burning is obviously the result of the Congo pepper. Traditionally, buljol is served for breakfast or a Sunday brunch in Trinidad.

8 ounces salt codfish (or substitute any cooked, flaky white fish fillet)	1 Congo pepper (or habanero), seeds and stem removed, chopped fine
1 large onion, chopped fine	Freshly ground black pepper
1 large tomato, chopped fine	3 tablespoons olive oil
1 seasoning pepper (or substitute a Yellow Wax Hot), seeds and stem removed, chopped fine	Lettuce leaves
	Sliced hardboiled eggs for garnish
	Sliced avocado for garnish

If using salt cod, place the fish in a bowl and pour boiling water over it. Allow it to sit for an hour, pour off the water, and repeat. Drain the fish, remove any skin or bones, and squeeze out all the water.

    Combine the fish with the onion, tomato, seasoning pepper, Congo pepper, black pepper, and the olive oil and mix well. Place this mixture on lettuce leaves and garnish with the eggs and avocado.

Serves: 4

Heat Scale: Hot

Hearts of Palm Salad with Dry Jerk Seasoning

We borrowed this excellent recipe from *Chile Pepper* food editor Nancy Gerlach. Hearts of palm are literally the heart of the tender shoots of the palm trees that are found throughout the Caribbean. Florida is the only place other than the Caribbean where these can be found fresh. However, good fortune has it that locating canned hearts of palm is not a problem—and your guests will never know!

	Dry Jerk Seasoning (recipe follows)	1	14-ounce can hearts of palm, drained, sliced
2	tablespoons vegetable oil	1	large tomato, sliced
	Juice of 1 lime		Lettuce

Whisk the seasoning, oil, and lime juice together.

Arrange the hearts of palm and tomato slices on the lettuce. Drizzle the dressing over the top and serve.

Serves: 2

Heat Scale: Mild

Dry Jerk Seasoning

½	teaspoon ground dry habanero chile	1	teaspoon ground cloves
1	tablespoon onion powder	½	teaspoon ground black pepper
1½	teaspoons ground allspice	½	teaspoon garlic powder
1½	teaspoons ground thyme	¼	teaspoon ground nutmeg
1	teaspoon ground cinnamon		

Combine all the ingredients.

Yield: 3 tablespoons

Heat Scale: Hot

Mango Fandango

Carmen Miranda would be jealous of this fruit extravaganza! Who wouldn't enjoy a tropical salad, with its juicy pineapple, fresh coconut, juicy mangoes, guava, bananas, and, of course, a hint of heat.

1	fresh pineapple, cut into chunks	2	ripe guavas, sliced
3	tablespoons rum	½	habanero, stem and seeds removed, diced
¼	cup brown sugar Juice of 1 lime	5	tablespoons grated fresh coconut meat
2	bananas, sliced	½	teaspoon freshly grated nutmeg
2	mangoes, sliced		

In a large nonreactive bowl, place the pineapple chunks, rum, and brown sugar. Mix well, cover, and chill in the refrigerator for 1 hour.

Remove the pineapple mixture from the refrigerator and add the lime juice, the rest of the fruit, and the habanero. Garnish with the grated coconut and nutmeg.

Serves: 4

Heat Scale: Hot

Cho-Cho Salad

This relative of the squash family goes by many names: cho-cho, chayote, tropical squash, and christophene. The fruit is pear-shaped and tastes very much like zucchini squash.

2	pounds christophenes (chayote squash)	1	clove garlic, crushed
	Water to cover	2	green onions, chopped (optional)
	Dash of salt	2	shallots, chopped
3	tablespoons corn or soy oil	½	teaspoon minced habanero chile
1	tablespoon white wine vinegar or distilled white vinegar		Freshly ground black pepper

Place the christophenes in a large saucepan filled with enough water to cover. Sprinkle with the salt, and boil until tender, about 20 minutes. When they are tender, remove them from the heat, drain, and set aside.

When the christophenes have cooled down, peel and halve them, discarding the seed and the skins. Cut the flesh into cubes and place them in a large mixing bowl.

In a small bowl, combine the oil, wine vinegar, garlic, green onions, shallots, habanero, and pepper to taste and mix well. Pour over the christophenes and chill before serving.

Serves: 4 to 6

Heat Scale: Medium

Chile–Conch Salad

This recipe was collected by *Chile Pepper* magazine's contributing photographer, Chel Beeson on one of his trips to the Bahamas. This very potent combination of conch, fresh vegetables, and habanero is usually served in a bowl.

2   goat peppers (habaneros), stems and seeds removed, minced

Meat of 6 conchs, pounded with a mallet until tender, then minced

3   small onions, chopped fine

4   stalks celery, chopped fine

2   bell peppers, chopped fine

8   ripe tomatoes, chopped fine

Juice of 3 limes

Juice of 1 pomelo (or substitute grapefruit)

Salt to taste

Combine all of the ingredients in a bowl and allow them to sit for at least 4 hours to blend the flavors. Divide the mixture into six or eight tall glasses and garnish with lime.

Serves: 6 to 8

Heat Scale: Hot

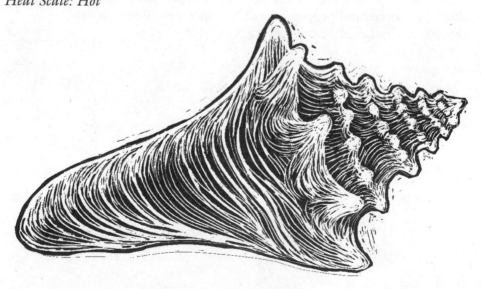

Quick Conch Salad

When you're in a hurry, this salad can't be beat. If you simply can't get your hands on some conch, chicken breast may be substituted.

3	conchs, pounded with a mallet until soft, cubed	1	tablespoon minced habanero chile
½	cup finely diced bell pepper	½	cup finely diced celery
½	cup finely diced cucumber	½	cup finely diced onion
¼	cup lime juice	2	fresh tomatoes, chopped
¼	cup pomelo (grapefruit) juice		Salt to taste

Mix all of the ingredients together and allow them to marinate in the refrigerator for at least 1 hour. Serve over greens, with chips.

Garnish with seashells for a beautiful display.

Serves: 6

Heat Scale: Hot

Curried Rice and Pigeon Pea Salad

Pigeon peas are similar to black-eyed peas and are also called *genteel* and *gung*. This African native bean, although less exotic than much of the island fare, is very low in fat and full of protein, fiber, and iron. Black-eyed peas may be substituted for the pigeon peas.

1 tablespoon margarine	1 pound thawed frozen or freshly cooked pigeon peas, drained
1 teaspoon West Indian Massala (see recipe, p. 20)	
¾ cup vegetable or chicken broth	¼ cup nonfat yogurt, plain
⅓ cup short-grain rice, uncooked	2 tablespoons cashews, toasted slivered
¼ cup celery, chopped	Salt and freshly ground black pepper to taste
2 tablespoons green onion, minced	
2 tablespoons chopped red bell pepper	1 ripe tomato cut into wedges
1 tablespoon freshly squeezed lime juice	1 hard-boiled egg, chopped
	Minced fresh cilantro for garnish

Melt the margarine in a large saucepan over medium high heat. Stir in the massala, then the broth. Bring the mixture to a boil, then reduce the heat to medium. Next, add the rice, and cover and simmer for 20 minutes until tender. Stir in the celery, green onions, bell pepper, and lime juice. Spoon the mixture into a storage container, and refrigerate until thoroughly chilled, about 2 hours.

Once the mixture is chilled, stir in the pigeon peas, yogurt, cashews, and seasonings. Spoon into serving bowls, arrange the tomato wedges and egg over salad, and garnish with the minced cilantro.

Serves: 4

Heat Scale: Medium Hot

Red Stripe Sweet Potatoes

Named after the famous Jamaican beer, this dish shows off the love of tubers in the Caribbean. Naturally, you're going to have to open a beer for this recipe, but what on earth do you do with what's left over in the bottle?

3   baked sweet potatoes

3   tablespoons Red Stripe Beer

2   ounces butter

2   tablespoons grated coconut

½   Scotch bonnet chile (or habanero), seeds and stem removed, minced

⅛   teaspoon cinnamon

Cut the potatoes in half and then scoop out the pulp, keeping the potato skin halves intact. Set the skins aside. In a large mixing bowl, crush the potato pulp with the beer and butter, then mix in the coconut and chile. Whip the potato mixture with an electric mixer for 2 minutes. Fill the potato skins with the mixture. Sprinkle the top of each potato with cinnamon. Heat the oven to 275 degrees and heat the potatoes through. Serve hot.

Serves: 6

Heat Scale: Medium

Banana Chips

Who says chips have to be bad for you? This healthy alternative to potato chips is a great way to introduce Caribbean food to kids. Oh heck—forget the kids! You'll like these, too.

6	green bananas peeled and sliced in ½-inch pieces	1	teaspoon salt
	Water to cover	1	teaspoon habanero powder
			Oil for deep frying

Place the banana slices in a large mixing bowl. Cover them with water and mix in the salt and the ground habanero. Soak the slices for 10 minutes. Next, drain the water and set aside. In a frying pan, heat the oil to 375 degrees. Deep-fry the slices until they are golden brown. Remove the chips with a slotted spoon and drain on paper towels.

Serves: 8

Heat Scale: Medium

Trotter Souse

There are very few things in the world that Melissa won't try. She thought pig's feet was one of them until she tried this dish in Barbados—and liked it! Pork stew meat may be substituted if you just don't have a foot fetish.

4	pounds pig's feet, cut into small pieces	1½	cups freshly squeezed lime juice
	Water	3	to 4 cups water
	Salt to taste	1	teaspoon salt
4	cloves garlic, minced	2	cucumbers, peeled and chopped
1	onion, sliced thin		
1	Congo pepper (habanero), seeds and stem removed, chopped fine	½	teaspoon freshly ground black pepper
			Watercress for garnish

Place the cut-up trotters in a pan, cover with salted water, and cook over medium heat until the meat is tender, about 2 hours. Remove the meat from the water, rinse in cold water, and drain.

Combine the meat with the remaining ingredients, except the watercress, and marinate for at least 6 hours (preferably overnight). Serve the marinated souse and the other ingredients cold in bowls, garnished with the watercress.

Serves: 8

Heat Scale: Hot

Frittering Away

"The fritter vocabulary of the Caribbean is immense, unprecedented in Europe and certainly in Spain, where the idea is mostly limited to desserts. But in the French islands one finds fritters based on taro, hearts of palm, chayote, breadfruit, pumpkin, black-eyed peas, minnows, crayfish, and, of course, salt cod. Jamaica calls its fritters, which are made from black-eyed peas (much like the West African original of these colonial fritters), *akkra*. On Curaçao, they call black-eyed pea fritters *calas*. Are these related to the New Orleans rice fritters of the same name? I bet they are. And then there are Trinidadian *phulouri*, split-pea fritters."

Raymond Sokolov

"Happy hour on any island would seem incomplete without the ubiquitous salt cod fritters. And ubiquitous they are. Salt cod fritters are enjoyed from one end of the Caribbean to the other. Jamaicans call them "stamp and go" (perhaps in reference to the speed with which they're eaten!); Spanish-speaking islanders affectionately refer to them as *bacalaitos* ("little codfish"). French West Indians enjoy them with rum punch, although they can't quite agree on the spelling—a*ccras, acras, achras, akkras, achrats,* and *acrats* are some of the versions I've seen. Bajans call them simply codfish balls and devour them by the dozens."

Steven Raichlen

Sopito to Sancoche:
Soups and Stews

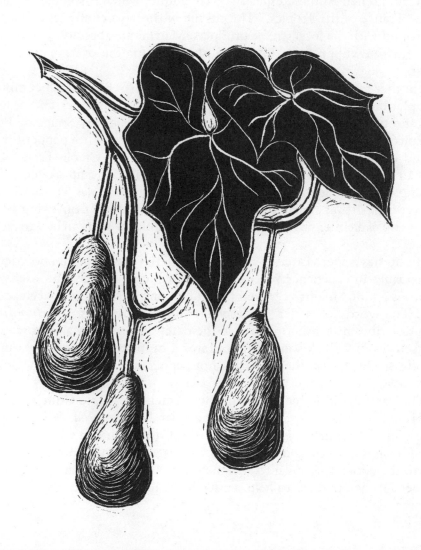

The soups and stews of the islands prove that a little meat can go a long way, provided they are accompanied by creative flavorings, hot peppers, and whatever vegetables happen to be plentiful. The first series of recipes centers around fish and shellfish. Sopito (Fish and Coconut Soup, p. 80) is a specialty of the Netherlands Antilles, and the soup is rich with fish, shrimp, and a touch of salted beef. Serve this dish with one of the breads from Chapter 8. Court Bouillon de Morue (Salt Cod in Court Bouillon, p. 82) is quite popular in the French Antilles, especially Martinique, which is sometimes nicknamed "France of the Tropics." The cuisine of this area combines its French background with the local Creole products. Martinique abounds with restaurants, and you will probably find this dish, or a variation of it, in a majority of them.

Another tasty soup is Bahamian Fish Chowder (p. 83), which combines green plantains, cinnamon, annatto, and fresh fish. It is quick and easy to make, and the short cooking time belies the taste it produces. Soupe de Poissons Épicé (Spicy Martinique Fish Soup, p. 84) is rich with hot peppers, fresh fish, and vegetables. The Martiniquan style of cooking is Creole–French and covers an extensive variety of dishes because the cooks are quite skilled at improvising. Even though this recipe calls for specific vegetables, cooks will use whatever is fresh and available at the time. This skill comes from living on an island—you can either be limited by what is available, or you can be extremely creative!

If you have ever visited the islands and have eaten conch chowder, it was probably an experience you have never forgotten. Conch Chowder with Tomatoes (p. 86) might very well have been one of those culinary experiences. The word "chowder" is derived from the French word *chaudiere*, which describes how fishermen made their stews from the sea. The word is also used for any thick soup that contains a number of coarsely chopped seafoods. In this recipe, the tomatoes, hot pepper, and allspice are the dominant flavors.

The last shellfish recipe is another conch creation, Conch Bisque (p. 88), and you might see the conch listed as lambie or *concha*, depending on where you are. Conch is eaten all over the Caribbean—raw in salads and cooked in stews, soups, and fritters. Conch is a shellfish that presents a challenge to the cook; it is similar to abalone, in that the meat is white and tough and needs to be pounded to help tenderize it. Take a heavy mallet, beat the living daylights out of the conch, and help release some built-up tension! The addition of the cream is what technically makes this dish a bisque.

Let's move on to two chicken stews that are both delicious and easy to prepare. Eastern Caribbean Chicken Stew (p. 90) includes ingredients that are probably in your cupboard right now; the big Caribbean difference lies in how these ingredients are used. The chicken is browned in a caramelized mixture of oil and sugar, which reflects the African method of cooking that was introduced to the Caribbean. This caramelizing gives a distinctive and unique flavor to West Indian dishes. The second chicken recipe is Guisado de Pollo con Arroz (Puerto Rican Chicken and Rice Stew, p. 92), which is a very traditional dish, with all of the ingredients at arm's reach: The oregano, hot pepper, and tomatoes add a real herbal tone. Even though this dish takes a little prior preparation, it is one that can be done ahead of time and served at a dinner party, where you can actually sit down, have a cooling drink, and visit with your guests before dinner is served.

Two lamb stew recipes are offered here, and the first one is incendiary! Lucy's Bequian Lamb Stew (p. 94) is extremely hot, although extremely tasty; however, Lucy claims it is not that hot. Peggy Barnes, who wrote about Lucy in *Chile Pepper*, recommends a lot of the Jamaican import, Red Stripe beer, to quench the flames. Trust Peggy—she's had Lucy's stew! Also, Peggy recommends that you serve this stew with a green salad and crusty bread.

The second lamb (or kid) stew is much tamer than Lucy's! Stoba di Cabrito (p. 96) is popular on the Lesser Antilles—Aruba, Curaçao, and Bonaire. The word *stoba* actually means a meat stew, and "kid" or young goat (*cabrito*) is generally used, but lamb can be substituted. Once again, the use of a small amount of salt beef harks back to the days of old. Another type of meat stew is Sancoche (p. 95), whose name derives from South American stews called *sancochos*. Another name for it is "plantation stew." The great Creole chef, Jean de Boissiere, noted: "This is the all-filling, midday meal of rich and poor alike on the plantations of Trinidad." Today it is still popular for a Saturday lunch in Trinidad and Tobago, with its rib-sticking vegetables and hot peppers. Another rich and filling soup is Spicy West Indian Oxtail Soup (p. 98). Some Jamaican cooks add cooked lima beans; Trinidadian cooks sometimes add dumplings to cook on top of this soup–stew dish. Because of the bony nature of oxtails, be sure to warn your diners!

We have included a recipe for Jamaican Pepper Pot Soup (p. 100) because of its widespread popularity throughout the Caribbean. As you might well expect, there are numerous permutations of this soup, including one that is called just "pepper pot" and uses cassareep, originating in Guyana and brought to the islands. The Arawaks discovered that if the poisonous juice of the cassava was boiled, it was then rendered into a harmless, thick substance that they called *cassareep*, which they added to the soup. A great legend has arisen surrounding pepper pot with cassareep: People claim that some pepper pot stews have continued cooking for years, if not generations, by the periodic additions of more ingredients and cassareep—the longest cooking one, according to legend, is over 100 years old.

However, one soup that is best served freshly made is Callaloo and Crab Soup (p. 99), which also has many variations. Connie and Arnold Krochmal say that "if there were an election to determine the West Indian universal dish, callaloo would win without a doubt." The constant ingredients are the callaloo (sometimes called dasheen, dachine, eddoe, taro, elephant ear, tannia, or yautia), hot peppers, and some type of salted meat—sometimes a salted pig's tail. The soup can be simple or extravagant with ingredients. Residents of Trinidad and Tobago believe that a woman can catch a husband by feeding him her best callaloo soup.

Another stew that might catch a man's heart (by way of his stomach) is Cuban Stew Bodaguita (p. 102). This stew is rich with meat, heat, and tropical vegetables, and is finished off with fresh lime juice and bananas—one more example of combining meat and fruit in the same dish, a common practice in the Caribbean. Many tropical vegetables are now available in grocery stores, specialty stores, and Latin American markets.

Another popular ingredient in West Indies dishes is peanuts, and a popular soup is Cream of Groundnut (p. 104). Actually, peanuts are a legume, not a nut. The term "groundnut" comes from the fact that after flowering, the plant bends down toward the dirt and buries its pods in the ground. Peanuts are a New World crop, taken by the Portuguese to Africa and introduced into the African diet. Africans were then transported as slaves to the Caribbean islands and, finding peanuts growing there, continued to cook with them in their own style. Peanuts are still a part of the African culinary traditions in the West Indies that continue to this day. Peanuts also have a place in Jamaican folk medicine; peanut root tonic is thought to increase virility.

The two soup recipes that follow are based on the pawpaw (papaya), a semitropical fruit that is eaten at all stages of its development: when it is green, it is cooked as a vegetable, and when it is ripe, it is eaten as a fruit. The seeds, which are usually thrown away, can also be made into a peppery salad dressing. A single seed can grow to a tree more than twenty feet high in only eighteen months. PawPaw Soup (p. 105) is rich, spicy, and unusual, through the creative use of some very common ingredients. Chilly Chile Papaya Soup (p. 106), a chilled fruit soup, is not too rich and can be served as a first course for a West Indies dinner. Sweet fruit soups are sometimes served as a dessert.

Pumpkin soup is another universal Caribbean dish. In Haiti, tradition states that it should be eaten on New Year's Day for good luck in the coming year. The recipe for Martinique Pumpkin Soup (p. 107) calls for a different kind of pumpkin than the one North Americans think of at Halloween time. West Indian pumpkin, or *calabaza*, can sometimes be found in Latin American markets. If it is not available, the best substitutes are Hubbard squash, butternut, or acorn squash. The West Indies pumpkin is also used in stews and in baking. You'll find this recipe convenient as well: It can be made ahead of time and frozen.

Along with the pumpkin, another versatile vegetable is the breadfruit, a South Pacific native brought to the islands by Captain Bligh of *Bounty* fame. It is a staple food in many West Indies countries, and it can be baked, boiled, or fried according to its ripeness. We've included two versions of breadfruit soup here—one hot and one chilled. Coconut and Scotch Bonnet Breadfruit Soup (p. 108) is smooth, rich, and hot all at the same time. Breadfruit Vichyssoise (p. 110) contains less coconut milk than the previous recipe, but is no less delicious with its zip of fresh nutmeg, cinnamon, and habanero peppers.

A native to the tropics and the subtropics, the avocado is also used in many dishes and is very popular. It's the avocado that gives Chilled Guaca–Chile Soup (p. 112) its rich, buttery taste and texture. Don't stint on the habanero hot sauce. The final recipe, Down Island Gazpacho (p. 113), combines the best of the Caribbean—fruits, vegetables, and hot peppers—and makes a dazzling first course. The chill of the soup is offset by the bite of Scotch bonnet pepper.

Sopito (Fish and Coconut Soup)

This soup, known as *sopito* in the Netherlands Antilles, has many variations. Some cooks add salted beef and/or salted cod, shrimp, cumin, fresh mint...and the list goes on. However, all cooks will agree on a few ingredients: the addition of at least 1 pound of fresh fish, some coconut milk, and hot peppers.

2	onions, 1 sliced and 1 chopped	¼	pound salted beef, diced into cubes
1	clove garlic, chopped		
1	bay leaf	2	whole cloves
2	stalks celery, chopped	1	cup Coconut Milk (see recipe, p. 14)
1	leek, chopped		
2	carrots, chopped	2	tablespoons cornmeal
1	tablespoon whole white peppercorns	1	cup whole shrimp, unshelled but washed
1	teaspoon chopped fresh basil	¼	teaspoon freshly grated nutmeg
½	teaspoon cumin seeds		Salt to taste
1	large habanero chile, seeds and stem removed, minced		Chopped fresh basil for garnish
5	cups cold water		
1	pound fresh, whole fish, cleaned and scaled		

Put the sliced onion, garlic, bay leaf, celery, leek, carrots, white peppercorns, basil, cumin, habanero pepper, and cold water in a large heavy casserole. Bring the mixture to a boil, lower the heat, cover, and simmer for 25 minutes.

Add the fresh fish to the simmering mixture and cook gently for 12 to 15 minutes, until the fish flakes easily.

Remove the casserole from the heat. Carefully remove the fish from the cooking liquid and skin and debone the fish, cutting it into 1-inch pieces. Reserve the fish.

Using a filter or fine cheesecloth, strain the cooking liquid into a clean soup pot and bring the stock to a boil. Add the chopped onion, salted beef, cloves, and coconut milk. Lower the heat, cover, and simmer for 40 to 50 minutes, or until the beef is tender.

Sprinkle 1 tablespoon of the cornmeal into the pot, stirring constantly for 1 minute. If the soup doesn't start to thicken, add 1 more tablespoon. Add the reserved fish, shrimp, and nutmeg, and cook it over low heat for 3 to 5 minutes, or until the shrimp is cooked. Salt to taste.

Serve with the fresh basil sprinkled on top.

Serves: 6

Heat Scale: Medium

A Feast in Guadeloupe

"After mass, the cooks demonstrated why fine cuisine is so deeply rooted in the culture, everyday life and even religious traditions of this most food-conscious of all Caribbean islands. In a nearby schoolyard, each cook brought a platter holding one of her specialties: tasty tidbits like codfish fritters and boudin Creole (Creole blood sausage) that are served as hors d'oeuvres along with either the traditional *'ti* (from the French word *petit*) punch or champagne; main courses featuring lobster, red snapper, baked ham in a rum-and-brown sugar glaze or roast chicken in curry sauce."

Jessica B. Harris

Court Bouillon de Morue (Salt Cod in Court Bouillon)

This exotic-sounding dish tastes every bit as exotic as its name. Even though fresh fish abounds in the Caribbean, the use of salt cod is still a favorite; it is a holdover from the days when fish had to be salted to be transported. Today, in markets, you can see slabs of salt cod, sometimes brought in from Canada. This dish is popular in the French Antilles, especially Martinique.

2   pounds salt cod
3   tablespoons olive oil or butter
3   cloves garlic, minced
2   cups onions, diced
4   scallions, chopped
3   tomatoes, peeled and chopped
1   teaspoon thyme

2   teaspoons chopped fresh parsley
1   habanero chile, stem and seeds removed, minced
Hot water to cover the mixture
Fresh slices of lime to garnish

Soak the salt cod all day (eight hours) in cold water in the refrigerator; change the water twice. Change the water a third time, and soak for two more hours. Drain and pick out the bones.

In a large, heavy skillet, heat the oil and add the garlic, onions, and scallions and sauté for 3 minutes. Add the tomatoes, thyme, parsley, habanero chile, and the pieces of desalted cod.

Add just enough hot water to cover the mixture; bring the mixture to a slow boil, then reduce the heat to a simmer and cook, uncovered, for about 15 minutes or until most of the liquid has evaporated. Serve garnished with the fresh lime slices.

Serves: 5 to 6

Heat Scale: Medium to Hot

Note: This recipe requires advanced preparation.

Bahamian Fish Chowder

The unusual ingredients in this recipe all work together to produce a pungent, spicy chowder that is a delight to the palate. The chowder is rich enough to serve as a main course for a luncheon or as a light entree for dinner, with crunchy garlic bread and a green salad.

2	tablespoons olive oil	½	teaspoon freshly ground cinnamon
4	cloves garlic, chopped		
2½	teaspoons Puerto Rican Sofrito (p. 29)	½	teaspoon ground annatto seed
1	fresh habanero pepper, seeds amd stem removed, chopped	2	pounds fish fillets (grouper, snapper, pompano)
1	cup onion, chopped	3	cups fish stock
½	cup celery, chopped	2	cups water
¾	cup green plantains, peeled and diced	1	cup milk
1	cup potato, diced		Salt and pepper to taste
			Chopped scallions for garnish

Heat the olive oil in a large, heavy casserole pot and add the garlic, sofrito paste, habanero pepper, onion, celery, plantains, and potato and sauté for 5 minutes over medium heat, stirring, until the onions start to wilt.

Then add the cinnamon, annatto, fillets, stock, water, and milk and stir gently to mix. Bring the mixture to a light boil, reduce the heat to a simmer, and simmer for 15 minutes, or until the fish flakes easily with a fork. Add salt and pepper to taste.

Serve the soup in warmed bowls and garnish with the chopped scallions.

Serves: 6

Heat Scale: Medium

Soupe de Poissons Épicé (Spicy Martinique Fish Soup)

Travel writers often refer to Martinique as being French first and Caribbean second. The style of cooking is Creole–French and covers an extensive variety of dishes. Kitchens are stocked with fresh herbs, garlic, chile peppers, and tomatoes, all of which appear in this recipe. This recipe "gets a lot of stuff thrown into the pot," so don't let the long list prevent you from making this soup—you probably have the majority of ingredients in your kitchen right now!

Marinated Fish

2   to 4 pounds of fish (snapper or grouper), cleaned, filleted, and sliced; reserve head

    Juice of 2 fresh lemons

2   cloves garlic, minced

2   tablespoons habanero chile, minced

1   teaspoon salt

1   tablespoon olive oil

1   teaspoon oregano

Fish Head Stock

1   fish head

7   cups water

1   teaspoon salt

4   cloves garlic, chopped

1   bay leaf

1   teaspoon thyme

6   whole black peppercorns

1   habanero chile, seeds and stem removed, chopped

Vegetables

3   tablespoons vegetable oil

2   tablespoons olive oil

2   leeks, white part only, chopped

4   scallions, chopped

2   cups onion, chopped

1   cup carrots, sliced

1   cup potatoes, cubed

½   cup turnips, cubed

4   tomatoes, peeled and chopped

    Salt and pepper to taste

2   cups crisp croutons for garnish

Place the fish pieces in a shallow glass pan and toss with the lemon juice, garlic, habanero, salt, olive oil, and oregano. Refrigerate for 1 hour.

Place the washed fish head in a heavy casserole with the water, salt, garlic, bay leaf, thyme, whole peppercorns, and the chopped habanero. Bring the mixture to a boil, then reduce the heat to a simmer, cover, and simmer for 1 hour.

Heat the oils in a heavy, large skillet and sauté the leeks, scallions, onion, carrots, potatoes, and turnips for 3 to 4 minutes. Place the sautéed mixture in a heavy casserole.

Strain the cooked fish head stock into the casserole containing the sautéed vegetables. Bring the mixture to a boil, reduce the heat to a simmer, cover, and simmer for 30 minutes.

Add the chopped tomatoes and the marinated fish pieces and cook slowly for an additional 15 to 20 minutes, until the fish is cooked and tender. Add salt and pepper to taste.

Serve the soup very hot, topped with crisp croutons.

Serves: 6

Heat Scale: Medium to Hot

Conch Chowder with Tomatoes

This chowder is popular on Saint Kitts and Nevis. The lime juice is used to "cook" the conch partially, which is very tough and needs to be thoroughly pounded and marinated before cooking. Some traditional Nevis cooks maintain that lots of ground black pepper should be used, and that peas should be added to the chowder before it is done.

2	pounds conch meat	2	tablespoons tomato paste
½	cup fresh lime juice	¼	teaspoon freshly ground allspice
	Water to cover		
1	teaspoon salt	2	bay leaves
6	cups water	1	teaspoon thyme
2	cups fresh tomatoes, peeled and diced	1	teaspoon oregano
1½	cups onion, chopped	¼	to ½ teaspoon freshly ground black pepper
½	cup celery, chopped	3	tablespoons dry sherry
2	teaspoons paprika		
1	whole fresh red habanero chile		

Pound the conch meat thoroughly with a mallet. Place the meat in a glass pan and pour the lime juice over it. Marinate the meat for 1 hour in the refrigerator.

Place the marinated conch in a large heavy casserole, cover with water, add the salt, and bring to a boil and cook for 5 minutes over medium heat. Remove the casserole from the heat and allow it to cool. Remove the conch and cut it into ½-inch pieces.

Discard the cooking water.

Rinse out the cooking pot and add the 6 cups of fresh water and bring that to a boil. Add the conch and the remaining ingredients (except the sherry) and bring the mixture to a boil, then reduce the heat, cover, and simmer over low heat for 1 hour, or until the conch is tender.

At the end of the cooking time, add the sherry and cook for 10 minutes more. Remove the whole habanero pepper and serve the soup hot.

Serves: 6

Heat Scale: Medium

Conch Bisque

A very popular dish in the Turks and Caicos, this conch bisque lacks the tomatoes so popular in most other conch dishes. The flavor comes from heavily pounded conchs, good white wine, thyme, and hot peppers. Since the soup tends to be rather rich, we suggest serving it as a light lunch or dinner entree.

6	conchs, cleaned, pounded with a heavy mallet to flatten, and diced into ½-inch pieces	2	cloves garlic, minced
5	cups water	2	teaspoons fresh thyme or 1 teaspoon dried thyme
1	cup dry white wine, plus more to be used for cooking liquid	2	medium potatoes, peeled and diced into ½-inch cubes
2	tablespoons butter and 2 tablespoons vegetable oil (or use all vegetable oil)	1	cup carrots, diced
		1	large habanero chile, stem and seeds removed, minced
1	cup onions, chopped	3	tablespoons chives, chopped
½	cup green bell pepper, chopped	1	cup half-and-half cream
1	cup celery, chopped		Salt and pepper to taste

Place the pounded conch, water, and 1 cup of wine in a heavy soup pot and bring the mixture to a hard boil. Lower the heat so the liquid is at a light rolling boil and boil for 45 minutes. Then, remove the mixture from the heat and strain and measure the liquid; add more white wine to make 6 cups of liquid and reserve the conch meat.

Wash out the soup pot and pour the 6 cups of liquid back into the pot and bring the liquid to a boil.

While the conch mixture is cooking, heat the oil/butter mixture in a heavy skillet and sauté the onions, bell pepper, celery, and garlic over low heat for 1 minute. Add the thyme and stir it through the sauté.

Add the sautéed mixture to the boiling conch liquid, and add the potatoes, carrots, habanero chile, chives, and the conch meat. Bring the mixture back to a boil, lower the heat, and simmer for 1 hour.

Remove the pot from the heat and let it cool slightly. Stir in the cream and reheat the soup, taking care not to let it boil. Salt and pepper to taste.

Serves: 6 to 8

Heat Scale: Medium to Hot

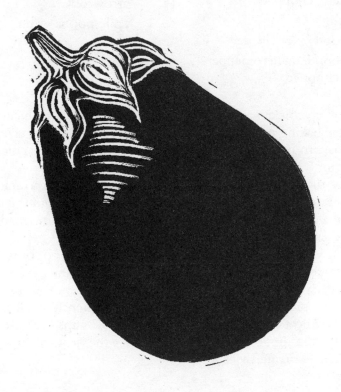

Eastern Caribbean Chicken Stew

This stew is popular all over the eastern Caribbean, particularly in Trinidad and Barbados. The herbs added to this soup should be very fresh and of high quality. If you ever eat this stew in Trinidad, it is likely that the herbs were grown in Maraval, where Paramin Village is located. Maraval's excellent drainage, and good distribution of rain and sun, account for the high quality of its herbs.

3	to 4 pounds of chicken, cut up	1	teaspoon salt
4	garlic cloves, minced	¼	cup corn oil
¾	cup chopped mixed fresh herbs (chives, thyme, oregano, and parsley)	2	tablespoons brown sugar
		2	cups chicken stock or water
¼	cup celery, chopped	2	teaspoons cornstarch or arrowroot
¼	cup rum	2	tablespoons water
1	tablespoon cider vinegar		
1	tablespoon habanero pepper, freshly chopped		

Wash the cut-up chicken and pat off excess water. Place the chicken in a large, shallow baking pan, and sprinkle the garlic, fresh herbs, celery, rum, vinegar, habanero pepper, and salt over the top. Marinate the chicken in the refrigerator for 2 hours.

Remove the chicken from the refrigerator, and allow it to stand at room temperature for 30 minutes. Remove the chicken from the marinade and put it in a colander over the baking pan, to catch any marinade that drips off. Reserve the marinade.

Heat the oil to a high temperature in a large, heavy pot or skillet, add the brown sugar, and stir the sugar until it starts to caramelize.

When the sugar is a rich, brown color, reduce the heat to medium and add the chicken pieces, a few at a time, turning frequently so all the sides brown evenly. Add the reserved marinade and the 2 cups of chicken stock or water. Stir the mixture, bring it to a boil, reduce the heat, cover, and simmer for 45 minutes—stirring twice.

Dissolve the cornstarch in the water, push the chicken to one side in the pan, and stir the cornstarch mixture into the chicken stock until it thickens. Pour the thickened sauce over the chicken and serve the chicken hot.

Serves: 4 to 6

Heat Scale: Medium

Note: This recipe requires advance preparation.

Guisado de Pollo con Arroz (Puerto Rican Chicken and Rice Stew)

Even though chicken and rice is a familiar theme throughout Caribbean cooking, each cook strives to make this a special dish—one that stands out from the rest—by adding secret ingredients. The delicious elements of this stew are a jazz of oregano, the fresh habanero chile, and the sprinkling of Parmesan cheese.

3	pounds chicken, cut into 8 pieces, washed, and patted dry	4	tomatoes, skinned, deseeded, and chopped
2	cloves garlic, minced	1½	cups long-grain rice
1	teaspoon oregano	7	cups chicken stock
½	teaspoon salt	¼	teaspoon freshly ground black pepper
3	tablespoons butter or olive oil	2	cups frozen peas
1	cup onion, diced	3	tablespoons grated Parmesan cheese
1	fresh habanero pepper, seeds and stem removed, minced		

In a large bowl, mix the garlic, oregano, and salt together; add the chicken pieces and toss the mixture. Marinate in the refrigerator for 1 hour.

Heat the butter or olive oil in a large, heavy skillet and brown the chicken pieces. Push the browned chicken pieces to one side of the skillet; add the onion and pepper and sauté for 3 minutes, until the onion is soft.

Mix in the chopped tomatoes and toss the mixture in the skillet. Reduce the heat to a simmer, cover, and simmer for 25 minutes.

Move the chicken to a platter and allow it to cool slightly. When it has cooled down, remove the meat from the bones and set aside.

Add the rice, chicken stock, and the black pepper to the skillet and bring the mixture to a boil. Reduce the heat to a simmer, cover, and cook the rice for 20 minutes. Then add the chicken pieces, the peas, and the Parmesan cheese. Simmer for 4 minutes until the chicken is heated through.

Serves: 5 to 6

Heat Scale: Medium

Lucy's Bequian Lamb Stew

This recipe is from Peggy Barne's friend on Bequia. "As far as Lucy is concerned, this peppery stew is 'not so very hot,'" says Peggy, who wrote about Lucy's "Caribbean Kitchens" in *Chile Pepper*. But she concluded: "I say, it creates enough heat to melt the polar icecap!"

2	pounds lamb, cut into ½-inch cubes	2	bay leaves
		¼	cup tomato paste
1½	cups red wine	4	habanero chiles, stems and seeds removed, coarsely chopped
3	tablespoons peanut oil		
4	cloves garlic, finely chopped		
1	large onion, coarsely chopped		Salt to taste

Marinate the lamb in wine for 3 hours. Remove the lamb and reserve the wine.

In a large skillet, heat the oil over medium heat. Add the lamb and sauté until lightly browned on all sides. Add the garlic and onion and sauté until the onion is translucent. Lower the heat and add the bay leaves, tomato paste, wine, habaneros, and salt.

Simmer until the lamb is tender, about 30 minutes. Remove the bay leaves and serve.

Serves: 4

Heat Scale: Extremely Hot

Sancoche

Depending on the cook, this rather amazing stew from the eastern Caribbean, particularly Trinidad and Barbados, can contain up to nine starchy ingredients, including yams, tannia, eddoes, taro, cassava, bananas, potatoes, pumpkin, and plantains. But since many of these ingredients are both hard to find and have similar tastes, we have adjusted the recipe somewhat.

½	pound corned beef, cut into 1-inch cubes	1	cup Coconut Cream (p. 14)
1	pound beef, cut into 1-inch cubes	1	pound sweet potatoes or yams, peeled and cut into 1-inch cubes
3	tablespoons vegetable oil	2	green plantains, peeled and thickly sliced
2	large onions, chopped		
2	quarts beef stock	2	pounds potatoes, peeled and cut into 1-inch cubes
1	tablespoon Trinidad Herb Seasoning Paste (p. 24)	1	Congo pepper (habanero), left whole
1	cup yellow split peas (or substitute black-eyed peas)		Salt and pepper to taste

Sauté the corned beef and the other beef cubes in the oil until slightly browned, then add the onions and sauté for 5 minutes, stirring occasionally. Add the beef stock, the herb seasoning, and the split peas; cover, and simmer for 1 hour.

Add the remaining ingredients, cover, and simmer until the potatoes are tender, about 30 minutes. Add more water if necessary.

Remove the Congo pepper, add salt and pepper to taste, and serve hot with one of the breads from Chapter 8.

Serves: 6 to 8

Heat Scale: Medium

Stoba di Cabrito (Curaçao-Style Lamb or Kid Stew)

This stew recipe includes a small amount of salted beef, another holdover from "the old days" when that was the only way to ship beef, and it is an ingredient found in almost all the recipes for this stew. The usual meat for the *stoba* is kid (goat or *cabrito*), but we have substituted lamb. If you have a source for goat, try it because it is delicious. Accompany this dish with Papaya Berde (p. 255). The annatto oil is commonly called *ruku*.

6   ounces salt beef, covered with water and soaked overnight in the refrigerator

4   cups fresh water

3   tablespoons vegetable oil

2   pounds young kid (*cabrito*) or lamb, cut into ½-inch cubes

2   cups onion, diced

2   garlic cloves, minced

1   medium green pepper, seeded and chopped

1   habanero chile, stem and seeds removed, minced

2   cups tomatoes, peeled and diced

1   teaspoon sugar

1   tablespoon fresh lime juice

¼   teaspoon freshly ground nutmeg

2   tablespoons annatto oil (see Note)

3   potatoes, peeled and cut into 1-inch cubes

Ruku or Annatto Oil

½   teaspoon annatto seed

1   cup vegetable oil (see Note)

Drain the soaked beef and place it in a heavy casserole with the 4 cups of water. Bring the mixture to a boil, reduce the heat to a simmer, cover, and cook for 1 hour. Remove the beef from the pot, cube, and reserve; strain the broth and reserve.

Heat the vegetable oil in the heavy casserole, add the lamb, and brown it. Add the onion, garlic, green pepper, and habanero pepper and sauté the mixture until the onion is wilted, about 3 to 4 minutes.

Stir in the tomatoes, sugar, lime juice, nutmeg, annatto oil, and the reserved cubed beef and simmer the mixture for 20 minutes.

Add the reserved beef stock and the potatoes and bring the mixture to a boil; reduce the heat and simmer for 30 minutes or until the potatoes are tender.

Serves: 6

Heat Scale: Mild

Note: To prepare the annatto oil: Heat the seeds and the oil in a heavy, small saucepan until the oil is hot. Remove the pan from the heat and let it stand until the oil absorbs the deep orange color of the seeds. Discard the seeds and reserve the oil. Yield: 1 cup.

Or, Have a Food Fight with It

A Caribbean natural pepper remedy supposedly will spice up your love life! In Guadeloupe, where the *chinense* species is called *le derrière de Madame Jacques*, that pepper is combined with crushed peanuts, cinnamon sticks, nutmeg, vanilla beans packed in brandy, and an island liqueur called Creme de Banana to make an aphrodisiac. We assume it's taken internally.

Spicy West Indian Oxtail Soup

We had one version of this dish in Trinidad, and it was rich and delicious. This particular recipe is actually a cross between a soup and a stew. If you cook down the liquids a little, then we guess it would qualify as a stew. Oxtail is very tasty, although very bony, and it is actually from a cow rather than an ox. This dish needs long, slow cooking to tenderize the meat and meld the flavorings.

2 tablespoons vegetable oil

3 pounds oxtail, washed, dried, and cut into 2-inch sections

2 onions, chopped

3 cloves garlic, minced

1 teaspoon dried thyme

3 carrots, sliced into ½-inch sections

5 cups water

5 cups beef stock

2 large tomatoes, peeled, seeded, and coarsely chopped

2 habanero chiles, seeds and stems removed, minced

2 cups potatoes, cut into ½-inch cubes

1 cup yam, cut into ½-inch cubes

Salt and pepper to taste

Heat the vegetable oil in a large, heavy casserole and, when it is hot, add the oxtails and stir to brown them a little. Then add the onions and garlic and sauté for 2 minutes, until the onion starts to wilt. Add the thyme, carrots, water, beef stock, tomatoes, and habanero peppers. Bring the mixture to a boil, reduce the heat to a simmer, cover, and cook for 2½ hours. Stir it once in a while, until the meat is tender and falling off the bones. Add more water if the level gets too low.

Add the potatoes, yams, and salt and pepper to taste. Simmer for an additional 15 minutes, or until the vegetables are tender.

Serve the soup very hot in large bowls.

Serves: 6 to 8

Heat Scale: Hot

Callaloo and Crab Soup

We ate this soup at every opportunity in order to sample its multiple variations, and even dined on it during our final dinner in Trinidad; it was the only thing that cheered us up as we thought about leaving the country. This recipe is a variation featuring crabmeat, a common and tasty addition.

2	tablespoons butter		1	cup sliced okra
1	medium onion, diced		1	teaspoon dried thyme
½	cup celery, chopped		¼	teaspoon freshly ground black pepper
1	clove garlic, minced			
1	quart chicken stock		1	Congo pepper (habanero), seeds and stem removed, minced
1	cup Coconut Milk (p. 14)			
½	pound smoked ham, diced, or 1 small ham hock		1	pound cooked crabmeat, chopped
2½	cups washed, coarsely chopped, firmly packed callaloo (dasheen), or substitute spinach leaves		1	tablespoon butter (optional)
				Salt to taste

Heat the butter in a large saucepan and sauté the onion, celery, and garlic for 2 or 3 minutes. Add the chicken stock, coconut milk, and ham and bring to a boil. Add the callaloo or spinach, the okra, thyme, black pepper, and the Congo pepper.

Reduce the heat to a simmer and cook, covered, for about 50 minutes, stirring occasionally, until the callaloo is thoroughly cooked.

Whisk the soup until very smooth, or purée it in small batches in a blender. Add the crabmeat and heat thoroughly. Add the butter, swizzled over the top, and taste for salt.

Serves: 8 to 10

Heat Scale: Medium

Jamaican Pepper Pot Soup

Variations of this recipe abound throughout the Caribbean. If you talk to a dozen people, you'll get a dozen different recipes, with each person claiming theirs is the way to create the perfect Pepper Pot Soup! We present to you a rather basic recipe, utilizing the ingredients that cooks will agree on; however, feel free to experiment. No matter what variation you try, it will always be good, hot, and satisfying.

2	cups onion, chopped	½	pound yams, peeled and diced into ½-inch cubes
½	pound salt pork, rind removed and diced; or 1 salted pig's tail	1	large fresh Scotch bonnet (or habanero), stem and seeds removed, and minced
2	garlic cloves, minced	2	tablespoons vegetable oil
1	teaspoon thyme	12	small okras, washed and sliced
7	cups water		
1	pound callaloo (or spinach), washed and chopped	1½	cups Coconut Milk (see recipe, p. 14)
½	pound coco (eddoe), or substitute white potatoes, peeled and diced into ½-inch cubes	1	cup cooked, chopped shrimp Salt and pepper to taste

Place the onion, salt pork, garlic, thyme, and water into a large, heavy soup pot or casserole, bring the mixture to a boil, skim away any froth that rises to the surface in the first 4 to 5 minutes of boiling, then reduce the heat to a simmer, cover, and cook for 1 hour.

Add the callaloo, coco, yams, and Scotch bonnet pepper to the soup, bring back to a boil, reduce the heat to a simmer, cover, and cook for another 45 minutes.

Heat the vegetable oil in a skillet and sauté the sliced okra until they are lightly browned, about 2 minutes, and then add them to the soup; simmer the soup for 5 more minutes, or until the okra is tender.

Stir the coconut milk and the shrimp into the soup and let it simmer 5 minutes, stirring occasionally.

Serve the soup in heated bowls.

Serves: 8

Heat Scale: Medium to Hot

Colorfully Named Jamaican Dishes

"Yet so many sojourners in the Jamaican island paradise are *deprived*. Many who have come not only once but several times never have an opportunity to know about ackees. Nobody bothers to introduce them to *Solomon Gundy* or to *Stamp and Go* (better known among the islanders as Stamps), or to *Stand and Rock* or *Dip-And-Fall-Back*. Year after year, some people return yet nobody tells them how a green banana should be dipped into a *Mackerel Run-Down*. Perhaps they never even hear about a *Run-Down*. Or *Firestick Coffee*. Or the big, gingery cookies called *Bullas* (an African word). How sad!"

Poppy Cannon

Cuban Stew Bodaguita

This recipe comes from R. Bruce Macdonald, who visited Cuba for *Chile Pepper*. The Bodaguita del Medio is the restaurant and bar made famous by Ernest Hemingway. Popular with both locals and tourists, the restaurant has resisted growing larger and still provides very traditional dishes such as this one.

½ pound pork, cubed	1 small eggplant, cubed
½ pound beef, cubed	½ cup whole-kernel corn
6 slices bacon, chopped	1 cup potato, cubed
Water	1 habanero chile, stem and
2 medium onions, chopped	seeds removed, chopped
4 cloves garlic, minced	¼ teaspoon saffron
¼ cup olive oil	¼ cup lime juice
1 sweet potato, peeled and cubed	2 small bananas, sliced
1 cup yuca, cubed (see Note)	Freshly ground black pepper
1 cup cubed chayote, or	White pepper
substitute zucchini (see Note)	Chopped parsley for garnish

Cover the pork, beef, and bacon with water and bring to a boil. Reduce the heat and simmer for 20 minutes, skimming off any foam that rises.

Sauté the onions and garlic in the oil until soft. Add to the meat. Add the sweet potato, yuca, chayote, eggplant, corn, and potato to the pot and simmer for 1 hour or until the vegetables are soft, adding more water if necessary.

Add the habanero to the pot.

Dissolve the saffron in the lime juice and add to the stew; then add the bananas and the black and white pepper and simmer for an additional 15 to 20 minutes.

Garnish with the parsley and serve.

Serves: 6 to 8

Heat Scale: Medium

Note: Available at natural foods supermarkets or Latin markets.

Island Haute

"Hilton's executive chef Lindell Williams, a Barbados native, is working to create an à la carte menu from Barbadian food products and dishes, adapting them to the American palate. At dinner one evening in the hotel's Fort Charles Grill, I sampled a delectable crisp sautéed flying fish stuffed with finely chopped local spinach and served with a butter–lime–orange sauce. The menu also offered a roasted Cornish game hen with a sauce of reduced cream and demi-glacé with fresh ginger; breadfruit vichyssoise; kingfish mousse poached in spinach leaves and napped with beurre blanc based on fresh lime juice; and a veritable rainbow of fresh tropical fruit sorbets."

Shirley Slater

Cream of Groundnut Soup

Peanuts are a popular ingredient in many West Indies dishes and are included here in a rather interesting manner—peanut butter in a soup. You'll find this soup all over the Caribbean, especially in Saint Kitts. The hot peppers and fresh ginger make it crunchy, spicy, and satisfying.

3	tablespoons unsalted sweet butter	1	teaspoon fresh ginger, grated
½	cup onion, minced	1	tablespoon brown sugar
3	tablespoons flour	1	tablespoon fresh lime juice
2	cups milk		
2	cups chicken stock	6	slices bacon, cooked to crisp, drained, crumbled for garnish
1	tablespoon habanero chile, minced	2	scallions, the white and some of the green, chopped for garnish
¾	cup crunchy peanut butter		

Melt the butter in a heavy casserole pot over a low heat. Add the onion and sauté for 30 seconds. Then sprinkle the flour over the onion–butter sauté and stir and cook the mixture until it is smooth, about 1 minute—taking care not to burn the butter.

Add the milk, all at once, and, using a whisk, stir the mixture until it is thick and smooth, about 2 to 3 minutes.

Then add the chicken stock, habanero, peanut butter, ginger, brown sugar, and lime juice. Heat the mixture, just barely to the boiling point, reduce the heat to low, cover, and simmer for 10 to 15 minutes.

Serve hot, garnished with the bacon and scallions.

Serves: 4

Heat Scale: Medium to Hot

PawPaw Soup

Popular in the Bahamas, this thick, creamy, spicy soup is served hot and is an unusual addition to any West Indies meal. Locals refer to habanero peppers as "goat peppers." No matter what they are called, they are always very hot! What's most important when making this soup is to find the perfect papaya—you need one that is slightly past the green stage, but not yet ripe.

1	tablespoon butter	2	tablespoons parsley, chopped
1	tablespoon vegetable oil	½	teaspoon salt
1	medium onion, sliced	¼	teaspoon freshly ground white pepper
1	14- to 16-ounce papaya, just slightly past the green stage, peeled, seeded, and thinly sliced	⅛	teaspoon freshly ground nutmeg
2	tablespoons goat pepper (or habanero), minced	3	cups cold milk
3	cups water	1	tablespoon arrowroot

In a small, heavy casserole pot, melt the butter, add the oil and onion, and lightly sauté for 1 minute. Add the papaya, goat pepper, water, parsley, salt, and white pepper. Bring the mixture to a hard boil, reduce the heat to a slight rolling boil, cover, and cook for 45 to 60 minutes, until the papaya is soft.

Pour the cooked mixture through a sieve into a clean pot, and, using a wooden spoon, press the solids through the sieve into the liquid.

Heat the soup and add the nutmeg.

Whisk the cold milk and the arrowroot together until the mixture is smooth. Add the mixture slowly to the heating soup, stirring constantly. Cook for 10 to 15 minutes over low heat, stirring several times, and do not allow the soup to boil. Serve hot.

Serves: 4

Heat Scale: Medium

Chilly Chile Papaya Soup

The abundance of fresh fruit in the Caribbean inspired us to create this unique recipe. The soup has some interesting flavors; the habanero chile is tempered by the addition of a little honey, and the yogurt smooths out the spiciness of the ginger beer. Serve it as a first course with a dinner of spicy grilled fish.

2	12-ounce ripe papayas, peeled and cut into chunks	2	tablespoons honey
½	cup unflavored yogurt	¾	cup chilled ginger ale
½	small habanero chile, seeds and stem removed	¼	cup chilled ginger beer
3	tablespoons fresh lime juice		Lime slices for garnish

Purée the papaya, yogurt, habanero pepper, lime juice, and honey in a blender or food processor until the mixture is smooth. Add enough of the ginger ale and the ginger beer to thin the mixture to a soup consistency.

   Refrigerate for at least 2 hours and serve in chilled, small soup bowls. Garnish with the lime slices.

Serves: 4

Heat Scale: Medium

Martinique Pumpkin Soup

This recipe comes from Peggy Barnes, who has traveled extensively in the Caribbean on her sailboat, stopping at some very interesting places! She says that most of the pumpkins that are served throughout the Caribbean are actually a large variety of squash, so Hubbard or other winter squashes stand in well for their island cousins. In this version of pumpkin soup from Martinique, there's yet another substitution: Chorizo sausage replaces fiery French *saucissons*.

1	chorizo sausage (about ¼ pound), or other hot sausage, casing removed, crumbled
1	large onion, coarsely chopped
1	stalk celery, coarsely chopped
1	quart chicken broth
2½	pounds Hubbard or banana squash, peeled, seeded, cut into ½-inch cubes (about 6 cups)
2	large carrots, peeled and coarsely chopped
1–2	tablespoons yellow or orange West Indies habanero hot sauce, such as Matouk's or one in Chapter 2
½	cup light cream (optional)
2	tablespoons butter (optional) Salt and ground white pepper

In a large, heavy saucepan, sauté the sausage for 1 to 2 minutes. Add the onion and celery and cook until the onions are translucent. Add the broth, squash, and carrots. Cover and simmer until the squash is tender. Remove from heat, cool slightly, then purée in small batches in a blender.

Return the soup to the saucepan, add the hot sauce, and reheat. If desired, add the cream and butter. Add salt and white pepper to taste and serve.

Serves: 6

Heat Scale: Mild

Note: This soup may be made ahead and frozen, omitting the butter, cream, and hot sauce. Add these when you are ready to serve.

Coconut and Scotch Bonnet Breadfruit Soup

This delicious hot version of breadfruit soup is frequently served at lunchtime in the West Indies, particularly in Jamaica. Sometimes, Trinidadian cooks will add corn and/or chopped carrots. If the soup is served as a first course for a dinner, keep the entree light and spicy with one of the fish selections from Chapter 7.

½   pound whole piece of ham, smoked ham hock, or salted beef (see Note if using salted beef)

4   cups water or chicken stock

2   cups breadfruit, diced

2   tablespoons butter or vegetable oil

1½   cups onion, diced

2   cloves garlic, minced

1   cup milk

3   cups Coconut Milk (see recipe, p. 14)

1   teaspoon dried thyme

2   tablespoons scallions, chopped

1   or 2 whole fresh habanero chiles

    Salt to taste

Place the meat and the water (or chicken stock) in a large heavy casserole, and boil the meat for 30 minutes. Remove the whole piece of meat from the stock, cool the meat slightly, chop it into small pieces, and set aside.

Bring the stock back to a boil, add the breadfruit, and boil for 15 to 20 minutes, until the breadfruit is soft. Using a potato masher, mash the breadfruit until it is smooth. Or, allow the mixture to cool slightly, and purée it in batches in a blender or processor and reheat the mixture.

Melt the butter or oil in a heavy skillet and sauté the onions and the garlic until the onions wilt, about 1 minute. Add the sautéed mixture to the mashed breadfruit mixture in the soup pot.

Add the reserved chopped meat, the milk, coconut milk, thyme, scallions, and habanero(s). Bring the mixture to a light boil, reduce the heat, and simmer (covered) for 30 minutes, stirring occasionally and carefully, so as not to break open the peppers.

Remove the peppers, add salt to taste, and serve hot.

Garnish with the parsley.

Serves: 4 to 6

Heat Scale: Medium to Hot

Note: If you are using salted beef, increase the water to 6 cups.

French Caribbean Spices

"At the market in Pointe-à-Pitre, you can buy all sorts of things for the table, from fresh fruit to live chickens, but the main attraction for the visitor is the wide range of spices. Some may be familiar, like the cumin and coriander which are reminders of the fact that Guadeloupe, like some other parts of the Caribbean, saw the importation of indentured labourers from India during the 19th century—colombo, a sort of curry, is a national dish. But along with the cinnamon stick and the vanilla pods, you can find things like roucou, which I had heard of for many years but never seen. It is said to have been used by the Amerindians of the Caribbean as a body paint—I now learnt that you can macerate the grains in oil and use the oil for making sauces as a substitute for tomato sauce. Something else I was seeing for the first time was bois bande—notorious around the region for its alleged aphrodisiac qualities."

John Gilmore

Breadfruit Vichyssoise (Chilled Breadfruit Soup)

This recipe is elegant and unusual to serve; it is served chilled, but it has the spicy bite of habanero sauce, so you get the chill and the spice. It is especially popular in Grenada. Our friend, Cathy Decker, an advertising executive who handles major resorts in the Caribbean (Ciboney and Sandals), says the vichyssoise style is one of her favorites. Even though it is a creamy soup, it is light enough to serve before a big West Indies-style dinner.

2	tablespoons butter or vegetable oil
1½	cups onion, chopped
2	cloves garlic, minced
2	cups breadfruit, peeled and diced into ½-inch cubes
4	cups chicken stock
1	cup coconut milk or half-and-half cream
2	tablespoons chopped fresh habanero chiles or one of the habanero pepper sauces from Chapter 2
¼	teaspoon freshly grated nutmeg
⅛	teaspoon freshly grated cinnamon
	Salt to taste
	Chopped parsley or scallions for garnish

Melt the butter or heat the vegetable oil in a small, heavy soup pot. Add the onion and the garlic and sauté over low heat for 1 minute.

Add the breadfruit, stock, coconut milk, peppers (or sauce), nutmeg, and cinnamon, and bring the mixture to a boil. Reduce the heat immediately, and simmer (covered) for 30 minutes, or until the breadfruit is tender.

Remove the soup from the heat and allow it to cool slightly. Add the semicooled mixture, in batches, to a blender, and purée the mixture until it is smooth. Add salt to taste.

Chill the puréed mixture for at least 2 hours before serving. Garnish with the parsley or scallions.

Serves: 4

Heat Scale: Medium

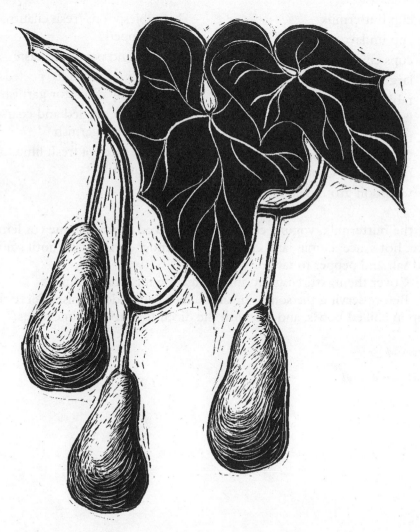

Chilled Guaca-Chile Soup

This chilled soup is another one that gets its kick from the addition of Caribbean hot sauce with its volatile peppers. The taste is always a culinary delight in Martinique and Guadeloupe, where the cooks don't stint on the peppers. The lime juice will keep the avocado from blackening while it is chilling, but the soup needs to be served the same day.

1   cup buttermilk
1   cup unflavored yogurt
2   cups chicken broth
1   large avocado, peeled and sliced
2   tablespoons fresh lime or lemon juice
2   tablespoons bottled habanero Caribbean hot sauce, or use a recipe from Chapter 2
¼   teaspoon ground cumin

2   tablespoons fresh cilantro, chopped
Salt and pepper to taste
1   medium avocado, peeled and coarsely diced for garnish
1   tomato, seeded and coarsely diced for garnish
4   thin slices of fresh lime for garnish

Put the buttermilk, yogurt, chicken broth, sliced avocado, lime (or lemon) juice, hot sauce, cumin, and cilantro in a blender and process until smooth. Add salt and pepper to taste.

Cover the mixture tightly and refrigerate for 2 to 3 hours.

Before serving the soup, stir in the diced avocado garnish. Serve the soup in chilled bowls, and top with the diced tomato and lime slices.

Serves: 4

Heat Scale: Hot

Down Island Gazpacho

Traditionally, gazpacho is thought of as a Spanish-style cold soup. However, this recipe takes the cold, uncooked soup idea one step further by including some of the fruit bounty available in the islands. The ultimate result is a soup that is cold, bold, and spicy—Island style.

2 cups pineapple or papaya juice	½ fresh Scotch bonnet (or habanero), seeds and stem removed
2 cups tomato juice	
¾ cup almost-ripe papaya, peeled and chopped into large cubes	3 tablespoons fresh lime juice
¾ cup fresh pineapple, coarsely chopped	2 tablespoons fresh cilantro, chopped
⅓ cup each green, red, and yellow bell pepper, diced	½ teaspoon whole black peppercorns, crushed

Place all of the ingredients in a blender and blend for 5 seconds. Refrigerate the mixture for 6 hours.

Serve the soup in icy cold bowls.

Serves: 4 to 6

Heat Scale: Medium

Curry and Jerk: Meat Dishes

This chapter starts off with three traditional goat curries from Trinidad, Jamaica, and Grenada, and one traditional pork curry from Martinique. The use of curry powder or *colombo* paste once again reflects the culinary influence of the East Indians on the islands. The East Indians were originally brought to the islands as a source of cheap labor, but they vastly influenced the cuisine and culture of the West Indies as time went on.

The first recipe, Trinidadian Coconut-Curried Goat (p. 120), utilizes the richness of a homemade curry powder, hot peppers, and a little coconut cream to round off the taste. Jamaican Curry Goat (p. 121) is a classic dish found in every nook and cranny of the island; despite many variations, the recipe usually contains some type of massala and Scotch bonnet peppers. Tony, one of our drivers, introduced us to this dish at a local lunch restaurant/hang-out in Ocho Rios. We found out very quickly that the cook simply chopped up the pieces of meat and threw everything, including the bones, into the pot. To avoid the bone splinters, we took very small bites of this most delicious dish! Some connoisseurs of the dish say that the best is found in Mandeville, far up in the mountains. A taste test for the best sounds like a good reason to go to Jamaica!

The recipe for Grenadian-Style Curried Goat (p. 122) differs in several ways from the other recipes; it uses fresh ginger and lime for a marinade, and the caramelized sugar and oil give the meat a golden-brown color, which is an African cooking technique. The fourth curry in this series is Pork Colombo from Martinique (p. 124). This interesting dish contains some ingredients not usually found in curries, such as wine, beans, and cabbage. The cabbage substitutes for the green tops of malanga, a tropical tuber. Once again, the ingenuity of island cooks comes into play here, as they use what's at hand to create an interesting and delicious dish!

Ingenuity is the key word for the presentation of Aruba Lamb Barbecue (p. 126). Yard-long beans, called *boonchi* in Aruba and *bodi* in Trinidad, are used to wrap the skewers before grilling and add a nutritional, as well as color-ful, touch. Also, the use of fresh pineapple and the many assorted vegetables on the skewers creates a real taste treat.

Another interesting lamb recipe is Curaçao-Style Roast Lamb or Kid (p. 128), which is usually prepared for a large cookout. Our friends tell us that this is a specialty barbecue that utilizes the *Passaat*, the tradewinds, because the winds move the smoke through the cooking meat and add to the flavor. Traditionally, whole, cleaned young lambs are used and are cooked on racks, windward of the coals. So, get two young, cleaned lambs and invite thirty or forty of your closest friends for an intimate dinner! Just kidding—we have adjusted the ingredients for a more modest feast. Chilindrón de Cordero (p. 130), our final lamb recipe, hails from Cuba, and it differs from the others because it is first marinated in a unique adobo sauce, and then simmered with spices and chiles. We were told that it is almost always served with cold beer; sounds like a party to us!

Pork is another popular meat in the Caribbean and is featured in Garlic Pork (p. 132), which is from Trinidad via Guyana and Portugal, according to our guide (of Portuguese ancestry) Michael Coelho. Michael said that back in the old days, this dish was traditionally prepared for Christmas dining and that it was never (or seldom) eaten after December 31.

Jamaica's popular North Coast Jerk Pork (p. 134) originated with the Maroons in Cockpit country. The Maroons, who were the runaway slaves, would hunt boar or wild pigs in the rugged Cockpit country and then smoke-dry, or *jerk*, the meat as a way of preserving it. As with most popular dishes, debate rages as to where to find the "best." Most people say that the best can be found only around Boston Beach, near Port Antonio; however, we found some richly flavored, tender, hot and spicy jerk pork at the Double V Jerk Centre in Ocho Rios, and it's hard to imagine any better!

Another traditional pork recipe, Tamal en Cazuela (p. 136), comes from Cuba. This "tamal in a pot" is flavored with hot chiles, lime juice, and sherry, and the addition of the corn and cornmeal almost likens this dish to some type of Italian polenta. Spicy fried pork cubes abound in Griot, or Hot Haitian Fried Pork (p. 138), which is served either as a snack or as an entree. The hot peppers in this dish are tempered by the addition of the fresh lime and orange juice used to marinate the meat. It is another one of those great Caribbean dishes that utilizes fruit juices to titillate the taste buds.

The last dish that calls for pork is Jug Jug (p. 140), another one of those great Caribbean dishes that claims a long history. It is a Barbadian dish usually made at Christmas time; some call it "transported haggis" in memory of the Scots who, after being exiled to Barbados after the Monmouth Rebellion of 1685, created a Caribbean version of their beloved haggis. The Caribbean recipe differs in several respects from the original haggis: Instead of stuffing the filling inside a sheep's stomach lining along with a minced mixture of the animal's organs, Barbadians use minced meat and mold the mixture in a bowl. Another difference: Islanders use either Guinea corn flour, cornmeal, or millet instead of the traditional Scots cereal oats. And what would an island dish be without the addition of hot peppers?

The final group of recipes consists of those that either feature or contain beef. Since the majority of Caribbean beef is imported on many of the islands, it tends to be very pricey. Ropa Vieja (p. 142) is a traditional Spanish dish of Cuba, and it is popular on all the Spanish-speaking islands of the Caribbean. The title literally means "old clothes," and the name comes from the shredded meat, which resembles ragged old clothes. The taste is anything but old; this palate pleaser contains hot peppers, spices, and pimientos.

The mere mention of Haiti conjures up an island with a troubled past— but plenty of spicy food. In Haitian cuisine, the hot stuff is usually served on the side so that each diner may create his own level of heat; however, Stuffed Haitian Fillet of Beef (p. 144) is stuffed and cooked with the hot peppers. Since cashews are grown in Haiti, it is not unusual to find them in many, many of the recipes.

Another spicy and delicious recipe is Trinidadian-Style Oxtail (p. 146). This particular recipe does not call for caramelizing the meat first, as many recipes do. The sugar and the oil are caramelized before browning or braising the meat, which harkens back to the African influence on the cuisine of these islands. In the plantation days, as well as today, in the hands of a skilled cook, this lowly cut of meat becomes a taste sensation. We ate oxtail several times when we were in Trinidad, and each version was different, but no less delicious.

A very different kind of beef recipe is from the island of Saint Croix, the largest of the U.S. Virgin Islands and a popular tourist destination. Beef Kebabs Tropicale (p. 148) would delight any sophisticated traveler, with its mixed tastes of fresh fruit and Scotch bonnet peppers. The fruit tends to cut the heat of the hot peppers, so don't stint on them! Another particularly spicy dish comes from the Dominican Republic, Carne Riplada (p. 150), or Spicy Flank Steak. In contrast to Haiti (with which it shares the island of Hispaniola), the Dominican Republic is luxurious and rich with its fine hotels, restaurants, casinos, and spas. It is also rich in food traditions, and this dish is found on many menus and is enjoyed by locals and tourists alike.

Cuban-Style Spicy Picadillo (p. 152) is practically the national dish of Cuba. This Cuban hash is rich with tomatoes, peppers, olives, and raisins. The contents of the dish can vary widely from one place to another; cooks will use whatever the region dictates. We think this dish would even be great served for breakfast or brunch topped with a poached or fried egg. Add some warm tortillas to sop up the great flavors, Cuban style.

The last recipe in the beef group was given to us by chef Joe Brown, owner of the Solimar Restaurant in Port of Spain. The Solimar Pasta Bowl (p. 154) is actually a plantain-based dish. Joe has worked in restaurants and hotels all over the world, and he always manages to give local foods a continental flair. Here is yet another example of how the cuisines of the islands are constantly being altered by new arrivals who incorporate traditional ingredients into new styles.

Trinidadian Coconut-Curried Goat

Goat meat, which is not commonly eaten in the United States (except in the Southwest), appears in many West Indian recipes. The Trinis sometimes eat curried goat Jamaican-style (as on p. 121), but this version with coconut is more customary in the eastern Caribbean.

2	tablespoons ghee (clarified butter) or vegetable oil	2	teaspoons red chile powder (powdered pure chiles, without spices)
1	onion, chopped fine		
2	cloves garlic, minced	1	teaspoon ground cumin
1	Congo pepper (or habanero), seeds and stem removed, chopped fine	1½	pounds lean goat meat (or substitute lamb), cut into ½-inch cubes
1	tablespoon freshly grated ginger	1½	cups water
2	teaspoons ground coriander	2	tablespoons Coconut Cream (see recipe, p. 14), or more to taste
1	teaspoon turmeric		
½	teaspoon freshly ground black pepper		Salt to taste

Heat the ghee or oil in a skillet, add the onion, garlic, pepper, and ginger, and sauté for 5 minutes, stirring occasionally.

Add the coriander, turmeric, black pepper, chile powder, and cumin and sauté for another 3 minutes, stirring constantly.

Add the meat and brown it, stirring occasionally. Add the water, cover, and simmer the meat until it is tender, about 1 hour. Add more water if the mixture becomes too dry. Stir in the coconut cream and cook for 5 minutes.

Add salt to taste and serve hot with a chutney from Chapter 2 and a side dish from Chapter 8.

Serves: 4

Heat Scale: Hot

Jamaican Curry Goat

Here is a classic Jamaican dish that is much beloved in that country. As usual, lamb may be substituted for the goat. Note the West Indian trait of using a massala without chile powder, and then adding chiles to the curry. The dish is traditionally served with white rice, mango chutney, and grated coconut.

2	pounds goat meat, cut into ½-inch cubes	2	onions, sliced
3	tablespoons West Indian Massala (see recipe, p. 20)	2	tomatoes, chopped
½	teaspoon salt	2	green onions, chopped
½	teaspoon powdered cardamom	2	Scotch bonnet (or habanero) chiles, seeds and stems removed, chopped
½	teaspoon freshly ground black pepper	2	tablespoons butter
2	cloves garlic, minced	¼	cup vegetable oil
		3	cups water

In a large bowl, combine the goat meat, massala, salt, cardamom, pepper, garlic, onions, tomatoes, green onions, and the chiles and mix well. Allow the meat to marinate for 1 hour.

Remove the meat from the seasonings and reserve the seasonings. Sauté the meat in the butter and oil in a large skillet until lightly browned. Add the water, cover, and simmer until the goat is very tender, about 1 hour, adding more water if necessary.

Return the seasonings to the meat mixture, cover, and simmer for 15 minutes.

Serves: 6

Heat Scale: Hot

Grenadian-Style Curried Goat

For this recipe, use a good-quality imported curry powder; the domestic curry powders just don't have the taste or the punch needed for this recipe. Serve this dish with rice and peas, fried plantains, or cooked yams.

2   pounds fresh goat (or lamb), cut into large pieces, washed

2   tablespoons fresh lime juice

4   tablespoons freshly grated ginger

1   teaspoon salt

4   tablespoons vegetable oil (use coconut oil if available)

4   tablespoons white sugar

2   Scotch bonnet (or habanero) chiles, seeds and stems removed, minced

6   cloves garlic, minced

2   cups chopped onion

1   tomato, peeled, seeded, and chopped

¾   cup tomato sauce

4   tablespoons imported curry powder, or substitute Trinidadian Curry Paste, p. 22

3   teaspoons dried thyme, or 4 sprigs fresh thyme

1   cup water, if necessary

Put the cut-up goat in a large, shallow glass dish. Drizzle the lime juice over the meat, and spread the ginger over the meat. Sprinkle the meat with the salt, then cover the pan and let the meat marinate in the refrigerator for 4 to 6 hours.

Heat a very large, heavy casserole to high heat, add the oil and sugar, and allow the mixture to caramelize. Add the meat, remove the casserole from the heat, and allow the meat to brown without stirring for 30 seconds. Return the pan to the heat, stir the meat, and finishing browning it.

Turn the heat down to medium and cook for 10 to 15 minutes, carefully turning and stirring the meat.

Add the chile peppers, garlic, and onion; reduce the heat to a simmer, cover, and simmer for 20 minutes, stirring twice. Then add the remaining ingredients, cover, and simmer for 1½ to 2 hours, or until the meat is tender. Stir the meat occasionally and check to make sure it doesn't burn. Add more water, if necessary.

Serves: 8

Heat Scale: Medium

Note: This recipe requires advance preparation.

A Masculine Feast

"It appears that there must be a presiding officer at a curry goat feed. He sat at the head of the table and directed the fun. There was a story-telling contest, reminiscences that were humorous pokes and gibes at each other. All of this came with the cock soup. This feast is so masculine that chicken soup would not be allowed. It must be soup from roosters. After the cock soup comes ram goat and rice. No nanny goat in this meal either. It is ram goat or nothing."

Zora Neale Hurston, 1939

Pork Colombo from Martinique

This recipe, curried with *colombo* paste, illustrates the Bengal influence in Martinique, particularly the northern part of the island. Why the Bengalis named their curry after Colombo, Sri Lanka—so far from Calcutta—is not known. Cooks can take their choice of cooking this curry with wine or coconut milk. This rather spicy dish is traditionally served with fried plantains.

2	pounds lean pork, diced	3	cloves garlic, crushed
¼	cup butter	1	Scotch bonnet (or habanero) chile, seeds and stem removed, minced
1	cup chopped cabbage		
2	onions, chopped		
1	green (or slightly ripe) mango, sliced	2	medium eggplants, peeled and chopped
1	cup white wine or coconut milk (see recipe, p. 14)	2	chayotes, peeled and chopped (or substitute small Hubbard squash)
2	tablespoons Colombo Curry Paste (see recipe, p. 21)	1	cup navy beans, cooked
2	teaspoons Tamarind Sauce (see recipe, p. 13)		

In a large skillet, brown the pork in the butter for 4 minutes over medium heat. Add the cabbage, onions, and mango and stir-fry for 3 more minutes. Add the wine or coconut milk and enough water to cover the meat mixture and bring to a boil. Immediately reduce the heat, stir in the curry paste, tamarind sauce, garlic, and habanero chile and cook, covered, over low heat for 1 hour, stirring occasionally.

Remove the cover and add the eggplants, chayotes, and navy beans. Cook, uncovered, over low heat for 1 hour, stirring occasionally. The curry sauce should be fairly thick.

Serves: 4

Heat Scale: Hot

A Plague of Livestock

"Within one generation of discovery, livestock threatened to overrun some of the Caribbean islands. Unprecedented quantities of meat and hides became available. By the 1520s, there were so many cattle on Hispaniola that officials petitioned for the establishment of a mesta (livestock guild) to control the herds. Wild dogs reputedly killed 60,000 cows a year in the 1560s, but this barely affected the size of the herds. The surplus protein was especially important for the maintenance of the fleets moving back and forth across the Atlantic. Pigs on the hoof were about as important as salted and smoked beef. Fed with maize stored onboard, pigs provided fresh meat for the return voyage."

John C. Super

Aruba Lamb Barbecue

This recipe is as upbeat and exciting as Aruba itself, with its casinos, nightlife, and more than a hundred international restaurants within its tiny seventy square miles! The presentation of this particular dish can be enticing and is unusual with its delicious flavors of curry and ginger, along with the zing of hot sauce and peppers. This version can serve from four to six people, depending on the size of the skewers and how much gets squeezed onto each!

1	cup onion, chopped	2½	pounds lamb, fat removed, cut into 1-inch cubes
3	cloves garlic, minced	3	bell peppers, cut into 1½ squares and parboiled for 1 minute
2	tablespoons freshly grated ginger		
2	teaspoons imported curry powder	20	pearl onions, precooked for 4 minutes, skins removed
1	tablespoon hot Hungarian-style paprika	20	cherry tomatoes, pierced once with a knife tip
½	teaspoon salt		
½	cup dry white wine	16	mild, pickled cherry peppers
2	tablespoons fresh lemon juice	1	small pineapple, cleaned and cut into cubes
2	tablespoons vegetable or peanut oil		
3	Scotch bonnet (or habanero) chiles, seeds and stems removed and minced	6	yard-long beans left whole, parboiled (if not available, omit)

Place the onion, garlic, ginger, curry powder, paprika, salt, wine, lemon juice, oil, chiles, and the lamb in a large shallow, glass baking pan, and mix them thoroughly. Pierce the meat cubes several times with the tines of a fork, so the marinade can penetrate. Cover the pan with plastic wrap and refrigerate the meat overnight.

Bring the meat marinade mixture to room temperature, about 20 minutes, and then drain the mixture in a colander, discarding the marinade.

On metal skewers, alternate pieces of the meat with the green peppers, onions, cherry tomatoes, pickled cherry peppers, and pineapple. Be careful not to pack the ingredients too tightly on each skewer, or they won't broil evenly. Wrap the beans around the skewers at an angle, and make sure to leave enough room at the ends of the skewers to tie the ends of the beans securely with several thicknesses of aluminum foil, so the beans won't fall off during the grilling.

The lamb can be grilled in an oven broiler or on an outdoor grill. If you are using an outdoor grill, we recommend using a hot burning wood, such as oak, and very little charcoal.

During the grilling/broiling, turn the skewers every 2 minutes, for 10 to 14 minutes, to ensure even cooking.

For a spectacular presentation, bring the grilled meat to the table on a warm platter, and remove the meat and vegetables in front of your guests.

Serves: 4 to 6

Heat Scale: Medium

Note: This recipe requires advance preparation.

Curaçao-Style Roast Lamb or Kid

This recipe originated with a big cookout (for thirty to forty people), but we have modified the recipe to serve eight to ten. The spicy sauce permeates the meat as it cooks very slowly over a grill, fueled with fragrant wood (such as pecan or apple), with just enough charcoal to keep the heat up. Or, slowly roast the meat in a 300-degree oven for 3 to 4 hours. We have been advised that the sauce should be made at least 2 to 3 days before the actual cooking.

Lamb and Marinade

4	to 5 pounds of lamb or kid (*cabrito*), cut into large pieces	2	teaspoons rosemary
½	cup olive oil	3	teaspoons oregano
½	cup gin or dry white wine	3	teaspoons thyme
		2	teaspoons basil

Sauce

1	cup tomato sauce	4	Scotch bonnet (or habanero) chiles, seeds and stems removed, chopped
½	cup white wine vinegar		
2	cloves garlic, minced		
2	whole cloves	2	cups onion, chopped
1	teaspoon salt	½	cup olive oil
½	teaspoon freshly ground black pepper	½	cup water

Place the washed pieces of lamb or kid in a large shallow glass pan, sprinkle the marinade ingredients over the meat, and turn the meat to coat it. Cover and refrigerate the meat for 24 hours.

To make the sauce, put the tomato sauce, wine vinegar, garlic, cloves, salt, and black pepper in a saucepan and bring the mixture to a boil, reduce the heat to a simmer, and simmer for 2 minutes. Remove the sauce from the heat and allow it to cool for 10 minutes. Pour the sauce into a large, glass, heat-proof jar with a cover, and add the hot peppers, onion, olive oil, and water. Regrigerate the sauce for 2 to 3 days before using it to baste the meat, shaking the jar several times to blend the ingredients.

Before cooking the meat, bring the sauce to room temperature.

To cook the meat, whether grilling or baking, drain some of the marinade off the meat and place the meat on the grill or in a very large glass baking pan; use the sauce to baste the meat about every 20 minutes while the meat is cooking.

Cut the hot meat into serving sizes (removing the bones), and serve it hot!

Serves: 8 to 10

Heat Scale: Medium

Note: This recipe requires advance preparation.

Chilindrón de Cordero (Cuban Lamb with Peppers)

Rudolfo de Garay and Thomas Brown, writing for *Chile Pepper*, uncovered this unique Cuban recipe. Although primarily made with kid, *chilindrón* also lends itself to lamb, rabbit, veal, and *lechón* (suckling pig). Because most people won't be able to find baby goat, we suggest using lamb and have included directions for making a rich stock to approximate the stronger flavor of kid.

Adobo

¼	cup olive oil	½	cup sour orange juice
2	cloves garlic, minced	3	pounds boned and trimmed lamb or kid (baby goat), leg, neck, or shoulder, cut into 1½-inch chunks
1	tablespoon salt		
1	tablespoon fresh ground black pepper		
¼	cup dry sherry		

Stock

	Bones and trimmings of meat	2	unpeeled garlic cloves, crushed
6	cups water	1	bay leaf
1	large unpeeled onion, quartered	2	allspice berries
1	green bell pepper, seeded and roughly chopped		

Chilindrón

The marinated meat

¼ cup olive oil

2 cups chopped seeded Cubanelle (or green bell) pepper

1 tablespoon garlic, minced

2 cups onion, chopped

½ cup tomato sauce

2 teaspoons salt

¼ teaspoon cinnamon

¼ teaspoon ground allspice

Reserved stock

5 or more rocotillo chiles or 1 or more habanero chiles, seeds and stems removed, minced

1 tablespoon distilled or white wine vinegar

Combine all of the ingredients for the adobo, mix well, and marinate the meat overnight.

To make the stock, brown the bones under a broiler. In a stock pot, add the bones and stock ingredients to 6 cups of water, and bring to a simmer. Let simmer until the liquid reduces to about a cup, about 2 to 3 hours. Strain and refrigerate the stock until a layer of fat hardens on top. Remove the fat and discard.

When the meat is finished marinating, drain it and reserve the adobo. Place the olive oil in a casserole over medium heat. When the oil is hot, add the meat and brown it. Turn the heat to high, add the chopped sweet peppers, garlic, and onions, and sauté until the onions are translucent. Add the tomato sauce and cook for 3 minutes. Add the salt, cinnamon, allspice, rocotillo or habanero chiles, the reserved stock, and the reserved adobo.

Cover and simmer for 45 minutes. The sauce should thicken and become a deep, rich reddish color. If the sauce is too watery, uncover the casserole, increase the heat, and reduce it. Test the sauce for seasonings and the meat for tenderness. Just before serving, stir in 1 tablespoon of distilled or white wine vinegar.

Serve with white rice, fried plantains (ripe or green), and a salad. *Chilindrón* is almost always served with beer, but sometimes with a young red wine.

Serves: 4 to 6

Heat Scale: Medium

Note: This recipe requires advance preparation.

Garlic Pork

This is a very traditional Portuguese island dish that probably originated in Guyana. Our main culinary guide in Trinidad, Michael Coelho, told us that years ago his father would slaughter a pig, cut it up, and marinate it in a huge mass of garlic, malt vinegar, and fresh thyme. After a *week*, the meat was cooked in a large pot, creating its own garlic oil. Nowadays, most Trinis forego the slaughtering and buy their pork at the Hi-Lo Supermarkets, but the taste is still strong and memorable!

30	garlic cloves	2	teaspoons salt
2	tablespoons minced fresh thyme or 4 tablespoons dried thyme		Juice of 1 lime
		2	cups white vinegar
2	onions, chopped	4	pounds boneless pork leg or shoulder, cut into 1-inch cubes
1	Congo pepper (or habanero), seeds and stem removed, chopped		Vegetable oil for frying

Combine all the ingredients except the pork and oil and purée in a blender in batches until smooth. Pour the mixture over the pork and marinate, covered, in a nonmetallic bowl in the refrigerator for at least 2 days.

Drain the pork (reserve the marinade) and pat it dry. Heat the oil in a frying pan and fry the pork cubes, a few at a time, turning often, until they are browned on all sides, about 5 to 7 minutes.

Drain the pork on paper towels, and keep it warm in an oven.

Variations: Some cooks brown the pork slightly and then finish the cooking in a 350-degree oven for about 30 minutes in a covered casserole, adding some water or marinade. For garlic lovers extraordinaire, simmer the marinade until thick and serve it over the pork cubes.

Serves: 6 to 8

Heat Scale: Mild

Note: This recipe requires advance preparation.

An Early Jerk Feast

"We had at dinner a land tortoise and a barbecued pig, two of the best and richest dishes that I ever tasted, the latter in particular, which was dressed in the Maroon fashion, being placed on a barbecue (a frame of wickerwork, through whose interstices the steam can ascend) filled with peppers and spices of the highest flavour, wrappt in plantain leaves and then buried in a hole filled with hot stones by whose vapour it is baked, no particle of juice being thus suffered to evaporate. I have eaten several other good Jamaica dishes, but not so excellent as this."

Matthew Lewis, 1834

North Coast Jerk Pork

The Jamaican jerk cooks use a technique of cooking best described as "smoke-grilling." It combines the direct heat of grilling with smoke produced by fresh pimento leaves and branches. While grilling, the meat is often covered with a piece of corrugated aluminum to keep the heat and smoke contained. This method can be approximated by using a Weber-type barbecue with a round drip pan filled with water, set in the center of the coals to catch drippings and prevent flare-ups. Although marinated pork can be smoked with cooler smoke in an indirect-heat smoker, the texture will not be the same as with smoke-grilling, and the traditional crust will not form. We prefer to smoke-grill over wood rather than charcoal, as the flavor is far superior.

5   to 6 pounds pork (roasts or chops, more needed if ribs), coarsely cut into pieces about 2 to 3 inches wide and 4 to 5 inches long, fat left on
2   cups North Coast Jerk Marinade (see recipe, p. 23)

Hardwood for the fire, such as apple, hickory, pecan, or oak hardwood chips for the smoke, soaked in water, or substitute fresh branches and leaves

Combine the pork and the marinade, toss well, and marinate the meat, covered, overnight in the refrigerator.

Build a fire, using hardwood, in the barbecue. It is permissible to start the fire with charcoal—just don't cook over it unless it consists of natural chunks of mesquite or oak charcoal, never briquets. When the wood has burned to coals, spread them apart and place a metal drip pan, half-filled with water, in the center of the fire. Place the marinated pork on the grill, directly over the pan, and as far from the fire as possible. Next, either use the barbecue cover to cover the meat, leaving a small vent for fresh air, or make a tent with aluminum foil to cover the meat and keep in smoke.

The trick for the next few hours is to add sufficient wood to keep the fire going while avoiding making it too hot. Every half hour or so, add some soaked hardwood chips to the coals to produce smoke. Feel free to drink some Red Stripe beer while tending the fire.

Cook the pork for 2 to 3 hours, depending on the heat of the fire, turning the meat occasionally on the grill. It can be basted with more marinade. The pork should be crispy on the outside and tender on the inside, almost to the point of falling apart.

Serves: 6 to 8

Heat Scale: Hot

Note: This recipe requires advance preparation.

Tamal en Cazuela
(Tamal in a Pot)

From Rudolfo de Garay and Thomas Brown, writing on hot and spicy
Cuban foods in *Chile Pepper*, comes this Cuban "polenta" made with pork.
If you want to make a vegetarian tamal, eliminate the pork, and add the gar-
lic, after the onions and lime juice, with the tomato sauce.

5	cloves garlic	½	cup chopped and seeded red bell pepper
½	teaspoon freshly ground black pepper	1½	cups chopped onion
2	tablespoons lime juice	¼	cup tomato sauce
1	pound pork, diced	1	small habanero chile or 5 piquins (or more, to taste), seeds and stems removed, chopped
2	cups uncooked corn kernels		
½	cup fine cornmeal		
⅓	cup sherry		
3	cups water	1	tablespoon distilled or white wine vinegar
2	teaspoons salt		Chopped parsley for garnish
3	tablespoons corn or vegetable oil		
1½	cups chopped and seeded Cubanelle (or green bell) pepper		

In a mortar, mash the garlic with ¼ teaspoon of black pepper. Add the lime
juice and stir to make the adobo. Marinate the diced pork in the adobo for
at least an hour, but overnight is better.

Purée 1½ cups of the corn kernels (reserve ½ cup of the kernels) with
the cornmeal, sherry, 1 cup water, salt, and the remaining black pepper.

Heat the corn oil in a saucepan over medium heat, and when it is hot,
add the pork and sauté until the pork begins to brown. Add the Cubanelle
and red bell peppers and onion, increase the heat, and sauté for about
5 minutes. Add the adobo and stir, scraping up any coagulated juices from
the bottom of the pan.

Add the tomato sauce and chiles and cook for a minute and a half. Add the puréed corn mixture, 2 cups water, remaining ½ cup whole corn kernels, and cook, stirring, for 5 minutes. Lower the heat and cook, stirring constantly, for 20 minutes. Stir in the vinegar. Pour onto a greased platter and garnish with chopped parsley.

Serve with a salad of avocado, watercress, and raw onions.

Serves: 4 to 6

Heat Scale: Medium

Habanero Quotes

American chefs and cookbook authors love to wax poetic about the unique flavor of the fresh *chinense* varieties. Chef Mark Miller described fresh habaneros as having "tropical fruit tones that mix well with food containing tropical fruits or tomatoes," and Scotch bonnets as possessing a "fruity and smoky flavor." Cookbook author Steven Raichlen agreed, describing the Scotch bonnets as "floral, aromatic, and almost smoky." As far as the dried habaneros were concerned, Miller detected "tropical fruit flavors of coconut and papaya, a hint of berry, and an intense, fiery acidic heat."

Griot (Hot Haitian Fried Pork)

This traditional Haitian dish of marinated, fried pork is one that still remains very popular in Haiti; it can be served as a snack or as the main meat dish for a spectacular dinner. Accompany it with beans and rice and/or fried plantains, add a salad of sliced cucumbers, and enjoy.

2 pounds pork loin, all fat removed, cut into ½-inch cubes	½ cup juice of Seville oranges, or substitute underripe Valencia oranges
2 cups onion, chopped	½ teaspoon salt
3 Scotch bonnet (or habanero) chiles, seeds and stems removed, minced	¼ teaspoon freshly ground black pepper
3 cloves garlic, minced	Water to cover
4 scallions, chopped (white part with a little of the green)	⅔ cup vegetable oil
Juice of 2 fresh limes (about ⅓ cup)	Paper towels

Combine the pork, onion, chiles, garlic, scallions, lime juice, orange juice, salt, and pepper in a large, shallow glass baking dish and marinate for 3 hours in the refrigerator.

Put the marinated meat in a large, heavy saucepan, add only enough water to cover, and bring the mixture to a boil. Reduce the heat to a simmer, cover, and simmer for 45 to 60 minutes until almost all of the liquid is evaporated.

Using a stack of paper towels as a blotter, spread the cooked meat on the towels to remove excess moisture.

Heat the oil in a large skillet, add the pork cubes, and fry the pork until it is quite brown. Drain the fried meat on additional paper towels. Serve this dish hot.

Serves: 5 to 6

Heat Scale: Hot

Note: This recipe requires advance preparation.

A Maroon after the Hunt

"Henry Gosse, writing in 1851, recalls the fine figure cut by the Maroon huntsman vending his wares: 'He was generally seen in the towns armed with a fowling piece and cutlass, and belts that suspended on one side a large plaited bag, known as a cuttacoo, and on the other a calabash, guarded with a netted covering, in which he carried his supply of water. On his back braced round his shoulders, and suspended by a bandage over the forehead, was generally seen the wicker cradle, that held inclosed a side of jerked hog, which he sold passing along, in measured slice to ready customers, as an especial delicacy for the breakfast table.'"

Barbara Klamon Kopytoff

Jug Jug

This transplanted dish from Scotland is very popular in Barbados at Christmas time, and variations of it have been handed down through many generations. It is usually served with roast chicken or ham. Fresh, dried, and canned pigeon peas are available in Latin American and Caribbean markets. Try this combination for your next Christmas dinner to give it a delightful Caribbean theme.

½   pound lean pork, cut into ½-inch cubes

½   cup lean corned beef, cut into ½-inch cubes

1   chicken leg, skin removed

1   pound fresh pigeon peas, or canned

Cold water to cover

3   tablespoons vegetable oil

3   onions, chopped

3   cloves garlic, minced

2   teaspoons dried thyme, or 3 sprigs fresh

2   Scotch bonnet (or habanero) chiles, seeds and stems removed, minced

2   tablespoons minced parsley

¼   cup minced celery

2   scallions, chopped, including some of the green

¼   teaspoon salt, or more to taste

¼   teaspoon freshly ground black pepper

½   cup cornmeal or ground millet

1   cup Coconut Milk (see recipe, p. 14)

½   to 1 cup reserved stock

1   tablespoon butter for buttering mold

Wash the meats, place them in a large, heavy casserole with the pigeon peas, and cover with cold water. Bring the mixture to a boil, reduce the heat to medium, cover, and cook for 45 minutes. Cool and strain the mixture, reserving the stock.

When the strained meat is cool enough to handle, remove the meat from the chicken leg, shred the chicken meat, and chop the meat and pea mixture.

Heat the oil in a large skillet and sauté the onion, garlic, thyme, chiles, parsley, celery, scallions, salt, and pepper until the vegetables are wilted, about 2 minutes.

Reduce the heat to a simmer, stir in the chopped meats and the peas, and let the mixture simmer, covered, for a few minutes.

In a saucepan, blend the cornmeal (or ground millet) with the coconut milk and gently heat the mixture, stirring constantly. As the mixture starts to thicken, add 2 tablespoons of the stock and stir it in thoroughly—add 2 to 4 more tablespoons of the stock, until the mixture doesn't stick to the pan. The process should take about 15 minutes.

Mix the cooked cornmeal in with the sautéed meat and vegetables and mix thoroughly. Spoon the mixture into a greased bowl and press down to eliminate any air bubbles.

Let the mixture sit for 15 minutes, turn the mold out onto a serving plate, and slice and serve.

Serves: 4 to 6

Heat Scale: Medium

Ropa Vieja

This spicy, shredded flank steak recipe originated in Cuba and has become popular on many of the Spanish-speaking islands of the Caribbean. In the end, the shredded meat should resemble ragged, old clothes; hence, its name "old clothes." The addition of annatto is very traditional in many Spanish and Cuban dishes, and it adds a slightly musky flavor to the dish. It should be used judiciously.

2½	pounds flank steak	2	cloves garlic, minced
2	bay leaves	1	green pepper, seeded and chopped
1	teaspoon salt	2	habanero chiles, seeds and stems removed, chopped
¼	teaspoon freshly ground black pepper	3	large tomatoes, peeled, seeded, and chopped
1	onion, cut into eighths	⅛	teaspoon ground cinnamon
1	carrot, sliced	⅛	teaspoon ground cloves
1	turnip, peeled and cut into quarters	2	canned pimientos, drained and chopped
	Water to cover	1	tablespoon capers
2	tablespoons olive oil		
½	teaspoon annatto oil		
2	leeks, chopped (white part only)		

Wash the flank steak and place it in a large casserole, and add the next seven ingredients. Bring the mixture to a boil, reduce the heat to a simmer, cover, and cook for 1½ hours, or until it is tender. Check the water level occasionally and add more if necessary.

Remove the steak to a plate to cool, and strain the cooking liquid into a bowl and set aside.

When the steak is cool enough to handle, shred it using two forks to tear the meat apart, and set aside.

Heat the oils in a large, heavy skillet and sauté the leeks, garlic, green pepper, and the chiles until the vegetables are tender, but not browned.

Add the tomatoes, cinnamon, and cloves and simmer the sauce, stirring, until it starts to thicken. Mix in 2 cups of the reserved stock, the reserved shredded meat, pimientos, and capers and simmer for 5 minutes longer.

Serve this dish with hot cooked rice and/or fried plantains.

Serves: 6

Heat Scale: Medium

Stuffed Haitian Fillet of Beef

This recipe presents a new twist on the usual baked fillet: When it is cut diagonally, the inside stuffing reveals the smells and sights of Haitian peppers, garlic, and cashew nuts. Since this is a rich entree, we suggest light side dishes, as well as a light, cooling dessert from Chapter 9.

3	pound beef fillet, tenderloin preferred	6	strips bacon
½	fresh lime	¾	cup chopped cashews
2	cloves garlic, minced		Salt and freshly ground black pepper to taste
1	thinly sliced onion		
2	habanero chiles, seeds and stems removed, cut in julienne strips		

Rub the outside of the fillet with the fresh lime half. Split the fillet open lengthwise, taking care not to cut all the way through. Rub the inside of the fillet with the fresh lime.

Spread one side of the butterflied fillet with the garlic; place the onion on top of the garlic, and follow with the habanero chiles, 3 slices of the bacon, and the cashews. Add salt and pepper to taste.

Put the fillet back together again and carefully wrap the fillet with the remaining 3 strips of bacon. Secure the fillet and bacon with toothpicks, so that the filling doesn't fall out. An alternative to the toothpicks is to wrap the fillet every few inches with cotton kitchen string. Refrigerate the fillet for 2 hours.

Preheat the oven to 450 degrees.

Allow the fillet to reach room temperature, about 20 minutes. Place the fillet in a lightly oiled shallow glass pan, place the pan in the oven, and immediately turn the temperature down to 350 degrees. Bake the fillet for 35 to 45 minutes, until brown and tender. To check on the doneness of the meat, you can (very carefully) separate the halves to check the interior.

Arrange the fillet on a heated serving dish, remove the toothpicks or string, carefully slice the meat into 1-inch pieces, and serve immediately.

Serves: 4 to 6

Heat Scale: Hot

Note: This recipe requires advance preparation.

Trinidadian-Style Oxtail

The first time we ever tasted this dish was in Trinidad, and we found that this cut of meat (although bony) is very tasty, rich, and quite succulent. The "oxtail" actually comes from a cow rather than an ox. It was served with dumplings and a side of green vegetables and lentils. It can also be served with yams or potatoes that are drizzled with butter and sprinkled with chopped parsley. In Jamaica, this dish is considered a special meal, with its own island variations, of course!

3	pounds oxtails (beef tails), washed, dried, and cut into 2-inch sections
2	tablespoons vegetable oil
2	onions, coarsely chopped
3	cloves garlic, finely chopped
1	teaspoon dried thyme
3	carrots, cut into 1-inch pieces
2	tablespoons habanero hot sauce (see recipes, Chapter 2, or use bottled sauce), or substitute ½ fresh Congo pepper (habanero), seeds and stem removed, minced

½	teaspoon freshly ground black pepper
3	cups beef stock
3	cups water
1	cup split peas or beans
1	tablespoon rum or 2 tablespoons sherry (optional)
	Salt to taste

Brown the oxtails in the oil. Add the onions and garlic and sauté for a minute. Add the thyme, carrots, hot sauce, and black pepper and sauté for 2 minutes. Add the beef stock and water and bring to a boil. Then, add the split peas or beans, reduce the heat, cover the pot, and simmer for 2½ hours, stirring occasionally and checking the level of the water to avoid burning. Add more water if necessary.

The meat should be falling off the bones, but if it isn't, simmer for another ½ hour. Just before serving, skim any fat off the top and add the rum or sherry and salt to taste. It can be served in a bowl if it is a little thin, or on a plate if you allow it to thicken more.

Variation: The Creole version of this dish calls for caramelizing sugar with vegetable oil until it is almost burned, then adding the oxtails and proceeding with the recipe.

Serves: 6 to 8

Heat Scale: Medium

Beef Kebabs Tropicale

These spicy kebabs can be found on the island of Saint Croix, as well as many other islands, where fruits abound. Because of the abundance of tropical fruits, the combination of meat and fruit is not that unusual—especially with the addition of a Caribbean habanero hot sauce or the peppers themselves. Serve the kebabs with a rice dish and a cool-down salad.

1	ripe mango, peeled and seed removed	3	tablespoons vegetable oil
1	clove garlic, peeled	3	pounds sirloin steak, fat removed, and cut into 1-inch cubes
3	scallions, peeled and white part reserved	1	large pineapple, peeled, cored, and cut into 1½-inch cubes
2	tablespoons brown sugar		
2	Scotch bonnet (or habanero) chiles, seeds and stems removed	3	small partially ripe papayas, peeled, seeded, and cut into 1½-inch cubes
2	tablespoons fresh lemon juice		
2	tablespoons fresh lime juice	3	sweet white onions, peeled and cut into quarters, layers separated
¼	cup dry white wine		
¼	cup passion flower fruit juice (available in most Latin American and Caribbean markets)		

In a food processor or blender, purée the mango, garlic, scallions, brown sugar, chiles, lemon juice, lime juice, white wine, passion flower juice, and oil to make a marinade. Spread out the cubed meat evenly in a large, shallow glass or Pyrex baking dish and pour the marinade over the meat. Pierce the meat with a fork, and then cover and refrigerate the mixture for 4 to 6 hours.

Remove the meat and marinade from the refrigerator and allow the meat to sit at room temperature for 10 minutes before putting the meat on skewers to grill.

On the skewers, alternate the meat, pineapple, papaya, and onion pieces. Broil the skewers in an oven broiler or on an outdoor grill, for 8 to 10 minutes (depending on how well you want the meat done). Serve hot off the grill.

Serves: 6 to 8

Heat Scale: Hot

Note: This recipe requires advance preparation.

Carne Riplada (Spicy Flank Steak)

This dish is popular on the Spanish-speaking islands of the Caribbean, especially in the Dominican Republic. Flank steak used to be considered an inexpensive cut of meat in the United States, but with the popularity of fajitas its price has risen accordingly. In the islands, Spicy Flank Steak is served shredded and is accompanied with cooked rice or mashed potatoes.

Steak and Marinade

2½	pounds flank or skirt steak
1	onion, quartered
2	cloves garlic, sliced
2	tablespoons olive oil

1	Scotch bonnet (or habanero) chile, seeds and stem removed, coarsely chopped
	Water to cover, plus 2 inches

Vegetables

½	cup olive oil
¾	cup green bell pepper, chopped
1	cup onion, chopped
2	cloves garlic, minced
½	teaspoon salt
¼	teaspoon freshly ground black pepper

1	Scotch bonnet (or habanero) chile, seeds and stem removed, minced
2	fresh tomatoes, peeled, seeds removed, and coarsely chopped

Place the washed flank steak in a large, heavy casserole and add the onion, garlic, olive oil, one of the chiles, and water. Bring the mixture to a boil, turn the heat down to a simmer, cover, and simmer for at least 2 hours.

Check the water level occasionally, and add more water if necessary.

When the meat is tender, remove it from the casserole and drain it; cool the meat, and then shred it or chop it very finely, and set aside. Strain and reserve 1 cup of the cooking water.

Heat the olive oil in a large skillet and sauté the bell pepper, onion, and garlic until the onion wilts—about 2 minutes. Add the salt, pepper, another chile, and the tomatoes and simmer for 1 minute. Then stir in the shredded meat and simmer the mixture until the meat is heated through, about 15 minutes. The meat should be a little moist (not dry), and if the meat mixture starts to dry out, add several tablespoons of the reserved cooking liquid. Serve hot.

Serves: 6

Heat Scale: Medium Hot

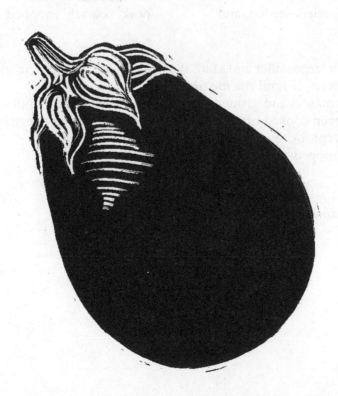

Cuban-Style Spicy Picadillo

This spicy dish can use either beef or pork; we have heard many friends claim that one or the other meat makes a superior picadillo. Try both versions and choose for yourself! Picadillo is traditionally served with Moros y Cristianos (Black Beans and Rice, p. 237), fried plantains, and a cucumber salad.

2	tablespoons vegetable oil	¼	teaspoon ground cloves
1	bell pepper, seeded and chopped	1	cup chopped green olives
1	cup chopped onions	¼	cup raisins
2	cloves garlic, minced	1	tablespoon white vinegar
2	habanero chiles, seeds and stems removed, minced		Salt and pepper to taste
4	tomatoes, peeled, seeded, and chopped	2	pounds boiled lean, boneless beef (chuck or brisket) or pork, coarsely chopped

Heat the oil in a large skillet and sauté the bell pepper, onions, garlic, and chiles for 3 minutes or until the mixture is soft.

Add the tomatoes and ground cloves and stir the mixture until most of the liquid has been cooked off, about 8 minutes. Then stir in the remaining ingredients, except for the meat, and simmer for 1 minute.

Add the chopped meat and heat thoroughly.

Serves: 6

Heat Scale: Medium

Oh, Those Profligate Planters!

"Just how dietary differences influenced nutrition and health is not clear. Today, the poor suffer from their diets. In the sixteenth centry, and even into the eighteenth, it is possible in some cases to argue that the diet of the poor was nutritionally comparable and in some cases superior to that of the wealthy. Portuguese and English planters, for example, loved imported foods and drinks as much as they did imported clothes. For dinner, they ate pickled and salted beef, pork, and fish, served with hardtack, conserves, and sweetmeats. It was the lucky barrel that arrived at Bahia or Kingston without deteriorating under the tropical sun. Europeans went ahead and ate the stinking imported foods, ignoring the cheap, readily available, and fresh local replacements. English planters in the Caribbean might have been the most profligate and extravagent of colonial diners. They consumed such quantities of food and drink that "their own intemperance" led to early sickness and death. As a rule, colonial elites preferred food and drink from home when they could get it. This might have led to the paradoxical situation of the most poorly fed being the best fed. In Brazil, blacks and poor people ate local foods rich in nutrients instead of expensive imported foods."

John C. Super

Solimar Pasta Bowl

This is an unusual pasta bowl, indeed, since chef Joe Brown of the Solimar Restaurant in Port of Spain, Trinidad, has substituted ripe plantains for the pasta. The melding of tastes and textures gives this dish an exotic twist. The casserole can be assembled 1 or 2 hours before serving, and then the egg and cheese mixture can be added and the casserole baked.

¼ cup soy oil or canola oil

2 pounds beef, minced (not hamburger)

4 seasoning peppers or substitute 4 Yellow Wax Hot chiles, seeds and stems removed, chopped

2 cloves garlic, crushed

1 tablespoon chopped Shadow Bennie (culantro) or substitute cilantro

1 large onion, chopped

1 large tomato, diced

¼ cup tomato paste

¼ cup beef or chicken stock

5 large, ripe plantains

½ pound bodi beans (or substitute fresh green beans), cut in 2-inch lengths and blanched for 2 minutes

4 eggs

½ cup cheddar cheese, grated

Heat the oil and fry the meat for 1 minute. Add the peppers, garlic, Shadow Bennie, and onion and sauté until the meat starts to brown.

Add the tomato, tomato paste, and beef or chicken stock and cook over medium heat for 10 minutes.

Slice the plantains lengthwise into thin strips and place one layer on the bottom of a greased 9- by 13-inch baking dish. Alternate layers of the meat mixture, beans, and plantains, ending with plantains.

Beat the eggs and add the cheese. Pour this mixture over the casserole and bake in a 350-degree oven for about 30 to 40 minutes, or until the top is golden brown.

Serves: 6 to 8

Heat Scale: Medium

At the Jerk Beach

"The activity in Boston Beach starts at around 6 a.m. with the killing of the pigs and chickens for the day. The meat is then prepared and seasoned and on the grill by 10:30 so it will be ready in time for lunch. To place an order customers point to the chunk of meat they want and gesture with their hands to show how large a portion is desired. The serving is whacked off and wrapped up in newspaper to take away. From a bright orange shack a woman sells the traditional jerk accompaniment, hard dough bread. The dense, white and relatively tasteless bread serves as an excellent antidote to the red-hot repast, as does a cold Red Stripe beer."

Kathleen Beckett-Young

"In two separate visits to Boston Beach, we discover that Jamaican jerk is a lot like the barbecue back home in Texas in at least one respect—you have to time your visit carefully. Lunch at 2:30 p.m. was disappointing because the meat, which had been cooking since the morning, was overly dry. A repeat visit the next day a little before noon was much more satisfying. Like Texas barbecue, jerk is served on a sheet of butcher paper and eaten with your hands. There's plenty of beer and soda available and the starchy breadfruit and festival will fill you up quickly. The jerk pork is our favorite and we are also fascinated by the coarse sausage. But the most interesting exercise in Boston Beach is trying to figure out the recipe for the famous wet jerk rub. We buy several bottles and stick our fingers in each to try and deduce the ingredients."

Robb Walsh

Rum-Drenched and Twice-Cooked: Poultry

Whether barbecued, sautéed, fried, or stuffed, poultry has been a delicious culinary addition to island fare. In fact, it is the perfect ingredient to combine with the exotic and powerful tastes from the Caribbean. Columbus, always the consummate tourist, wrote on his first voyage to the West Indies, "I saw so many islands, I didn't know where to go first." We believe you'll feel the same way about the pleasing poultry recipes in this chapter.

Our first recipe, Chicken Breast Stuffed with Spiced and Peppered Lobster (p. 160), is from the Bahamas, where resort chefs often fuse the old with the new to create new island tastes. And speaking of new tastes, how about grilling up a few? Island grilling may be new to you, but barbecuing has been a part of Caribbean cooking from the time the Spanish arrived there to find the Amerindians cooking fish, poultry, and meat on wooden racks over an open fire. Our recipes reflect this tradition of outdoor cooking. From Spice-Infused Barbecued Chicken (p. 162), to Tart and Hot Grilled Chicken (p. 164) and Grenadian Grilled Chicken (p. 165), these recipes demonstrate the islanders' love of barbecuing as well as their devotion to developing their own heated marinades.

There's almost nothing that tastes better than chicken cooked in the milk of a coconut, or as one Caribbean explorer called it, the nectar of the gods. Our rendition of Goat Pepper Coconut Chicken (p. 166) won't disappoint, but rather, will inspire you to try our other fruit-infused poultry dish, Patito con Piña (Ducking with Pineapple, p. 168). As in most cultures, duckling is an island delicacy, often saved for holidays or other festive occasions. Rum-Drenched Duckling (p. 167) offers a party unto itself, with its use of rum as a sauce base.

The next two recipes offer a treat from Trinidad, often combining the spices thyme and chives as well as the well-respected heat of the habanero. Twice-Cooked Spicy Chicken (p. 170) is a popular fast food in Trinidad, and is the less spicy of the two. Our second culinary concoction from Trinidad is a caramelized chicken of sorts called Pelau (p. 171). The caramelized sugar has made this a classic dish, as islanders are known for their sweet tooths!

Our next stop is Jamaica, where chicken is not only likely to get fried but jerked around, too. Spicy Plantation Chicken (p. 173) was collected by Dave and Mary Jane on a trip to Ocho Rios. The secret to this recipe (besides the Congo pepper, of course) is to baste it frequently throughout the cooking time. Montego Bay Chicken (p. 174) is also called "yardie" chicken, after the people who often cook it in the shanty town area of the city. Fancy

Fricasseed Chicken (p. 176) is a hot addition to any meal with its use of two Scotch bonnets. Feel free to cut down on the chiles if you are worried about overheating your guests. And no cookbook featuring the Caribbean would be complete without a jerk recipe or two. Jerk is often thought of as the most Jamaican way to cook. But it is the marinade, a spiced-out combination of scallions, onions, thyme, allspice, cinnamon, chile peppers, and salt, that makes it special on dishes such as our Jamaican Jerk Chicken Wings (p. 178).

Spicy sauces are the key ingredients to our next recipes. Our first one is a great spicy dish from Cuba called Pollo Glazeado con Salsa de Habanero (Glazed Chicken with Habanero Sauce, p. 180).

And according to Peggy Barnes, culinary magic is within your grasp with the seductive Caribbean Chicken with Black Ginger Sauce (p. 182), which balances the heat of the habanero with rum and soy sauce. Colombo de Poulet (Chicken Colombo, p. 184) is an intricate adaptation of French and Caribbean cuisine served often on the island of Guadeloupe.

Our final four recipes all highlight the spiciness and heartiness of the Caribbean cuisines. From Calypso Ginger Chicken Breasts (p. 185) to Bajan Fried Chicken (p. 186), Stir-Fried Cashew Chicken (p. 187) and the famous Chicken Victoria (p. 188), these poultry picks will put a twinkle in your eye and the need for a trip to the islands in your heart!

Chicken Breast Stuffed with Spiced and Peppered Lobster

Chile Pepper Food Editor Nancy Gerlach was treated to this entree by Joy Williams at the Radisson Grand Resort during her culinary tour of the Bahamas. This dish is representative of one that combines traditional foods—in this case minced lobster—with nontraditional foods to produce a new dish.

Stuffing

1	small onion, sliced	1	goat pepper (or habanero) chile, stem and seeds removed, minced
2	tablespoons butter or margarine		
3	tablespoons tomato paste	1	6-ounce lobster tail, boiled and minced
1	teaspoon thyme		
2	cloves garlic, minced		Salt

Chicken

2	boneless, skinless chicken breasts		Lime juice, fresh preferred
	Garlic salt	¼	cup grated Parmesan cheese
	White pepper	½	cup flour
			Vegetable oil

To make the stuffing, sauté the onions in the butter until soft. Add the tomato paste, thyme, garlic, and chile and continue to sauté for an additional 2 minutes. Stir in the lobster, season with salt, and heat through.

To make the chicken, season the chicken with the garlic salt, white pepper, and lime juice. Combine the cheese with the flour, dip the chicken in the seasoned flour, and shake off any excess.

Heat the oil in a frying pan and cook the chicken until golden brown on both sides. Remove.

Let the chicken cool, then split and stuff the chicken with the minced lobster stuffing. Heat before serving.

Serves: 2

Heat Scale: Medium

Dog Days

During the Depression, times were tough in Trinidad. The great calypso singer, The Tiger, opined that Trinis were worse off than dogs!

A dog can walk about and take up bone
Fowl head, stale bread, fish tail, and pone.
If it's a good breed and not too wild
Some people will take it an' mind it like a child.
But when a hungry man goes out to beg
They will set a bulldog behind his leg.
Forty policemen may chuck him down too
You see where a dog is better than you.

Spice-Infused Barbecued Chicken

Direct from Saint Lucia, this dish is a tribute to the lush and fertile soils of this island. For over 150 years the English and French battled for control of Saint Lucia. Fortunately, today, they coexist nicely and have blended the heritage of their cuisines. The spices, chicken, and vegetables all combine well with the heat of the habanero.

8	large garlic cloves, minced		6	yellow summer squash, cut into ½-inch-thick rounds
2	teaspoons ground coriander			
2	teaspoons ground turmeric		4	chayote squash, halved lengthwise, cut into ¼-inch-thick slices, or 4 zucchini, cut into ½-inch-thick rounds
2	teaspoons dried mustard			
2	teaspoons ground cloves			
2	teaspoons habanero powder			
1	teaspoon anise seed		1½	cups olive oil
2	pounds boneless skinless chicken breasts, cut into 1-inch pieces		⅓	cup fresh lime juice
			12	bamboo skewers
				Salt and pepper to taste
1⅓	pounds boneless skinless chicken thighs, cut into 1-inch pieces			

In a small bowl, combine the garlic, coriander, turmeric, dried mustard, ground cloves, chile powder, and anise seed. Place the chicken in a glass baking dish and the vegetables in another. Sprinkle each with half of the spice mixture. Add half of the olive oil and half of the fresh lime juice to each and mix to coat well. Cover and refrigerate 6 to 8 hours.

Soak the skewers in water for 30 minutes. Drain the skewers and thread each one with alternating pieces of chicken and vegetable.

Prepare the barbecue or preheat the broiler to a medium heat. Season the kebabs with salt and pepper. Grill until the chicken is cooked through, about 5 minutes per side. Transfer to a platter. Serve with the Mango Fandango (p. 66) in Chapter 3.

Serves: 4

Heat Scale: Medium

Note: This recipe requires advance preparation.

Tart and Hot Grilled Chicken

According to *Chile Pepper* author Arnold Krochmal, this dish is sold in the suburbs in Puerto Rico and the Dominican Republic, where it is the local equivalent of fast food. The street vendors do a great job, and the aroma is enticing.

¾	cup vegetable oil	2	teaspoons oregano
	Juice of 3 limes	1½	tablespoons minced cilantro
6	cloves garlic, minced	3	pounds boneless chicken
1½	teaspoons ground black pepper		breasts
2	tablespoons commercial habanero hot sauce, or a recipe from Chapter 2		

Combine the oil and remaining ingredients except the chicken in a glass bowl and mix well. Add the chicken, toss well, and allow to marinate in the refrigerator for 2 to 3 hours.

Grill the breasts for about 12 minutes on each side, basting with the marinade. Serve with any of the rice dishes in Chapter 8.

Serves: 6

Heat Scale: Medium

Note: This recipe requires advance preparation.

Grenadian Grilled Chicken

Shirley Jordan, writing in *Chile Pepper*, reported that Islanders love to cook outdoors, and most cooks in the Caribbean take pride in developing their own spicy marinades. Here is a tangy one that works well with pork as well as chicken.

1	Scotch bonnet chile (or habanero), seeds and stem removed, minced	2	tablespoons butter or margarine
1	green bell pepper, stem and seeds removed, finely chopped	3	tablespoons tomato paste
1	teaspoon dried thyme	½	cup dry white wine
1	teaspoon Worcestershire sauce	¼	cup white wine vinegar
2	cloves garlic, minced	1	chicken, cut in serving-size pieces
2	shallots, minced		

Combine the chile, bell pepper, thyme, and Worcestershire sauce and mix well.

Sauté the garlic and shallots in a saucepan with the butter until lightly browned. Stir in the tomato paste, wine, and vinegar. Add the chile mixture and bring to a boil, reduce the heat, and simmer for 5 minutes. Allow to cool.

Marinate the chicken in the sauce for 3 to 4 hours in the refrigerator.

Preheat the barbecue. Arrange the chicken on the hot grill and cook, turning pieces often and basting with sauce, until done, about 10 to 15 minutes.

Serves: 4 to 6

Heat Scale: Mild

Note: This recipe requires advance preparation.

Goat Pepper Coconut Chicken

Coconut goes with almost everything in the Bahamas. Its water is used in drinks, the flesh is made into milk and cream, and it is also grated and dried to use in various dishes.

Purchase the freshest coconut possible when preparing this dish. Choose one that's heavy in size and sounds full when shaken. One fruit will yield 3 to 4 cups of grated coconut.

1	onion, finely chopped	2	teaspoons West Indian Massala (see recipe, p. 20)
½	cup butter	1	tablespoon sugar
1	chicken, cut into 8 pieces	½	teaspoon saffron
1	goat pepper (or habanero), seeds and stem removed, minced	2	cups chicken stock
	Salt and black pepper to taste	1	cup freshly grated coconut

In a large frying pan, soften the onion in the butter and brown the chicken pieces. Add the chile pepper, salt, pepper, massala, sugar, and saffron, stirring until the chicken is golden. Remove the chicken from the pan and keep warm.

Add the stock to the pan and heat slowly for 15 minutes. Put back the pieces of chicken and simmer, uncovered, over low heat for 25 minutes.

Add the coconut and simmer for another 10 minutes. If possible, serve each portion separately in half a coconut shell.

Serves: 4

Heat Scale: Medium

Rum-Drenched Duckling

Rum is frequently used in the Caribbean as part of a marinade and to add an accent to cooking; it's also used in many exotic drinks. Rum is also considered a medicinal brew. Its production is believed to have started in the early 1600s. To produce 30 gallons of rum, a ton of sugar is needed. And to get a ton of sugar, 10 tons of sugar cane must be harvested. This recipe calls for dark rum, often found in Jamaica, Barbados, and Martinique.

5-	to 6-pound duckling	¼	teaspoon each sage, thyme, and marjoram
2	tablespoons unsalted butter		
	Salt and freshly ground pepper	1	bay leaf
1	medium onion, finely chopped	2	cups chicken stock
1	clove garlic, chopped	1	whole habanero chile
1	sprig parsley	½	cup dark rum

Pull any loose fat from the cavity of the duck and prick the fatty parts with a fork. Heat the butter in a heavy casserole large enough to hold the duck comfortably and lightly brown the bird all over. Discard all but 2 tablespoons of the fat.

Season the bird with salt and pepper. Add the onion and garlic to the casserole and sauté until the onion is tender. Return the duck to the casserole with the parsley, sage, thyme, marjoram, and bay leaf tied in a square of muslin or cheesecloth (bouquet garni). Add the chicken stock and the habanero, cover, and simmer gently until the duckling is tender, about 1½ hours. Discard the bouquet garni and habanero, and remove any fat that has accumulated. While keeping the duck warm, reduce the sauce until slightly thick.

Heat the rum, pour it over the duck, and flame it. Serve the duck on a bed of rice, with the sauce served separately.

Serves: 6

Heat Scale: Medium

Patito con Piña (Duckling with Pineapple)

The pineapple that Columbus saw for the first time in the West Indies has spread all over the world, and he would be amazed at how it is being used now. It can be found in everything from meat dishes to drinks to salads. It flourishes in the Caribbean and is Puerto Rico's largest export crop. Serve this with a rice dish from Chapter 8.

4½	pound duckling		1	cup chicken stock
	Salt and freshly ground pepper		2	cups fresh or unsweetened canned pineapple, chopped
2	tablespoons unsalted butter			
¾	cup dark rum		2	teaspoons arrowroot
1	cup unsweetened pineapple juice, fresh if possible		¼	cup cold water
1	habanero chile, seeds and stem removed, minced			

Pull any loose fat from the cavity of the duckling and prick the fatty parts with a fork. Season with salt and pepper. Heat the butter in a heavy casserole large enough to hold the duckling comfortably. Brown the bird all over, lift out, and discard all the fat.

Return the duckling to the casserole with ½ cup of the rum and ½ cup pineapple juice. Cover and cook in a 325-degree oven for 1 hour and 15 minutes. Remove the duckling to a serving platter, carve it, and keep it warm.

Discard all the fat from the casserole. Add the remaining ¼ cup of rum, stir, and scrape up all the brown bits. Pour into a saucepan. Add the rest of the pineapple juice, habanero, and the chicken stock, and cook over brisk heat until the liquid is reduced to 2 cups. Adjust the seasoning, add the chopped pineapple, and cook for 5 minutes longer over very low heat.

Mix the arrowroot with the cold water and stir into the sauce. Cook just long enough to thicken slightly. Serve separately to accompany the duckling.

Serves: 4

Heat Scale: Medium

Twice-Cooked Spicy Chicken

This is a great dish for those who can't handle a lot of heat.

Chicken dishes are very popular all over the Caribbean, especially in Trinidad and Tobago—as evidenced by the number of fast-food shops selling it. The best "fast-food" chicken we ever had was at one of Marie Permenter's Royal Castle Restaurants in Trinidad. However, in this recipe, it is prepared home style, and the phrase "twice-cooked" refers to the browning and then the baking.

½ cup plus 1 tablespoon Trinidad Herb Seasoning Paste (see recipe, p. 24)

1 cup water

1 chicken, cut up

3 tablespoons vegetable oil

2 tablespoons butter

1 tablespoon brown sugar

2 cloves garlic, crushed

1 tablespoon Worcestershire sauce

2 tablespoons tomato paste

2 seasoning peppers (or substitute Yellow Wax Hots), seeds and stems removed, chopped

2 onions, sliced into rings

½ cup dry sherry

Combine ½ cup of the seasoning mixture and the water to make a marinade. Pierce the chicken pieces with a fork and then toss them in the marinade. Allow the chicken to marinate for at least 4 hours.

Remove the chicken from the marinade and pat dry. In a frying pan, heat the oil and butter and add the brown sugar. Cook, stirring constantly, for 1 minute. Add the chicken and sauté until brown, about 5 to 7 minutes.

Add the remaining ingredients plus 1 tablespoon more of the seasoning paste, stir well, and cook over medium heat for about 5 minutes.

Transfer the mixture to a casserole dish and bake, uncovered, in a 350-degree oven until well browned, about 30 to 40 minutes.

Serves: 4

Heat Scale: Mild

Note: This recipe requires advance preparation.

Spicy Plantation Chicken

If you are ever in Ocho Rios, we highly recommend that you eat one of Andre's meals. Chef Andre Niederhauser of the Harmony Hall Restaurant in Ocho Rios recommends cooking this chicken on a rotisserie, but roasting it in the oven will also work. The key to success with this dish is to baste the chicken as many as 20 times during the cooking.

½   cup scallions, chopped

3   whole cloves

1   medium chicken, left whole
    Salt to taste

1   tablespoon ground Jamaican
    pimento (allspice)

¼   cup honey

¼   cup lime or lemon juice

1   Scotch bonnet chile (or
    habanero), seeds and stem
    removed, minced very fine

½   cup butter, melted

2   cloves garlic, minced

1   tablespoon demi-glacé

Combine the scallions and cloves and spread them over the chicken, inside and out. Place the chicken, covered, in this mixture in the refrigerator overnight. Remove the chicken and season lightly with salt.

Combine the pimento, honey, lime or lemon juice, and Scotch bonnet to make a basting sauce. Brush some of the baste on the chicken; skewer the chicken on a rotisserie or place it in a roasting pan in a 350-degree oven. Cook the chicken for about 40 minutes, basting often.

Remove the chicken and cut it up into serving pieces.

In a small saucepan, heat the butter and sauté the garlic for 1 minute. Add the remaining basting sauce and the demi-glacé and cook until slightly thickened. Serve this sauce over the chicken.

Serves: 4

Heat Scale: Medium

Note: This recipe requires advance preparation.

Pelau

Caramelizing meat is an African practice that became part of the Creole culinary tradition. The process gives the *pelau* its dark brown color—a sure sign of a good *pelau*. The brown layer that forms on the bottom of the pot is called *bun-bun*, and for some people it's their favorite part of this meal. This recipe comes from Johnny's Food Haven in Port of Spain, Trinidad.

3	tablespoons vegetable oil	3	cups water
¾	cup sugar (white or brown)	1	cup Coconut Milk (see recipe, p. 14)
1	chicken, cut up (about 2½ to 3 pounds)	2	cups fresh Hubbard squash, cubed
1	onion, chopped	2	carrots, chopped
1	clove garlic, minced	¼	cup chopped parsley
1	Congo pepper (habanero), seeds and stem removed, minced	1	teaspoon dried thyme
1½	cups pigeon peas, soaked overnight, or substitute black-eyed peas	1	bunch scallions or green onion, chopped, including the greens
2	cups rice (do not use instant rice)	¼	cup ketchup
		3	tablespoons butter

Heat the oil in a heavy pot or skillet. With the heat on high, add the sugar and let it caramelize until it is almost burned, stirring constantly. Add the chicken and stir until all the pieces are covered with the sugar. Reduce the heat to medium, add the onion, garlic, and Congo pepper and cook, stirring constantly, for 1 minute.

Drain the pigeon peas and add them to the pot along with the rice, water, and coconut milk. Reduce the heat and simmer, covered, for 30 minutes.

Add the remaining ingredients, stir until well mixed, then cover and cook until the vegetables are tender, about 20 to 30 minutes. The *pelau* should be moist at the end of the cooking time.

Serves: 4 to 6

Heat Scale: Mild

Advice for 19th Century Tourists Who Wish to Cook Poultry

"Poultry ought not to fetch more than 9d. per lb. in the towns; 6d. in the country parts. In and about Kingston the people hawk them about asking exhorbitant prices; it is always best to weigh them. Ducks vary from 10 1/2d. to 1s. per lb.; turkeys 1s. per lb.; pigeons 1s. 6d. a pair for the large. Wild guinea birds 2s. 6d. each, or 5s. to 6s. per pair."

John Kenneth McKenzie Pringle, 1893

Montego Bay Chicken

Here is a classic fricasseed chicken recipe from Montego Bay, Jamaica. The people who live in the shanty-town area of Montego Bay cook this "yardie" dish often. One of the secrets, they say, is to use the freshest chicken possible.

1	red bell pepper, seeds and stem removed, chopped	1	Scotch bonnet chile (or habanero), seeds and stem removed, minced
1	yellow bell pepper, seeds and stem removed, chopped	2	cloves garlic, minced
1	large onion, chopped	1½	tablespoons fresh thyme
8	green onions, chopped, including the greens	3	chicken legs with thighs attached
2	carrots, peeled and sliced ¼ inch thick	1½	cups milk
¾	cup celery tops, finely chopped		Flour for dredging
8	fresh okra, sliced ½ inch thick		Vegetable oil
2	tomatoes, chopped	2	4-ounce jars sliced pimientos, drained
1	cho-cho (chayote squash), peeled and chopped, or substiute zucchini		

Combine the peppers, onions, carrots, celery tops, okra, tomatoes, chayote, Scotch bonnet, garlic, and thyme in a bowl. Place the chicken in a glass dish, cover with the mixture, and marinate for 3 hours.

Remove the chicken and scrape off any vegetables. Pour the oil into a pan to a depth of 1 inch and heat. Dip the chicken in the milk and then the flour, shaking off any excess. Pan-fry the chicken until golden brown, about 20 minutes. Remove and drain off all but 1 tablespoon of the oil.

Reduce the heat and pour a half-cup of the milk in the pan to deglaze it. Add the vegetable mixture and braise for 2 minutes. Push the vegetables aside in places and put the chicken back in the pan. Add enough milk to come half-way up the chicken.

Simmer the mixture for 25 minutes, stirring the vegetables occasionally, and taking care not to knock the breading off the chicken. Turn the chicken pieces, add the pimientos, and continue to simmer, stirring occasionally, for 20 minutes or until the chicken is done.

If the gravy is too thick, thin it with additional milk; if the gravy is too thin, raise the heat and reduce it until it thickens.

Serves: 6

Heat Scale: Medium

Note: This recipe requires advance preparation.

Fancy Fricasseed Chicken

This is one of the most delicious ways of cooking Caribbean chicken, as it is marinated before it is cooked, then cooked twice. The marinade is rich and spicy, and the dish ends up that way as well. This dish does well with rice and peas, fried plantains, and Mango Fandango (p. 66).

1	4-pound chicken	2	Scotch bonnet chiles (or habanero), seeds and stems removed, minced
	Juice of 1 lime		
	Salt	¼	cup vegetable oil
	Freshly ground black pepper	2	to 3 cups water
1	clove garlic, crushed	1	whole green Scotch bonnet chile (or habanero)
1	sprig fresh thyme		
2	onions, chopped		
2	tomatoes, chopped		

Wash and dry the chicken. Rub it all over with the lime juice. Cut the chicken into pieces and place them in a bowl. Season the chicken with salt and plenty of black pepper.

In a separate bowl, combine the garlic, thyme, onions, tomatoes, and minced Scotch bonnet. Mix well, then coat each piece of chicken thoroughly with the spice mixture. Let the chicken marinate, covered, for 1 hour in the refrigerator.

Remove the chicken pieces from the bowl and pat dry, reserving the marinade. Fry in the oil (or a half-and-half mixture of oil and butter) over moderate heat until very brown. Fry as many pieces as the pan will hold without overlapping, and when they are all browned remove them from the pan.

Take the pan off the heat for a minute or so, and let it cool a little. Then lower the heat, put the pan back on, and add the reserved marinade. Stir for a minute or so, then pour in the water, bring to a boil, and add the chicken pieces and the whole Scotch bonnet. Reduce the heat, cover the pan, and simmer for 45 minutes to 1 hour or until the chicken is tender but not falling apart. Be careful not to break the whole Scotch bonnet.

Taste the juices for salt and, if the gravy is too liquid, reduce it by increasing the heat, leaving the cover off, until the excess liquid evaporates. The juices from the chicken together with the seasonings will produce a thick, delicious gravy. Remove the Scotch bonnet carefully before serving.

Serves: 4

Heat Scale: Medium

Jamaican Jerk Chicken Wings

Jamaican jerk huts are everywhere in Jamaica, especially in Kingston, where many a steel drum has been converted to a grill. The controversy continues as to what part of Jamaica (and what particular place) has the best. So far, the unofficial taste troop has designated Boston Beach. Use the marinade below or substitute North Coast Jerk Marinade (p. 23) if you have some prepared.

1	onion, chopped
⅔	cup scallions, finely chopped
2	garlic cloves
½	teaspoon dried thyme, crumbled
1½	teaspoons salt
1½	teaspoons ground allspice
¼	teaspoon nutmeg, freshly grated
½	teaspoon cinnamon
½	teaspoon habanero chile, minced
1	teaspoon freshly ground black pepper
10	drops commercial habanero hot sauce, or to taste
2	tablespoons soy sauce
¼	cup vegetable oil
18	chicken wings (about 3¼ pounds), wing tips cut off and reserved

In a food processor or blender, purée the onion, scallions, garlic, thyme, salt, allspice, nutmeg, cinnamon, habanero, black pepper, habanero hot sauce, soy sauce, and oil.

In a large shallow dish, arrange the chicken wings in one layer and spoon the marinade over them, rubbing it in. Let the wings marinate, covered and chilled, turning them once, for at least 1 hour, or preferably overnight.

Arrange the wings in one layer on an oiled rack set over a foil-lined roasting pan, spoon the marinade over them, and bake the wings in the upper third of a preheated 450-degree oven for 30 to 35 minutes, or until they are cooked through.

Serves: 4 to 6

Heat Scale: Medium

Kingston's Favorite Jerk

"Although jerk pork originally led the field, jerk chicken is now the most popular. In Kingston the demand for jerk chicken on the weekends is incredible. The steel drums coverted to grills are ubiquitous. They line the streets and, on weekends in certain sections of Red Hills Road, so much smoke emerges from the line of drums that, except for the smell, one could be forgiven for thinking that a San Franciscan fog had come to Jamaica."

Caribbean Week

Pollo Glazeado con Salsa de Habanero (Glazed Chicken with Habanero Sauce)

This chicken dish is from Rodolfo de Garay and Thomas Brown, who wrote about spicy Cuban dishes in *Chile Pepper*. They noted: "This recipe also works well as a barbecue. Make sure the chicken is half-cooked over the coals before beginning to brush on the habanero sauce." Sour orange juice can be approximated by mixing orange juice and lime juice in equal proportions.

½ cup sour orange juice
½ teaspoon freshly ground black
    pepper
1 teaspoon garlic, minced
1 teaspoon salt
8 pieces chicken
1 habanero chile, seeds and stem
    removed, quartered

1 teaspoon lemon juice
1 teaspoon white vinegar
¼ teaspoon salt
2 tablespoons tomato sauce
2 tablespoons onion, chopped
    Vegetable oil for sautéing

Combine the sour orange juice, black pepper, garlic, and salt to make an adobo and marinate the chicken for at least 2 hours (and preferably overnight).

   When ready to begin cooking, preheat the oven to 400 degrees. Place the habanero, lemon juice, vinegar, salt, tomato sauce, and chopped onion in a blender or food processor and blend to make a sauce. Add a little water if necessary. (If habaneros are not available, a commercially bottled sauce may be used instead.)

Remove the chicken from the adobo and reserve the liquid. Put about ⅛ inch of oil in a frying pan over medium–high heat. Brown the chicken until golden on both sides.

Mix the remaining adobo with the habanero sauce. Place the chicken pieces on a pan and brush with the sauce. Bake for about 6 minutes, then turn the chicken over, brush the other side with sauce, and continue baking for another 6 minutes. Repeat this until the sauce has been used up and the chicken is finished cooking, about 30 minutes. This dish may be served hot or cold.

Serves: 4 to 8

Heat Scale: Medium

Note: This recipe requires advance preparation.

Caribbean Chicken with Black Ginger Sauce

Peggy Barnes collected this Antiguan recipe for *Chile Pepper* magazine. In this dish, imported pickled ginger and soy sauce combine with local rum to turn chicken into black magic. Peggy wrote: "Local cooks choose a sweet soy sauce, like Kikkoman, to balance the heat generated by the habanero peppers. Serve with steamed white rice topped with the ginger sauce, and a quick stir-fry of snow peas or zucchini slices."

2½	pounds bone-in, skinless chicken breasts	1	teaspoon ground black pepper
1	cup white rum	2	teaspoons cornstarch
¼	cup vegetable oil	1	cup soy sauce
1	large onion, coarsely chopped	½	cup Japanese pickled ginger (available in Asian markets)
1	habanero chile, seeds and stem removed, minced	2	tablespoons slivered scallions (green part only) for garnish
4	garlic cloves, finely chopped		
2	tablespoons fresh ginger, grated		

Marinate the chicken in the rum for several hours or overnight.

Remove the chicken and reserve the rum. Preheat the oven to 350 degrees.

In a large skillet, heat the oil and cook the chicken until golden brown. Remove and keep warm. Add the onion and cook for 1 minute. Add the habanero, garlic, fresh ginger, and ground black pepper. Cook for 2 minutes.

In a medium bowl, dissolve the cornstarch in the soy sauce, then add the reserved rum and the onion–garlic mixture and combine well to make a sauce.

Place the chicken in a baking pan, pour the sauce over the chicken, and bake for 1 hour. Turn the chicken several times during baking to coat with the sauce. Five minutes before serving, top the chicken pieces with the pickled ginger, turn off the oven, and let the dish stand for 10 minutes. Garnish with the scallions before serving.

Serves: 4

Heat Scale: Medium

Note: This recipe requires advance preparation.

Colombo de Poulet (Chicken Colombo)

This recipe hails from Guadeloupe, where they are not afraid to hit the peppers. Shaped like a butterfly, the two islands of Basse-Terre and Grande-Terre are separated by the Rivière Salée. Guadeloupe sports a 74,000-acre Parc National, full of waterfalls, lakes, rain forests, and even a volcano. This curry is as lush as the landscape and should be served over white rice.

¼	cup peanut oil	1	tablespoon minced fresh parsley
2	pounds chicken pieces	¼	cup dried chickpeas, soaked overnight and drained
1	medium onion, finely chopped		
2	green onions, finely chopped	1	large carrot, diced
2	cloves garlic, minced	2	chayotes or zucchini, peeled and sliced
2	tablespoons Colombo Curry Paste (see recipe, p. 21)	1	habanero chile, seeds and stem removed, minced
½	teaspoon ground allspice		
2	cups water		
1	tablespoon white wine vinegar		
3	sprigs thyme, finely chopped, or 1 teaspoon dried thyme		

Heat the oil in a large, deep saucepan over high heat and brown the chicken. Reduce the heat to medium high, add the onion and garlic, and cook until soft. Add the curry paste, allspice, water, vinegar, thyme, parsley, and chickpeas. Reduce the heat to low, cover, and cook for 40 minutes. Add the carrot, chayote or zucchini, and habanero and cook until the vegetables are tender, about 10 to 15 minutes. Serve hot.

Serves: 4

Heat Scale: Medium

Calypso Ginger Chicken Breasts

True to its name, this recipe will make you sing. With key ingredients featuring liqueurs and pawpaw (better known as papaya), this recipe truly combines the rich flavors of the islands.

6	large chicken breasts	1	onion, chopped
	Juice of 1 lemon	½	cup chicken stock
	Salt and pepper	½	cup La Grenade liqueur
2	callaloo leaves or substitute	1	teaspoon Worcestershire sauce
	6 spinach leaves	2	tablespoons butter
6	to 8 slices papaya	1	teaspoon cornstarch
½	teaspoon minced Scotch bonnet chile (or habanero)	1	teaspoon rum
		4	teaspoons soy sauce
3	chives, chopped	½	teaspoon nutmeg, grated
2	pieces ginger, grated		

Remove the skin from the chicken breasts and wash them with lemon juice. Flatten the chicken breasts with a mallet and season them with salt and pepper.

Spread the callaloo or spinach leaves on the bottom of a shallow buttered baking dish. Spread the breasts over the leaves, add the papaya slices, habanero, chives, ginger, and onion. Cover the dish with aluminum foil and bake in a 350-degree oven for 30 minutes.

In a saucepan, combine the chicken stock, La Grenade liqueur, Worcestershire sauce, butter, cornstarch, rum, soy sauce, and nutmeg, and cook over medium heat for 5 minutes to make a sauce.

Remove the chicken breasts from the dish and arrange them on a platter over a bed of rice. Pour the sauce over them and serve hot.

Serves: 6

Heat Scale: Medium

Bajan Fried Chicken

From Barbados, this chicken is famous because of its tasty seasonings. But beware if you're a tourist in Barbados. What may be pitched to you as authentic "Bajan" seasoning may actually be only dried green onions!

1   cup Bonney Bajan Seasoning (see recipe, p. 26)

2   pounds chicken parts, pricked all over with a fork

2   cups vegetable or corn oil for frying

1   cup all-purpose flour

½   teaspoon baking powder
    Salt

½   teaspoon freshly ground black pepper

Combine the Bonney Bajan Seasoning and the chicken in a bowl and marinate for 1 hour or longer in the refrigerator.

Heat the oil in a frying pan until hot. Combine the flour, baking powder, salt, and pepper. Pat the chicken pieces dry with paper towels. Separate some of the skin from the chicken pieces and place some of the marinade between the skin and meat. Coat the chicken with the flour mixture.

Fry the chicken over medium heat until cooked and golden brown on both sides, 15 to 20 minutes. Serve hot.

Serves: 4 to 6

Heat Scale: Medium

Note: This recipe requires advance preparation.

Stir-Fried Cashew Chicken

Cashews are a cash crop of the Caribbean. The cashew tree produces both a nut and a fruit, and, strangely enough, it is related botanically to both mangoes and poison ivy. This recipe illustrates the Asian influence on the Caribbean.

¼	cup peanut oil	1	cup mushrooms, sliced
3	boned chicken breasts, thinly sliced	1	8-ounce can bamboo shoots, drained and chopped
½	cup chopped onion	2	teaspoons salt
3	scallions, white and green parts, chopped	2	tablespoons commercial habanero hot sauce, or select a recipe from Chapter 2
1	cup cucumber, peeled and coarsely chopped	¾	cup whole roasted cashews
1	cup carrots, coarsely chopped		Butter or oil
1	8-ounce can water chestnuts, drained and sliced		

Heat the peanut oil in a heavy frying pan or wok and stir-fry the chicken over high heat for 3 minutes. Add the onion, scallions, cucumber, carrots, water chestnuts, mushrooms, bamboo shoots, and salt, then cook, stirring constantly over brisk heat, for about 5 minutes longer. Pour the hot sauce over the mixture and cook without stirring for 1 more minute.

Meanwhile, sauté the cashews in a little butter or oil until golden brown.

Pile the chicken–vegetable mixture into a warmed serving dish and top with the cashews. Serve with rice.

Serves: 4

Heat Scale: Medium

Chicken Victoria

In 1838, Jamaica was emancipated from England. This recipe is in honor of Queen Victoria, who is remembered as "Missus Queen who set us free." This dish is great to make ahead for a dinner party, especially a buffet.

1	4-pound chicken, cut into serving pieces
1	tablespoon fresh lime juice
1	teaspoon salt
½	teaspoon freshly ground black pepper
1	medium onion, thinly sliced
1	clove garlic, crushed and chopped
1	green bell pepper, seeded and chopped
1	tablespoon commercial habanero hot sauce, or select a recipe from Chapter 2
3	tablespoons vegetable oil
½	teaspoon annatto seed
2	cups long-grain rice
1	cup mushrooms, sliced and sautéed in butter
1	tablespoon tomato sauce
1	2- to 3-inch piece of lemon peel
1	tablespoon lime juice
1	teaspoon sherry
4	cups concentrated chicken stock
3	tablespoons gold Jamaican rum

Squeeze the fresh lime juice over the chicken pieces, then sprinkle them well with the salt and pepper. Add the onion, garlic, green bell pepper, and the hot sauce to the chicken pieces. Cover and refrigerate for up to 24 hours.

When ready to cook, shake the seasoning off the chicken and reserve. Pat the chicken pieces dry with paper towels.

Heat the oil and annatto seeds in a heavy-bottomed casserole until the oil becomes red. Discard the seeds. Sauté the chicken pieces until browned, then remove and set aside.

To the casserole, add the uncooked rice, the reserved seasoning, and sauté, stirring until the oil is absorbed. Be careful that the rice does not burn. Add the mushrooms and return the chicken pieces to the casserole. Add the tomato sauce, lemon peel, lime juice, sherry, and chicken stock. Taste for seasoning and make any necessary corrections. Cover and simmer gently until the rice is cooked, the chicken is tender, and the liquid has been absorbed. This should take about 40 minutes. Add the rum last and cook uncovered for about 5 minutes longer.

Serves: 6

Heat Scale: Medium

Note: This recipe requires advance preparation.

Jamaican Pimento

"Familiarly called allspice or Jamaican Pepper, this exceptional spice is grown almost exclusively in Jamaica where it was in use by the Tainos before 1494. The name allspice derives from the likeness to a combination of cinnamon, nutmeg and cloves. The tree is particularly handsome with glossy aromatic evergreen leaves (used for an essential oil) and has a smooth, light coloured almost barkless trunk. Every part of the tree is aromatic with a unique pungent fragrance pleasing to humans but obnoxious to insects. The spice comes from the green berries that resemble black pepper when dried. Pimento dram liqueur is made from the ripe berries while the famous Jamaican jerk barbecue depends on burning the aromatic pimento wood and leaves to impart the irresistible smokey savour that was a speciality of the intrepid Jamaican Maroons."

Valerie Facey

Blue Backs, Shrimp, and Pounded Conch: Seafood

In 1492 and during subsequent voyages, Colombus sailed the Caribbean and discovered its tropical treasures. And a vast treasure it is. The sea covers more than 75,000 square miles, 2,600 of which make up the chain of islands that stretches from Florida to Venezuela to enclose the Caribbean. About 2,000 islands make their home in these waters, although some are as humble as a few rocks in the sea. Some are large, such as Cuba, whose size allows it the title of the largest Caribbean island, followed by Hispaniola, Jamaica, and Puerto Rico.

But it is the host of delectable dinners that live below this sea of emerald green and turquoise that is of interest in this chapter. The brilliantly colored fish of this area are not only beautiful to look at, they are delicious to eat.

In the Caribbean, one is usually only a few minutes away from the water, and thus a tasty, fresh seafood treat. The first recipe in this chapter, Keshi Yena coe Cabron (Baked Cheese with Prawn Stuffing, p. 194), is a classic "stuffed cheese" recipe from Dutch Curaçao. The next two recipes hail from Cuba, known as one of Ernest Hemingway's favorite islands. Of course, one of the things that drew the novelist to Cuba was the sea and, most likely, the divine dishes it produced. We begin our expedition with Camarones Enchilado (Shrimp Enchilado, p. 196), a stunning sauté of seafood and peppers, and continue with Pescado Sobre Uso (Sofrito for "Reused" Fish, p. 198), which actually refers to a preservation method using *sofrito*.

In Columbus's New World, much of the Indians' diet consisted of fish. The same is true today, with each island offering its own specialties. We collected no less than five interesting recipes from the Bahamas. The Grouper Soup in Puff Pastry (p. 200) is a simple but elegant dish, and we'll definitely get your goat with the Flash in the Pan Snapper (p. 201), which features minced serranos as well as the hot goat pepper. Kingfish for a Day (p. 202) is positively regal with its combination of spices, fish, and heat. The Coconut–Hot Sauce Shrimp (p. 203) offers a smooth transition for those who like to take control of their heat level. This recipe allows you to choose your favorite hot sauce and serve it on the side with these crispy crustaceans. And if you like unusual shellfish such as escargot, chances are you'll love our Bahamian Curried Conch (p. 204). It marries the sea with the exotic tastes of India for a spectacular taste explosion.

Sir Francis Drake was one of the early explorers of the Caribbean, and a folktale about his run-in with crabs is legendary. It is said that while he and his troops lay in wait on Hispaniola to do battle with the Spanish army, they heard what they thought was the movement of hundreds of troops. This noisy ensemble panicked Drake and his troops so badly that they ran off. The story has it that the loud, scary noise was actually the scurrying of four-legged soldiers—that is, crabs—marching through the undergrowth! Our next four recipes feature these daring creatures, although we promise none of the dishes will scare you away, and most likely will heat up your day. After trying French Caribbean Crabs (p. 205), Blue Crab Backs (p. 206), Caribbean Crab Gumbo, and Resurrection Crab Supper (p. 209), we think you'll agree that crab is one of the true delicacies of the islands, especially when laced with the fruity but heated taste of habaneros.

For most of their history, the islands have been dominated by various European powers. For example, Jamaica was Spanish for 146 years, then British for 307 more before achieving independence in 1962. These cultural influences have worked themselves into the cuisines of this land, as exhibited in the sea-faring recipes we found on our Jamaican search. Get out some extra napkins for our first recipe, Black River Swimp (p. 210), better known as crayfish, as it is a peel-and-eat extravaganza. The luscious Spiny Lobster in Sizzling Sauce (p. 211) is a rare treat for most islanders, as the lobsters are much more valuable when sold rather than eaten. However, we highly suggest you splurge and try this dish! And finally, from Jamaica comes Escovitched Fish (p. 212), which was brought to this island during its Spanish domination as a way to preserve food.

Our last six recipes represent an eclectic mix of old and new, hot and sweet. We named the first recipe Chinese-Style Swordfish with Crispy Slaw and Soy Vinaigrette (p. 214), as it offers an interesting blend of Caribbean and Asian attributes. The Crispy Slaw with Soy Vinaigrette can be served as a good stand-alone dish. Pucker Up and Snap (p. 216) features the ever-popular red snapper as the main ingredient. A great variation of this recipe uses grapefruit juice to add a tangy taste. "Hot fish onboard" could be the sign that accompanies our next recipe, "Poisson" Catch of the Day (p. 218), as it calls for several habanero chiles. The Hot Prawns in Curry Cream Sauce (p. 220) is extremely rich but, hey, anyone can splurge now and then. However, we have lightened it up a bit by using half-and-half. We urge you to try the last two recipes—Drunken Seafood, Creole Style (p. 222) and *Jolly Roger* Flying Fish (p. 223)—with rum punch or the Coors of the Caribbean, a Red Stripe beer or two. It won't put out the heat, but after a few drinks you may not notice it as much!

Keshi Yena coe Cabron (Baked Cheese with Prawn Stuffing)

This somewhat complicated but classic recipe from Dutch Curaçao is worth the extra trouble, and the presentation and taste are as spectacular as the island itself. This dish features Dutch Edam cheese along with the flavors of the sea.

1	4-pound Edam cheese Water	12	ounces raw prawns, shelled and deveined (or substitute jumbo shrimp)
1	tablespoon softened butter		
1	tablespoon firm (chilled) butter	3	tablespoons soft fresh bread crumbs
2½	teaspoons vegetable oil	6	small pimiento-stuffed olives, drained and finely chopped
¼	cup onions, finely chopped		
1	firm, ripe tomato, peeled, seeded, and chopped	2½	teaspoons finely chopped sweet gherkin
½	teaspoon habanero powder	1½	tablespoons seedless raisins
½	teaspoon salt	1	egg, well beaten
	Freshly ground black pepper		

Peel the red wax off of the cheese and cut a 1-inch-thick slice off the top. Scoop out the center of the cheese with a spoon, leaving a boat-like shell about ½ inch thick. Hollow the slice from the top in the same way to make a lid for the shell. Place the lid and shell in a large pan or bowl, pour in enough cold water to cover them by at least 1 inch, and let them soak for 1 hour.

While the cheese is soaking, grate enough of the scooped-out cheese to make 1¾ cups cheese, then set it aside. When the cheese shell and lid have soaked for 1 hour, remove them from the water and invert them on paper towels to drain.

Preheat the oven to 350 degrees. Using a pastry brush, spread the softened butter evenly over the bottom and sides of a round baking dish at least 5 inches deep and just large enough to hold the cheese snugly. It is very important to choose a baking dish that is the right size, or the the cheese will collapse during baking.

Melt the remaining butter and the vegetable oil in a heavy frying pan over medium heat. Sauté the onions, stirring frequently, until they are translucent. Add the tomato, habanero powder, salt, and a little black pepper. Cook the mixture quickly, stirring constantly, until almost all of the liquid in the pan has evaporated; what remains should have a very thick consistency.

Transfer the contents of the pan to a deep mixing bowl. Add the grated cheese, prawns, bread crumbs, olives, gherkin, and raisins, and toss together until thoroughly mixed. Taste for seasoning, then stir in the beaten egg. Place the cheese shell in the prepared baking dish, then spoon the prawn mixture into the cheese shell, and top it with the cheese lid.

Bake the shell uncovered on the middle shelf of the oven for about 30 minutes, until the top is bubbly and lightly browned. Serve the Keshi immediately, straight from the baking dish.

Serves: 6

Heat Scale: Medium

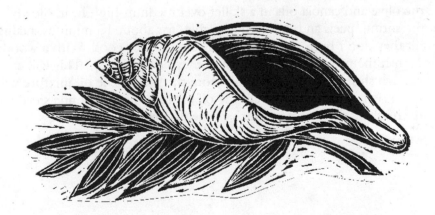

Camarones Enchilado (Shrimp Enchilado)

This recipe is from Rodolfo de Garay and Thomas Brown, who wrote about Cuba in *Chile Pepper* Magazine. They noted: "The word *enchilado* as used in Cuba refers to chiles, not to the Mexican dish of a rolled and stuffed tortilla. This dish is a sauté of seafood and peppers; lobster is often substituted for shrimp."

¼	cup extra virgin olive oil	2	tablespoons minced garlic
¾	cup canola oil	½	teaspoon oregano
1½	pounds large fresh shrimp, peeled and deveined (save the peels, and heads if available)	2	bay leaves
		1	teaspoon salt
1	cup Cubanelle (or green bell) pepper, chopped	1	teaspoon freshly ground black pepper
1	cup red bell pepper, chopped	½	cup tomato purée
1	cup yellow bell pepper, chopped	½	cup fine dry sherry
1½	cups onion, chopped	4	tablespoons white vinegar
1	habanero chile, seeds and stem removed, thinly sliced	1	cup Spanish olives stuffed with anchovies (optional)

Place the olive and canola oils in a skillet over medium-high heat. Slowly sauté the shrimp peels and heads (if available) for about 15 minutes, taking care that they don't burn. They will turn color as they cook. With a wooden spoon, crush them as much as possible as they become crisp. This will extract as much shrimp flavor as possible from the shells. The oil mixture will darken to a rich, dark amber. Strain the oil mixture through a fine sieve, pressing the shells to extract as much of the flavored oil as possible.

Place ¼ cup of the shrimp-flavored oil in a large sauté pan, heat, and sauté half the Cubanelle or green bell peppers and onions until the onions are translucent. Then add the remainder of the peppers and onions. Add the habanero, garlic, oregano, bay leaves, salt, and pepper, and sauté until the onions are soft and the pan is almost dry.

Add the tomato purée and the sherry. Increase the heat and cook to reduce the liquid by half. Add the peeled shrimp and cook only until the shrimp turn pink, no more than 3 to 5 minutes. Add the vinegar and, if desired, stuffed olives, and heat through for an additional minute.

Serve with white rice and beer and, if desired, fried ripe plantains and shrimp toast (made with the remainder of the shrimp-flavored oil).

Serves: 4

Heat Scale: Medium

Jamaican Black Crab

"In his celebrated 1756 treatise on the *Civil and Natural History of Jamaica*, Patrick Browne says of the Jamaican black crab: 'When the black crab is fat and in a perfect state, it surpasses every thing of the sort, in flavour and delicacy. They are frequently boiled and served up at the more sumptuous tables…' The Jamaican black crab, a seasonal land crab that is actually dark red, should not be confused with the common Jamaican white land crab, which is also edible. To this day the black crab is regarded by Jamaicans as a choice treat and these crabs are usually spicily prepared with loving care. Though not as delicate in flavour, sea crabs may be substituted."

Valerie Facey

Pescado Sobre Uso
(Sofrito for "Reused" Fish)

The name of this Cuban dish may not sound too appetizing, explained
Rodolpho de Garay and Thomas Browne in *Chile Pepper* magazine, but it
actually refers to the poorer households where lack of refrigeration required
that an entire catch of fish be cooked immediately. Later that day or the
next, the leftover fish would be fixed with a sofrito to be eaten. This sofrito,
of course, can be spooned over fish you've just cooked and is delicious with
most kinds of fish. Use pure or refined olive oil. Do not use extra virgin
olive oil, as it will take away from the traditional taste of this sofrito.

6	firm white fish fillets	2	habanero chiles or 6 rocotillo chiles, seeds and stems removed, and splint lengthwise
1	cup olive oil		
1½	cups onions, sliced		
½	cup Cubanelles or green bell pepper, chopped and seeded	1	tablespoon vinegar (hot chile vinegar may be used for extra heat)
5	cloves garlic, minced		
1	teaspoon salt		
¼	teaspoon freshly ground black pepper		

Fry the fillets in the olive oil until they are done and slightly brown. Remove
the fillets, reserve them, and keep them warm. Strain the olive oil.

In a saucepan, heat the reserved oil. When hot, add the onions and sauté until they begin to wilt. Add the Cubanelles or green bell pepper, garlic, salt, and black pepper and cook for about 2 minutes. Add the habaneros or rocotillos and cook for 2 minutes. Stir in the vinegar and remove from the heat.

With a slotted spoon, ladle the sofrito over the fillets. (Plenty of oil will come with the onions and peppers, so a slotted spoon should be used to keep from ladling on too much oil.)

Serves: 6

Heat Scale: Hot

A Trinidadian Fish of Legend

"The Amerindians also ate much river fish, including the cascadura about which legend has it that he who eats this fish shall always return to Trinidad. Though its magical quality did not save the Amerindian race from extinction here, we go on eating the cascadura and would allow no visitor to leave without sampling its delicate flavor."

Therese Mills

Grouper Soup in Puff Pastry

The recipe for this soup, created by chef Philip Bethel at the Graycliff Hotel in the Bahamas, was given to Nancy Gerlach, who included it in her *Chile Pepper* article, "The Blistering Bahamas." "It is not only tasty," she wrote, "but makes a truly elegant presentation."

1   pound fresh grouper fillet
    Juice of 2 fresh limes or lemons
    Salt to taste
4   slices bacon, diced
2   small potatoes, peeled and diced
1   stalk of celery, diced
1   onion, diced
1   quart (4 cups) water

2   fresh cayenne chiles, stems and seeds removed, diced; or substitute 1 habanero
2   tablespoons pimientos, diced
    Salt to taste
4   6-inch circles of puff pastry
1   egg, beaten

Preheat the oven to 350 degrees.

Dice the grouper and season with salt and the fresh juice of one lemon or lime. Place equal portions of the fish in four small ovenproof cups and set aside.

Fry the bacon for a couple of minutes, add the potatoes, cover, and simmer over medium heat for 5 minutes. Add the celery and onion and continue to cook for another 5 minutes. Add the water and bring to a boil. Lower the heat, season with the remaining lemon or lime juice and the chiles, and simmer until the potatoes are done.

Divide the ingredients, including the broth, into the cups and add the pimientos.

Brush one side of each pastry circle with beaten egg and place the circles, egg side down, over the cups. Brush the top sides with the remaining egg and place the cups in the oven. Bake for about 10 minutes until the dough rises and is golden.

Serve the soup hot.

Serves: 4

Heat Scale: Medium

Flash in the Pan Snapper

You'll find this quick-fried dish in the Bahamas. An interesting ingredient is lime salt, which is, simply, minced bird peppers or piquins mixed with salt and sprinkled with lime juice, and set out to dry.

2	whole small red snappers, cleaned, scaled, head and tail left on	2	teaspoons fresh goat pepper (or habanero), minced
	Juice of 1 lime	½	cup vegetable oil
	Juice of 1 lemon	2	cups water
1	teaspoon crushed black peppercorns	2	teaspoons fresh serrano chiles, minced
2	teaspoons fresh piquin chile, minced	1	small white onion, minced
	Lime salt	2	teaspoons ground allspice

Score the skin of the snapper in a checkerboard pattern, then sprinkle it with lime and lemon juice, crushed black peppercorns, and the piquin. Marinate the fish overnight.

Remove the fish from the marinade and rub it with the lime salt and goat pepper.

Heat the oil in a deep skillet, add the fish coated with the goat pepper, and fry the fish until the skin is brown, approximately 5 minutes per side over a hot flame. Turn the fish only once.

When the fish is done, remove it from the pan and keep it warm; reserve the pan juices. Add the water, the minced serranos, the onion, and the allspice, and boil the mixture until it's thick. Serve the gravy over the fish.

Serves: 4

Heat Scale: Hot

Note: This recipe requires advance preparation.

Kingfish for a Day

This fish dish is another Bahamian treat. We had a wonderful lunch of fresh mangoes, kingfish, and Red Stripe beer on one of the beautiful beaches of that country of many islands. Try this as a lazy-day luncheon or dinner. And don't forget the beer!

1	goat pepper (or habanero), seeds and stem removed, minced	1	pound kingfish fillets, boiled and flaked
1	cup flour	4	chives, minced
2	eggs, beaten	½	teaspoon thyme
½	cup milk	3	cloves garlic, minced
			Cooking oil for frying

In a mixing bowl, make a batter by mixing together the minced goat pepper, flour, eggs, and milk, followed by all the other ingredients. Form the batter into fingers. In a separate frying pan, heat the oil. Deep-fry the fingers until golden brown, about 10 minutes.

Serves: 4

Heat Scale: Hot

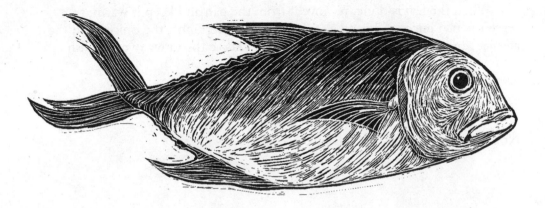

Coconut–Hot Sauce Shrimp

Chile Pepper photographer Chel Beeson collected this easy recipe while he was in the Bahamas. Melissa is known to cook this dish when time is short and guests will be arriving soon! Another added bonus is that you serve it with the commerical hot sauces of your choice. Better yet, have each guest bring a different hot sauce to share!

2 cups flour	2 cups flaked coconut
4 eggs, beaten	Cooking oil for deep frying
1 cup Coconut Milk (see recipe, p. 14)	Commercial habanero hot sauce, or select a recipe from Chapter 2
2 pounds jumbo shrimp, shelled and deveined	

Make a batter with the flour, eggs, and coconut milk. Dip the shrimp in the batter, then roll them in the coconut flakes. Deep-fry until they are brown, about 5 minutes. Serve with the hot sauce (preferably habanero) of your choice.

Serves: 4

Heat Scale: Hot

Bahamian Curried Conch

Conch has been described as the escargot of the West Indies. The conch has been a mainstay of the Bahamian diet, as well as the economy, for many years. Conch just needs to be pounded forever to make it tender. Prepare a conch dinner to release all of your pent-up frustrations!

3　stalks celery, chopped

2　large onions, chopped

1　clove garlic, minced

2　to 3 tablespoons butter

4　tablespoons Trinidadian Curry Paste (see recipe, p. 22)

1　teaspoon ground allspice

1　goat pepper (or habanero), seeds and stem removed, minced

3　bay leaves

2　pinches thyme leaves

1　pound conch meat, pounded until tender, and minced

In a medium-size frying pan, sauté the celery, onions, and garlic in the butter until soft. Add the curry paste and allspice and sauté another 3 minutes. Add the remaining ingredients and water to barely cover them and cook, uncovered, for about 15 minutes over low heat. Serve over white rice.

Serves: 4

Heat Scale: Medium Hot

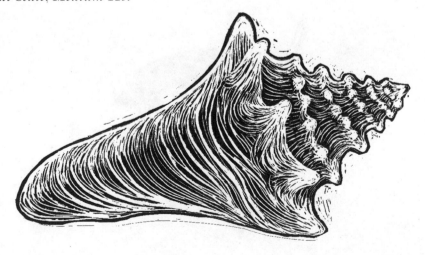

French Caribbean Crabs

We dined on this delectible crab dish while on the island of Martinique. Since this dish offers wonderful French flavors, we suggest you complement your meal with a nice bottle of Muscadet and a loaf of French bread. *Bon appétit!* If you can't find land crabs, sea crabs will do nicely.

10	land crabs	1	sprig parsley, chopped
	Water	½	cup boiling water
⅓	cup olive oil	1	bay leaf
1	Scotch bonnet chile (or habanero), seeds and stem removed, minced		Juice of one lime
			Salt and pepper to taste
2	cloves garlic, finely chopped	6	cups cooked white rice
1	purple onion, finely chopped	2	chives, chopped for garnish
½	teaspoon thyme		

Brush the crabs and throw them into boiling water for 10 minutes. Remove and cut the crabs into small pieces; break off the claws and remove as much of the meat as possible. Brown all these pieces in very hot oil with the chopped Scotch bonnet, garlic, onion, thyme, and parsley. Add boiling water to cover the pieces and add the bay leaf, lime juice, and salt and pepper.

Allow the mixture to simmer for 10 minutes. When the time is up, mix the pieces of crab and the sauce with white rice, and garnish with the chopped chives.

Serves: 6 to 8

Heat Scale: Medium

Blue Crab Backs

This entree is known by many names, but one of the most popular renditions of the dish comes from Trinidad, where it is called Crab Backs. In the West Indies, crab backs are made with the small blue-backed land crabs that live in the swamps and coconut fields. However, if you can't get to a coconut field right away, blue crabs from the market will work just fine!

4 cooked blue crabs, about ¾ pound each, split open	2 teaspoons Worcestershire sauce
2 tablespoons butter	1 tablespoon fresh pineapple juice
1 onion, minced	2 tablespoons rum
3 scallions, trimmed and minced	Pinch of grated nutmeg
1 habanero chile, seeds and stem removed, minced	1 teaspoon salt
	Freshly ground black pepper
2 tablespoons fresh chives, minced	2 cups soft white bread crumbs

Preheat the oven to 350 degrees. Clean the crabs, removing and discarding the stomach, digestive tract, and the gills (dead man's fingers). Pick out all the crab meat from the shell, discarding any skin or cartilage. Reserve the shells. Crack open the claws and combine all the meat together in a large mixing bowl.

Melt the butter in a skillet, add the onion and scallions and sauté, stirring constantly over medium heat for 5 minutes, until soft and golden.

Turn off the heat, then stir the onion and scallions into the crab meat. Add the habanero, chives, Worcestershire, pineapple juice, rum, nutmeg, salt, and freshly ground pepper. Stir in 1¾ cups bread crumbs, then mix the ingredients thoroughly.

Spoon the filling into the reserved shells and place the shells on a baking sheet. Cook in the center of the oven for 15 minutes.

Remove the crabs from the oven and sprinkle with the remaining bread crumbs. Return to the oven for a further 15 to 20 minutes, until the crumbs are a golden brown. Serve hot.

Serves: 2 to 4

Heat Scale: Medium

Trinidadian Seafood, Anyone?

"King fish usually dominates the day's ocean catch. A meaty fish similar to swordfish, it's often fried, curried a lot, and a favorite in fish broths. Red snapper, shark, grouper, bonito, yellow tuna, and salmon also fill the fishermen's nets. There are also good shrimp, chip-chip (a tiny, clam-like crustacean), lobster, and oysters."

Knolly Moses

Caribbean Crab Gumbo

Okra, of course, is a key ingredient of this rich gumbo, which is both tasty and nutritional. Variations of this recipe can be found all over the West Indies. The African slaves introduced okra to the islands, as well as callaloo and taro.

2	tablespoons butter	½	pound okra, trimmed and sliced
1	tablespoon vegetable oil		
1	onion, chopped	2	habanero chiles, left whole
1	pound tomatoes, peeled, drained, and chopped	2½	cups boiling water
		2	cups cooked crab meat
1	tablespoon fresh basil, chopped		Salt and freshly ground pepper
2	tablespoons fresh parsley, chopped		

Heat the butter and oil in a large saucepan over medium heat. Add the onion and fry for 5 minutes. Stir in the tomatoes, basil, and parsley, and cook for another 5 minutes.

Add the okra and habanero, and pour in the boiling water. Add the crab meat, season with salt and freshly ground pepper, then lower the heat and simmer for 45 minutes.

Discard the habaneros, spoon the gumbo into warmed soup bowls, and serve with fresh bread.

Serves: 4

Heat Scale: Medium

Resurrection Crab Supper

Surprise your family this year and substitute this traditional Easter feast from "down de islands" for the traditional ham or lamb. Team it with the Hearts of Palm Salad from Chapter 3 to make a memorable party.

1	cup cooked crab meat	2	sprigs thyme, finely chopped
	Juice of ½ lime	2	sprigs parsley, finely chopped
1	tablespoon pineapple juice	2	medium tomatoes, quartered
2	tablespoons butter	3	cups rice rinsed until water runs almost clear
1	small onion, minced		
2	green onions, finely chopped	4	cups water
2	habanero chiles, seeds and stems removed, minced	1	teaspoon nutmeg, grated
		2	bay leaves
6	cloves garlic, crushed		Salt and black pepper

Sprinkle the crab meat with the lime and pineapple juices.

Melt the butter in a saucepan over medium-high heat. Add the onion and green onions, habaneros, garlic, thyme, parsley, and crab meat, and sauté for 4 minutes.

Add the tomatoes, rice, water, nutmeg, bay leaves, and salt and pepper to taste. Bring to a boil, then lower the heat and cook, covered, until the rice is tender and has absorbed all of the liquid, about 25 minutes. Serve hot.

Serves: 6

Heat Scale: Hot

Black River Swimp

Michael Baim collected this recipe for *Chile Pepper* magazine while he was traveling in Jamaica. "Swimp are fresh water crayfish cooked," he wrote, "in a fiery concoction that would have blistered our lips if it weren't for the fact that they were in bite-sized portions." Baim recreated the recipe from swimp he bought from roadside vendors in plastic baggies. This is a peel-and-eat delight!

2   Scotch bonnet chiles (or habaneros), seeds and stems removed, coarsely chopped

2   cloves garlic, crushed

3   green onions, coarsely chopped

⅛   teaspoon ground thyme

10   black peppercorns

½   teaspoon salt

2   quarts water

2   pounds unshelled shrimp or fresh water crayfish

Combine all the ingredients, except the shrimp, in a large pot, bring to a boil, and boil for 5 minutes. Add the shrimp or crayfish and cook until they just turn pink, about 3 to 5 minutes. Rinse under cold water to stop the cooking and to chill them.

Serves: 4 to 6

Heat Scale: Hot

Escovitched Fish

This recipe is definitely in a pickle! This tasty preserving technique was brought to the Caribbean courtesy of the Spanish. While this method is popular on most of the islands, this dish is one of the highlights of visiting Old Harbour and Port Royal in Jamaica, where the "fish ladies" compete for business.

1 Scotch bonnet chile (or habanero), seeds and stem removed, minced

3 green bell peppers, seeded and sliced

2 medium onions, thinly sliced

3 carrots, peeled and thinly sliced
   Bay leaf

1 ½-inch slice fresh ginger root, finely chopped

6 peppercorns
   Salt

2 cups water

2 tablespoons olive oil

6 tablespoons vinegar

3 tablespoons olive oil for frying

2 pounds kingfish (or substitute snapper), skinned and filleted
   Stuffed olives for garnish

In a medium saucepan, combine the chile, bell peppers, onions, carrots, bay leaf, ginger, peppercorns, and salt with the water. Cover the pan and simmer for about 30 minutes.

Add the 2 tablespoons of olive oil and the vinegar and simmer for a minute or two longer. Turn off the heat and set aside.

Heat 3 tablespoons of olive oil in a large, heavy frying pan and sauté the fish fillets until they are lightly browned on both sides; be careful not to overcook. Drain the fish and arrange it in a warmed, shallow serving dish; pour the hot sauce over the dish, garnish with stuffed olives, and serve warm.

Serves: 4

Heat Scale: Hot

Spiny Lobster in Sizzling Sauce

One could definitely baste the night away with this incredible dish. This recipe does take a little extra effort, but it's worth it. We suggest using the spiny lobster found in Caribbean waters, which are also known as *langosta* in the Spanish Caribbean. They are available in U.S. fish markets.

2	uncooked 1½- to 2-pound lobsters, split in half lengthwise	2	tablespoons finely chopped habanero chile
2½	tablespoons vegetable oil mixed with 1 teaspoon liquid annatto	1	teaspoon salt
		1	teaspoon fresh basil
½	cup dry white wine		Lemon and lime slices for garnish
1¾	cups Puerto Rican Sofrito (see recipe, p. 29)		

Remove and discard the gelatinous sac in the head of the lobster and the long intestinal vein attached to it. Cut off the tail section of each lobster directly at the point where it joins the body. Twist off the claws and cut the flat underside of each large claw with a sturdy, sharp knife. Cut off and discard the small claws and the antennae.

Heat the oil–annatto mixture over high heat in a large, heavy frying pan until a light haze forms above it. Add the lobster bodies, tails, and large claws and, turning them constantly, fry them for 3 to 4 minutes, until the shells begin to turn pink. Transfer the lobsters to a large platter.

Pour off all but a thin layer of oil from the pan, add the wine, and bring to a boil over high heat. Stir in the sofrito, chiles, salt, and basil. Next, put the lobsters and any juices around them back into the wine mixture. Turn the pieces over in the sauce to coat them evenly, then reduce the heat to medium. Cover the pan tightly. Cook the lobsters for 8 to 10 minutes, basting the shellfish from time to time with the sauce.

To serve, place the lobsters on a large platter, garnished with lemon and lime slices. Offer the sauce on the side.

Serves: 2

Heat Scale: Medium

Jamaican Seafood, Anyone?

"A rich section of the Pringles' own private family cookery book is devoted to fish, with talk of snappers and mullet-of-the-mountain, kingfish, old wife, and calepeaver (sometimes called the salmon of Jamaica—a very rich, delicately flavored fish). There is June fish and lobster in a dozen ways. Turtle is preferred not only in soup but also in cutlets, balls, steak, and stew. Black crabs are baked in the back. Saltfish appears not only with ackees, but also with rice, in fritters, and curried."

Poppy Cannon

Chinese-Style Swordfish with Crispy Slaw and Soy Vinaigrette

This recipe celebrates the Asian influences that abound in Caribbean cooking. Chinese people were introduced to the islands through the practice of indentured servitude after slavery was abolished. Happily, the only practices that survived that era are the wonderful culinary contributions of both cultures.

Crispy Slaw

1   cup cabbage, finely shredded
½   cup snow peas, julienned
½   cup carrots, julienned

Swordfish

4   ½-inch-thick swordfish, tuna, or halibut steaks (6 ounces each)
2   teaspoons coarsely ground black pepper
1   habanero chile, seeds and stem removed, minced

3   tablespoons peanut oil
2   tablespoons fresh ginger, chopped
½   teaspoon habanero powder (optional)

Soy Vinaigrette

¼   cup low-sodium soy sauce
2   tablespoons vegetable oil
2   tablespoons rice vinegar
2   tablespoons sweet rice cooking wine
4   teaspoons fresh lime juice

2   wonton wrappers, cut into thin strips

4   teaspoons fresh lemon juice
3   teaspoons sugar
2   teaspoons grated fresh ginger
2   teaspoons sesame oil
2   cloves garlic, minced

Tomato wedges and bean sprouts to garnish

Combine the shredded cabbage, snow peas, and carrots in a small bowl, cover, and refrigerate.

Sprinkle both sides of the fish with the pepper and habanero, cover, and refrigerate 1 to 4 hours.

Combine all vinaigrette ingredients in a small bowl (see Note).

Heat the peanut oil in a heavy skillet over medium-high heat. Add the ginger and fry until it is a golden brown, about 30 seconds. Remove the ginger and reserve.

Add the fish and fry it until it is brown and cooked through, about 3 minutes per side. Transfer the fish to a plate. Add half of the vinaigrette to the vegetable slaw. Toss well. Divide the slaw among four plates. Sprinkle the ginger and the wonton strips over the slaw. Spoon the remaining vinaigrette over the fish. Garnish with the tomato wedges and sprouts.

Serves: 4

Heat Scale: Medium

Note: This recipe requires advance preparation. The vinaigrette can be prepared up to 2 days ahead.

Pucker Up and Snap

This tangy, marinated dish from Curaçao marries the land and the sea with its perfect use of citrus as well as the plentiful and mild red snapper. Snapper enjoys great culinary respect on this island, where it is made everywhere—from the fanciest resorts to the most humble homes.

2½	cups water	3	cloves garlic, finely chopped
¼	cup grapefruit juice	1	teaspoon habanero chile, minced
2½	teaspoons salt		
2	red snappers, about 1 pound each, cleaned, heads and tails left on	4	parsley sprigs
		½	teaspoon dried thyme
½	cup onions, finely chopped		Mangoes and papayas for garnish, sliced

Put 1½ cups of the water, all but 1 tablespoon of the grapefruit juice, and 1 teaspoon of the salt into a large, shallow glass baking dish, stirring until the salt dissolves completely.

Wash the fish under cold running water and place them in the juice mixture. The liquid should cover the fish completely; add more water if necessary. Let the fish marinate for about 1½ hours in the refrigerator. Then drain and discard the marinade.

Pour the remaining 1 cup of water into a heavy, medium-sized frying pan and add the onions, garlic, habanero, parsley, and thyme. Bring the mixture to a boil over high heat, then reduce the heat to low, cover tightly, and simmer for 5 minutes.

Add the fish to the pan and bring to a boil again. Reduce the heat to the lowest possible point, cover, and simmer for about 8 to 10 minutes, turning once or twice.

Using a slotted spoon, transfer the fish to a deep, heated dish. Add the remaining tablespoon of the grapefruit juice to the cooking liquid, and taste for seasoning. Pour the broth over the fish and serve at once. Garnish with sliced mangos and papayas.

Serves: 2

Heat Scale: Medium

Note: This recipe requires advance preparation.

Just Make Sure It's a Turtle, Not a Mako

"One of the Amerindians' most ingenious fishing techniques was used for the green turtle, of which they were very fond. They realized that a certain fish called the remora or sucker-fish fed by attaching itself to sharks or other large fish, such as the big blue parrotfish, by a sucker the size of a large plate on its forehead. The Arawak would catch the remora, feed and tame it, then accustom it to carrying a light cord tied to its tail and gill frame. When a turtle came near their canoe, they released the remora, which would swim to the turtle and suck on its carapace. Then they could haul it into the boat."

Cristine Mackie

"Poisson" Catch of the Day

We promise there is not any poison in this dish! *Poisson* is the French word for fish, and this fish dish from Martinique and Guadeloupe delivers quite a punch. Bring a fire extinguisher to this meal (or at least a dairy product or two) to put out the delicious flames.

Marinade

1	medium onion, sliced		Salt and freshly ground black pepper	
2	cloves garlic, crushed			
¼	teaspoon ground allspice	1½	to 2 pounds monk fish fillets (or other firm, white fish)	
2	habanero chiles, seeds and stems removed, crushed		Starfruit and parsley sprigs for garnish	
	Juice of 2 limes			
2	tablespoons water			

Basting Sauce

2	tablespoons white vinegar	1	teaspoon habanero chile, minced	
¼	cup water		Salt	
⅛	teaspoon ground allspice			
½	teaspoon thyme			

Combine the marinade ingredients in a bowl, add the fish and coat it with the marinade. Cover and refrigerate the fish for 1 to 2 hours.

Prepare the barbecue or preheat a broiler or grill. Remove the fish from the marinade, allow it to stand at room temperature for 10 minutes, and broil at moderate heat until golden brown and cooked on both sides, about 10 minutes.

While the fish grills, combine the basting sauce ingredients in a small, nonreactive saucepan and simmer over low heat for 1 minute. Pour the basting sauce over the fish just before serving.

Garnish the platter with starfruit and parsley sprigs.

Serves: 4

Heat Scale: Hot

Note: This recipe requires advance preparation.

The Remora Revisited

"The Indians of Jamaica, says an old Spanish historian, go fishing with the remora, or sucking-fish, which they employ as falconers do hawks. The owner of one on a calm morning carries it out to sea, secured to his canoe by a small but strong line many fathoms in length, and the moment this creature sees a fish in the water, though at a great distance, it darts like an arrow and soon fastens upon it. The Indian, meantime, loosens and lets go the line, which is provided with a floating buoy. When he considers the game to be nearly exhausted, he gradually draws the line in toward the shore, the remora still adhering with such tenacity to hold its prey that it is with great difficulty it is made to quit its hold."

F. A. Ober

Hot Prawns in Curry Cream Sauce

Prawns, also known as the Caribbean lobsterette, are been considered quite a delicacy. This recipe is a seafood lover's delight created on the island of Anguilla, where cooks have mixed a bit of habanero, fresh herbs, and tropical fruits to make a most succulent entree.

3	tablespoons olive oil	½	cup dry white wine
2	shallots, chopped	1	tablespoon fresh lemon juice
2	cloves garlic, chopped	2	pounds medium uncooked prawns, peeled and deveined (or substitute jumbo shrimp)
2	Scotch bonnet chiles (or habaneros), seeds and stems removed, minced	2	ripe mangoes, peeled, pitted, and chopped into fine pieces
½	teaspoon West Indian Massala (see recipe, p. 20)	½	cup half-and-half
	Pinch ground turmeric	4	cups cooked rice
	Pinch saffron threads		Minced fresh dill for garnish

Heat the oil in a large, heavy skillet over medium heat. Add the shallots, garlic, chiles, massala, turmeric, and saffron and sauté for 2 minutes. Add the wine, lemon juice, and the prawns. Simmer until the prawns are just cooked through, about 4 minutes. Using a slotted spoon, transfer the seafood to a large bowl and cover with foil to keep warm.

Boil the sauce in a skillet until it is reduced to ¼ cup, about 3 minutes. Add the half-and-half and simmer until the mixture has thickened to a sauce consistency, about 5 minutes, stirring occasionally. Do not allow the mixture to boil.

Scoop the cooked rice onto four warmed plates, divide the shellfish among the plates, and pour the sauce over the rice and prawns. Garnish with dill.

Serves: 4

Heat Scale: Hot

Flying Fish Facts

"In Barbados, this exquisite purple-backed denizen of the sea with silver sides and winglike pectoral fins is a versatile and delicious Bajan delicacy. Eaten at all meals, the succulent flying fish is a culinary star found everywhere from gourmet restaurants to roadside stands throughout the island. Though flying fish can be found in tropical waters throughout the world, they are particularly plentiful off Barbados, especially from December to June. In fact, flying fish account for up to 60 percent of the weight of all fish caught on the island. Experts attribute this abundance to high concentrations of the plankton varieties flying fish feed upon in Barbados's waters."

Kay Shaw Nelson

Drunken Seafood, Creole Style

Red Stripe beer is the magical ingredient in this ship-shape dish from Antigua. Make sure you buy extra beer for the cook; that way, you may get to have the big piece of lobster during dinner!

1 clove garlic, minced	2 1-pound lobster tails, shelled, lobster meat chopped
¼ cup onion, chopped	
¼ cup green bell pepper, diced	3 tablespoons tomato paste
1 habanero chile, seeds and stem removed, minced	½ cup celery, diced
	1 beef boullion cube
2 tablespoons butter	½ pound freshly cooked crab meat, or substitute canned crab meat, drained and picked over for pieces of shell
1 cup rice	
2 cups Red Stripe beer	
½ pound raw medium shrimp, shelled and deveined	

In a medium-size frying pan, sauté the garlic, onion, bell pepper, and habanero in the butter. Add the rice, beer, shrimp, lobster, and the rest of the ingredients, except the crab. Bring the mixture to a boil, stirring occasionally. Cover the pan and cook over medium heat until the rice is done, about 15 minutes.

When the rice is done, stir in the crab meat, heat for a minute or two, and serve on a heated platter.

Serves: 4

Heat Scale: Medium

Jolly Roger Flying Fish

Melissa experienced this dish while playing tourist in Barbados. She took a ride on the *Jolly Roger* pirate ship, walked the plank, and dined on fried flying fish all in the same afternoon. This is a famous dish in Barbados that is served with the Piri Piri Oil in Chapter 2, but be careful not to use too much—or you may end up drowning the heat in rum punch as Melissa did. Try saying "fried flying fish" three times in a row after you've had some of that punch. It can't be done.

6	small, boned flying fish	2	whole cloves
1	tablespoon lime juice	2	teaspoons white flour
1	garlic clove, crushed		Vegetable oil for frying
¼	teaspoon salt		Piri Piri Oil (see recipe, p. 31)
¾	teaspoon freshly ground black pepper		
1	teaspoon fresh thyme, chopped		

In a shallow glass baking dish, marinate the fish in the lime juice, garlic, salt, ¼ teaspoon of the black pepper, thyme, and cloves for at least 1 hour in the refrigerator.

Remove the fish from the marinade, and dry them well with paper towels.

In a separate bowl, mix the flour with the remaining ½ teaspoon of freshly ground black pepper and then dredge the fish in this mixture, shaking off any excess.

Heat enough oil to cover the fish in a large frying pan. Fry the fish until they are golden brown, then serve immediately.

This dish can be served with hot rice, piri piri oil, and lots of rum punch.

Serves: 6

Heat Scale: Varies

A Bahamian Conch-Cracking

"The highlight of the festival was the conch cracking competition. Cracking conch is done with a metal tool that's a cross between a hammer and a small ax. The local fishermen are highly proficient at penetrating the hard shell and extracting the meat, which takes plenty of strength, skill, and dexterity. To Bahamians, conch cracking is a macho pastime, similar to bullfighting in Spain, where the matador presents the bull's ears to an adoring fan. Here, the winners tossed conch meat into the crowd (usually in the direction of a special friend). Afterwards, rum still flowing, celebrants climbed onto the stage and danced and partied well into the afternoon."

                                        Carl and Ann Purcell

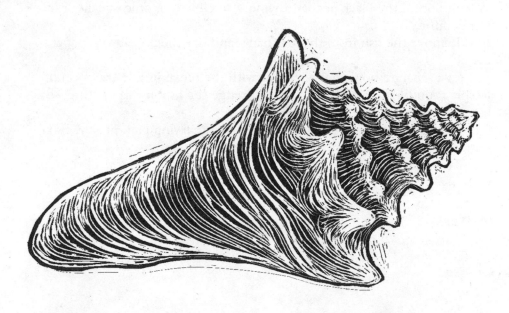

Reggae Rice: Accompaniments and Side Dishes

Welcome to the world of accompaniments and sides dishes—the likes of which you have probably never encountered before, unless you are an intrepid Caribbean visitor and have eaten your way through the islands! The first accompaniment is Split Pea Bara Bread (p. 229), which is commonly used to make doubles, a kind of Trinidadian East Indian sandwich with fillings. Some recipes for this bread contain garlic and some do not; it is almost impossible to find a consensus on what is the best recipe for this bread. That would be like trying to get Texans to agree on the best chili con carne recipe!

Sizzling Nevis Cornbread (p. 231) can be found all over the islands, from fancy restaurants and old plantation houses to ordinary homes. Since it is such a substantial side dish, we suggest serving it with one of the lighter soups from Chapter 4 or one of the grilled fish dishes from Chapter 7.

Norma Shirley's Callaloo—Scotch Bonnet Strudel (p. 232) is a blending of local ingredients (Scotch bonnet peppers and callaloo), combined with goat cheese and phyllo dough to give the dish a continental flair. It is a rich, delicious, and substantial strudel.

Rice, either on its own or mixed with spices or combined with other substantial ingredients (for example, beans or vegetables), is found throughout the Caribbean. Spiced Indian Fried Rice (p. 233) demonstrates the influence of East Indian cooking in the Caribbean and is especially popular in Trinidad. Reggae Rice (p. 234) is a rice dish with an attitude! The addition of the Scotch bonnet pepper makes this a very lively side dish that would be perfect to serve with grilled fish or seafood. Before the days of refrigeration, salting was one way to preserve meat, and to this day, even with refrigeration, many people still prefer the addition of salted meat. Island-Style Okra and Rice (p. 235) reflects this tradition in Barbados.

Sometimes the nomenclature of a recipe can be deceiving, such as Jamaican Rice and Red Peas (p. 236). The red peas are actually red kidney beans, and in Jamaica, the two terms are used interchangeably. This is, perhaps, one of the most common dishes in Jamaica, and it is frequently called Jamaican Coat of Arms. Another recipe with an interesting Spanish name is Black Beans and White Rice (p. 237); it's usually called "Moros y Cristianos," referring back to the conflict of the Spaniards and the Moors in Spain. This Cuban dish is still very popular today, and the name Moros y Cristianos has not changed.

Two other black bean recipes, Frijoles Negros (p. 238) and Spicy Caribbean Black Beans (p. 240), show the proliferation and popularity of black beans in the West Indies. Frijoles Negros contain the mildly hot ro-cotillo chile, and the beans can be served on their own or over rice. Spicy Caribbean Black Beans, with its infusion of vinegar, wine, and chile, can serve as a side dish, or it can also be prsented as a thick soup.

The exotic vegetables that abound in the West Indies also make delicious side dishes. Spicy Chayote Gratin (p. 241) demonstrates the versatility of this vegetable, which looks like a green pear-shaped squash. It can be stuffed, creamed, steamed, or added to soups and stews. Its uses are as numerous as its many names: chayote, cho-cho, christophene, and (on the French islands) mirliton. In Jamaica, it is still used medicinally in folk medicine to relieve and reduce hypertension.

Although breadfruit has no traditional use in folk medicine, it does have high nutritional value, and it certainly has a tradition in history, especially with Captains Cook and Bligh. Both captains brought the breadfruit trees from Tahiti to Jamaica and Saint Vincent, and since then breadfruit has spread all over the Caribbean. When you serve Breadfruit Creole (p. 242), redolent with garlic and habanero peppers, remind your diners that they are truly eating a part of history. Breadfruit Oiled-Down (p. 243) demonstrates another traditional method of preparation used throughout the islands, and the addition of salt pork once again harkens back to the West Indies' early culinary history.

Another tasty side dish is French Caribbean Ratatouille (p. 244), which has its roots in Provence, but this variation is definitely Caribbean. Sometimes the ingredients are sautéed separately and then combined (classic Julia Child), or they can be combined and simmered, as they are in this recipe. Unlike its French classic counterpart, the ingredients in this Caribbean ratatouille vary, according to the bounty of the many small garden plots that proliferate the islands.

Less exotic and more familiar vegetables are also cooked frequently. Even the lowly cabbage becomes a star in Caribbean Cabbage and Green Peas (p. 246), with the creative addition of hot peppers and fresh herbs. Cabbage grows easily and is eaten both raw and cooked. In Trinidad, we found that sweet and spicy coleslaws were extremely popular; just add a dash of sugar and some minced hot peppers.

Trinidadians also like to add curry to their vegetables, as demonstrated in the next two recipes. Fresh ginger gives Trinidadian Curried Cauliflower, Potatoes, and Peas (p. 247) some punch. The second example, Curried

Potatoes (Aloo Curry, p. 254), brings zest and flavor to an unusual side dish. Even common vegetables get a new twist in the hands of skillful Caribbean cooks!

Potatoes are also used in fritters, and fritters of all kinds are ubiquitous in the Caribbean. They are served as snacks, street food, and accompaniments. One variation on the codfish fritter theme is the recipe for Sizzling Shrimp and Potato Fritters (p. 248), which is an interesting accompaniment to any meal. The taste sensations come from the judicious use of herbs, hot peppers, and cheddar cheese.

Another New World crop, the sweet potato (a native of the tropical areas of the Americas), is featured in the recipe Jammin' Jamaican Sweet Potatoes (p. 250). Yams are also very popular in the West Indies and can be used in this recipe. Sweet potatoes are often found baking in the coals in the jerk shacks that proliferate throughout Jamaica. Since Jamaica provides most of the world's supply of allspice, it is not surprising to see it in many Jamaican recipes. It is a very pungent spice, and a little bit goes a long way.

Another staple in Caribbean cooking is the plantain, which is used both ripe and green. Ripe plantains (the ones with a lot of black on the peel; they are not rotten, merely ripe) taste sweet, and they can be fried, eaten as a vegetable, added to breads, and made into desserts. When it is green, plantain can be fried or used in stews. The African slaves used green plantains to make *foo foo*, pounded plantain balls that were used as a substitute for dumplings in soups or stews, much like a potato would be used. In West Indies Plantains with Cheese (p. 252), the plantains of the West Indies are united with continental overtones—a light cream sauce and a dusting of cheese.

The last recipe in this chapter features papaya, another "fruit" that is often used in its green state as a vegetable. Papaya contains a valuable enzyme, papain, that aids digestion and is also used to tenderize meat. This recipe from Curaçao, part of the Netherlands Antilles, for Papaya Berde (Stewed Green Papaya, p. 255) is most frequently served there as an accompaniment to Curaçao-Style Lamb or Kid Stew (p. 96). However, we found variations of cooked green papaya served throughout the Caribbean.

Sizzling Nevis Cornbread

On this fifty-eight square mile island in the Caribbean we found a traditional recipe for cornbread, also called batter bread. Since the island has been invaded by the Spanish, English, and French, and was home to imported slave labor, the recipe probably represents an amalgam of all of these influences. It is easy to prepare and delicious to eat!

¼   cup bacon, chopped

2   eggs, beaten

1   cup buttermilk

1   fresh Scotch bonnet chile
    (or habanero), seeds and stem
    removed, minced, or substitute
    ½ teaspoon dried, ground
    habanero powder

½   teaspoon salt

1   teaspoon sugar

1   cup cornmeal

½   cup boiling water

Fry the bacon in an 8- or 9-inch round, heavy, oven-proof skillet. When it is almost browned, reserve the bacon pieces and 1½ tablespoons of the fat and discard the remaining fat. Keep the skillet hot over medium heat.

Mix the eggs, buttermilk, hot pepper or habanero powder, salt, and sugar together. Stir in the cornmeal and the boiling water just to blend. Pour this mixture into the hot skillet and bake at 375 degrees for 15 to 20 minutes, or until it is slightly browned on top.

Cut the bread into squares and serve hot.

Serves: 4 to 5

Heat Scale: Medium

Split Pea Bara Bread

This is one version of the bread used to make Trinidadian "Doubles" (see recipe, p. 50). You can prevent the dough from sticking to your hands by keeping your hands lightly floured, or by dipping your hands in water as you make each piece of *bara*. Serve the bread along with one of the soups or stews from Chapter 4.

1   cup ground split pea flour (see Note)

½   cup flour

3   teaspoons baking powder

½   teaspoon salt

¼   teaspoon ground cumin

½   teaspoon turmeric

1   clove garlic, minced

1   Congo pepper (habanero) seeds and stem removed, minced (optional)

¼   cup lukewarm water

Canola or soy oil for frying

In a large bowl, mix the split pea flour, flour, baking powder, salt, cumin, and turmeric. Then add the garlic and the minced Congo pepper.

Add the water and mix thoroughly. The mixture should be of a soft dough consistency; if it is too thick, add more water by tablespoons. Be sure to mix thoroughly after each addition of water so that the dough does not get sticky. Cover and let the dough sit for 30 to 45 minutes, until it starts to puff up.

In a small skillet, pour in the oil to a depth of 1 inch and heat it.

Take a large tablespoon full of dough and flatten it with your hands until it is about ¼ inch thick, and about 3 to 4 inches in diameter. You can cheat a little and gently roll out each bara with a rolling pin if you wish.

When the baras are rolled, fry them, one at a time, in hot oil for about 30 seconds to 1 minute before turning. It's best to try one first for timing before frying the rest.

Drain the finished baras on paper towels and keep them warm until serving.

Serves: 6 to 8, depending on the size

Heat Scale: Medium

Note: If split pea flour is not available at your local health food store or natural foods supermarket, buy dried split peas and soak them overnight in water. Drain off the liquid and grind the peas in a blender, adding back some water if necessary. Then add the remaining ingredients and proceed. The peas can also be boiled in water until barely soft and then ground in the blender.

Rastafarian Vegetarianism

"Rastas believe that everything a man or woman does becomes a part of what he or she is. When Jah created the first people, he specified that all herbs bearing seed and trees bearing fruit would be as meat to them. The orthodox Rasta follows this dictate and refuses to soil and desecrate his or her system by consuming dead flesh; only life can give life. 'He shall not make his stomach a cemetery,' says the Rasta."

Tracy Nicholas

Callaloo–Scotch Bonnet Strudel

This was the most unusual recipe we tasted during our latest sojourn in Jamaica. It is not surprising that it is chef Norma Shirley's creation; after all, she received her culinary training in New York state. Norma notes that this side dish can be served with bechamel sauce.

3	ounces butter or vegetable oil		Salt and black pepper to taste
1	medium onion, diced	4	ounces cream cheese
¼	to ½ teaspoon finely chopped Scotch bonnet chile (or habanero)	2	ounces Montrachet (or goat) cheese, softened
8	to 10 cups callaloo or spinach leaves (washed)	1	tablespoon fresh chives, chopped
		6	to 8 sheets phyllo dough

In a skillet, melt 2 ounces of the butter, add the onion, and sauté until transparent. Add the Scotch bonnet (if using) and callaloo or spinach, and sauté until it wilts (do not overcook). Add salt and pepper to taste. Set aside to cool.

Mix the cream cheese, Montrachet cheese, and chives together; set aside. Melt the remaining butter.

Preheat the oven to 350 degrees. Place one sheet of phyllo dough on a cool pastry board. Brush lightly with the melted butter or vegetable oil. Repeat the process until all phyllo leaves are used. Place the callaloo mixture in the middle of the phyllo dough and top with cheese mixture. Fold the edges of dough to form a log. Brush with the melted butter. Place on a baking sheet and bake for 15 to 20 minutes until golden brown.

Serves: 6

Heat Scale: Medium

Spiced Indian Fried Rice

This side dish from Trinidad resembles a pilaf, and, in fact, it can be baked rather than cooked on top of the stove. The key to the taste is the mixture of spices, which reflects the East Indian influence in West Indies cooking.

¼	vegetable oil or *ghee* (clarified butter)	½	teaspoon ground cloves
1	large onion, minced	½	teaspoon ground cardamom
2	cups long-grain white rice	½	teaspoon ground cinnamon
½	teaspoon cayenne powder	½	teaspoon ground cumin
		4	cups water

Heat the oil in a pan, add the onion, and sauté until soft. Add the rice and sauté until it is golden brown. Stir in the spices, add the water, and stir again.

Cover the pan and cook over low heat for about 20 minutes. Remove from heat, stir the rice, and let sit for 5 or 10 minutes before serving.

Variations: Transfer the rice mixture to a ceramic baking dish and bake, covered, in a 350-degree oven for about 40 minutes. Remove the top during the last 10 minutes for a crispier rice. Chicken or beef stock may be substituted for the water to match the rice to a main dish. Substitute Trinidadian Curry Paste (see recipe, p. 22) for the spices, add a tablespoon of minced Congo pepper (habanero), and you have Hot Curried Fried Rice.

Serves: 6 to 8

Heat Scale: Medium

Reggae Rice

Similar rice recipes are found all over the Caribbean, just like reggae music, even though Jamaica claims the music! We hope the rice makes your taste buds dance with delight. Serve this spicy side dish with jerk-style meat or grilled fish.

2	tablespoons vegetable oil	2	cups rice
½	cup onion, chopped	4	cups boiling water
2	cloves garlic, minced	1	teaspoon salt
½	cup carrot, grated	¼	teaspoon freshly ground white pepper
¼	cup bell pepper, chopped		
1	Scotch bonnet chile (or habanero), seeds and stem removed, minced		

Heat the oil in a large, heavy skillet and sauté the onion, garlic, carrot, bell pepper, and Scotch bonnet for 2 minutes.

Add the rice, stir it into the sautéed mixture, and toss and stir for 1 minute.

Put the sautéed mixture into a large saucepan, add the boiling water, salt, and pepper, and bring to a boil. Reduce the heat to a simmer, cover, and cook for 20 minutes, or until all of the water is absorbed.

Serves: 6

Heat Scale: Medium

Island-Style Okra and Rice

This traditional Barbadian dish, with its use of salt beef and salt fish (or salted codfish), harks back to the days when salting was used to preserve food, and salted meats and fish are still a part of the food tradition on many of the Caribbean islands. Just boil and rinse, boil and rinse, and you will be able to remove the excess salt. You can also substitute minced beef and fresh grouper or snapper, but the dish will not taste like the traditional Barbadian recipe.

4	ounces salt beef, cut into ½-inch pieces	6	cups boiling water
½	pound salted codfish, soaked overnight in refrigerator	6	okras, cut crosswise into 4 pieces
2	tablespoons vegetable oil	1	habanero chile, seeds and stem removed, minced
2	cups onion, chopped	2	cups rice
2	cloves garlic, chopped		

Bring two separate pots of water to a boil, and put the beef in one and the soaked codfish in the other. Reduce the heat to a simmer, and simmer for 15 minutes. Drain the pots and remove the bones from the cod. Reserve the beef and the fish.

Heat the oil in a large, heavy pot and sauté the onion and the garlic for 1 minute. Add the boiling water, okras, and reserved salt meat and cover and simmer for 15 minutes.

Add the chile, rice, and the reserved codfish; cover the pot and simmer for 20 minutes, until the rice is cooked.

Serves: 4 to 6

Heat Scale: Mild

Note: This recipe require advance preparation.

Jamaican Rice and Peas

This dish is sometimes referred to as the "Jamaican Coat of Arms" because it is a very common dish that is cooked everywhere by everyone. The "peas" are actually red kidney beans; the coconut milk is a very traditional ingredient, and the dish simply wouldn't be Jamaican without it! If you do not want to make your own coconut milk, it can be purchased in Latin or Asian markets, but be careful—do not buy the sweetened coconut cream used for piña coladas.

1	cup dried red kidney beans Water to cover
2	ounces salt pork, minced, or 2 slices bacon, chopped
2	cloves garlic, minced
2	scallions or 1 leek (white part), chopped
½	teaspoon dried thyme or 1 spring fresh thyme
¼	teaspoon freshly ground black pepper
1	Scotch bonnet chile (or habanero), seeds and stem removed, minced
2	cups Coconut Milk, commercial or home made (see recipe, p. 14)
2½	cups water
2½	cups raw white rice Salt to taste

Wash and clean the kidney beans, then put them in a heavy pot and cover with the water. Bring the beans to a boil, and then reduce the heat to a simmer and cover. Simmer the beans for about 2 hours, or until they are almost tender.

Stir in the remaining ingredients and bring the mixture to a light boil; reduce the heat to a simmer, cover, and cook for 20 to 25 minutes, until all of the liquids have been absorbed. If the mixture seems too dry, add a little water; if the mixture seems too wet, remove the cover to allow the liquids to evaporate slowly. Add salt to taste.

Serves: 6

Heat Scale: Medium

Moros y Cristianos (Black Beans and White Rice)

This recipe translates as "Moors and Christians," and refers to when the Spanish were trying to expel the Moors from Granada. This Cuban dish is still popular today, and the name has not changed. The dish is a tasty, healthy addition to grilled meats or fish.

1	cup black beans	1	large onion, chopped
3	cups water	2	cups partially cooked white rice
2	tablespoons olive oil	1	teaspoon salt
1	habanero chile, stem and seeds removed, minced		Freshly ground black pepper to taste
3	cloves garlic, minced		

Wash the beans and pick out any extraneous material. Pour the beans into a large bowl and cover with cold water; refrigerate overnight. Or, clean the beans and put them in a large, heavy casserole pot, covered with cold water. Bring the beans to a boil, cover, and boil for 2 minutes. Remove the pot from the heat and let it stand for 1 hour.

Drain the beans, rinse them, and place the rinsed beans in a large, heavy saucepan. Add the 3 cups water and bring the mixture to a boil; reduce the heat to a simmer, cover, and cook over low heat for 40 to 50 minutes. The beans should be tender but not mushy.

Heat the oil in a large, heavy skillet and sauté the chile, garlic, and onion until the onion is tender. Add this mixture to the beans, along with the rice, salt, and pepper; stir to mix all of the ingredients.

Increase the heat to medium, and cook until most of the water is absorbed, about 10 minutes; then reduce the heat to low and cook until the remainder of the liquid has been absorbed, stirring frequently to avoid burning.

Serves: 6

Heat Scale: Medium

Frijoles Negros (Black Beans, Cuban Style)

This recipe is from Rudolpho de Garay and Thomas Brown, writing in *Chile Pepper*. They noted: "Black beans are the classic Cuban dish and are eaten nearly every day. Most versions are not spicy with chiles, but some cooks like a little heat. This recipe calls for rocotillo chiles, but habanero and your favorite chiles can be substituted, as there are enough black bean recipes to fill a book. This version may also be puréed and served cold with pepper fritters as a garnish."

1	pound dry black beans	1	cup Cubanelle (or green bell) pepper, seeded and chopped
9	cups water	1	cup red bell pepper, seeded and chopped
2	bay leaves		
1	teaspoon ground cumin	10	rocotillo chiles, stems removed, seeded and chopped (or substitute 1 habanero chile and 5 Yellow Wax Hot chiles)
¼	teaspoon oregano		
¼	teaspoon thyme		
2	teaspoons salt		
½	teaspoon freshly ground black pepper	¼	cup dry sherry
1	teaspoon sugar	¼	cup olive oil
1	cup onion, chopped	¼	cup white vinegar
2	tablespoons garlic, chopped		Freshly chopped parsley

Inspect the beans, removing all stones and other foreign particles along with broken or discolored beans. Wash the beans thoroughly in cold water.

Bring 3 cups of water to a boil, add the beans, bring to a boil again, and boil uncovered for 3 minutes. Turn the heat off and let sit partially covered for 1 hour.

After the hour of standing, add 6 cups of water, bay leaves, cumin, oregano, thyme, salt and pepper, sugar, onion, garlic, and the chopped green and red peppers and chiles. Bring to a boil again, lower the heat, and simmer for approximately 2 hours. Add the rocotillos and simmer for another ½ hour or until done.

Add sherry, olive oil, and vinegar, and sprinkle parsley over each serving. Finely chopped raw onion may also be sprinkled over each serving. When serving with rice, use only white rice, never yellow.

Serves: 8

Heat Scale: Hot

I-tal Food

"But the food of the greatest worth to the cultists is vegetables of almost every kind. Like ganja, the earth brings forth all good things. Food is cooked with no salt, no processed shortening, and few condiments except in its I-tal form. If they need oil, they will make use of the dried coconut in which the richest oil is found. The word "I-tal" means the essence of things, things that are in their natural states. So, the Rastafarian food is now known as I-tal food. One of the staples of the Rastas is fish, but only of the small variety, not more than twelve inches long. All larger fish are predators and represent the establishment–Babylon–where men eat men."

Leonard Barrett

Spicy Caribbean Black Beans

This recipe is another variation of preparing black beans to be served with white rice; however, this is one of our personal favorites. It is not very spicy, but it is very traditional, and truly delicious. Feel free to add more peppers to suit your taste. Add the salt at the end of the cooking time; adding it sooner will make the beans tough.

1	pound black beans	1½	teaspoons oregano
	Water to cover	1	bay leaf
10	cups water	1	habanero chile, seeds and stem removed, minced
2	green bell peppers, diced		
3	tablespoons olive oil	1	tablespoon sugar
1	cup onion, diced	2	tablespoons vinegar
4	garlic cloves, minced	2	tablespoons white wine
½	teaspoon freshly ground black pepper	2	tablespoons olive oil
		1	teaspoon salt

Wash the beans and place them in a pot. Add cold water to cover, and bring the beans to a boil and boil them for 2 minutes, uncovered. Remove the pot from the heat, cover, and allow the beans to sit for 1 hour. Then drain the beans, rinse them, add the 10 cups of hot water, half of the diced green peppers, and bring the beans to a full boil. Turn the heat down to a simmer.

In a saucepan heat the olive oil and sauté the onion, garlic, and the remaining diced bell pepper. Add this sautéed mixture to the simmering beans, along with the black pepper, oregano, bay leaf, habanero pepper, and the sugar. Cover the pot and simmer for 45 minutes.

Stir the simmering beans and add the vinegar and the wine and simmer, covered, for an additional 45 minutes. At the end of the cooking time, stir in the olive oil and the salt.

Serves: 6 to 8

Heat Scale: Mild

Spicy Chayote Gratin

We frequently encountered this gratin dish, with its many variations, in Guadeloupe, and it shows the French influence on the island. Since the flavor of the chayote is delicate, we suggest serving this dish hot with some grilled fish.

4	medium chayotes, about 1 pound, hearts cut out Water	2	Scotch bonnet chiles (or habaneros), seeds and stems removed, minced
3	slices bacon, chopped	½	teaspoon salt
1	to 2 tablespoons of olive oil, if needed	½	cup coconut milk
1	cup onion, minced	2	teaspoons parsley, chopped
2	cloves garlic, minced	½	pound Gruyère cheese, grated
6	scallions, chopped	¼	cup bread crumbs

Place the cleaned chayotes in a large pot of salted, boiling water and boil them gently until they are easily pierced with a knife. Remove them from the water and allow them to cool before handling.

When the chayotes are cool enough to handle, carefully remove the pulp, mash it, set aside, and reserve the skins.

Sauté the bacon in a large skillet and add the onion, garlic, scallions, chiles, and salt for 1 minute. If there isn't enough bacon grease, add a little of the olive oil to the sauté mixture.

Mix the coconut milk and the reserved mashed chayote into the sauté mixture and simmer for 5 minutes. Remove the skillet from the heat and stir in the parsley and the cheese.

Carefully fill the reserved chayote skins with this mixture. Sprinkle with bread crumbs and top with butter. Place the stuffed skins in a shallow baking dish and bake at 350 degrees for 15 to 20 minutes, until the tops are browned.

Serves: 4

Heat Scale: Medium

Breadfruit Creole

Another variation for breadfruit is this traditional recipe from "de islands." It's called Breadfruit Creole because it includes tomatoes. This easily prepared, tasty recipe is a good accompaniment to any kind of grilled meat or fish. It will add a touch of the Caribbean to your next dinner party!

1 large or 2 medium fresh, ripe breadfruits; peeled, seeds removed, and cut into 1-inch cubes	1 habanero chile, seeds and stems removed, minced
Water to cover	2 medium tomatoes, peeled and chopped
3 tablespoons vegetable oil	1 teaspoon dried thyme
3 cloves garlic, minced	½ teaspoon salt
1 cup onion, chopped	¼ teaspoon freshly ground black pepper

Place the cubed breadfruit in a large saucepan, add enough water to cover, and bring to a boil. Reduce the heat to a low rolling boil, cover, and cook until the breadfruit is tender—about 30 to 40 minutes. Place the breadfruit in a sieve and allow it to drain for 5 minutes.

Heat the oil in a large, heavy skillet and sauté the garlic, onion, and the chile for 2 minutes.

Add the breadfruit and the remaining ingredients to the sautéed mixture, and stir to blend. Partially cover the skillet and simmer for 15 to 20 minutes until the breadfruit is tender.

Serves: 6

Heat Scale: Medium

Breadfruit Oiled-Down

This recipe hails from Barbados, although breadfruit is cooked this way on other islands as well. Fresh breadfruit can be found at Latin and West Indian markets; if not, buy the canned variety and rinse it before using. The Barbadian (as well as many other islands) method is to cook it in a manner called "oiled-down." This method means the breadfruit has been cooked with coconut milk until all the liquid has been absorbed, leaving a small amount of coconut oil in the pan.

½ pound salt pork or smoked ham, cubed

4 cups cold water

1 tablespoon vegetable oil

1 cup onion, chopped

1 leek or 5 scallions, chopped, white part only

1 Scotch bonnet chile (or habanero), seeds and stem removed, minced

2 sprigs fresh thyme or 1 teaspoon dried thyme

4 cups Coconut Milk (commercial or see recipe, p. 14)

3 pounds fresh breadfruit, peeled and cut into 3-inch cubes

Salt and pepper to taste

Put the salt pork (or smoked ham) and the water in a small saucepan and bring to a boil. Lower the heat to a simmer and cook the meat for 10 minutes. Drain the meat, rinse, and set aside.

Heat the oil in a large, heavy skillet and, over a simmer, sauté the onion, leek, chiles, and thyme for 4 minutes.

Pour the coconut milk into the sautéed mixture and bring the mixture to a boil, then lower the heat and add the reserved salt pork and the breadfruit. Simmer the mixture, covered, for 25 to 30 minutes, or until the breadfruit is tender and the milk has been absorbed. There should be only a small amount of coconut oil left in the pan. Salt and pepper to taste.

Serves: 6

Heat Scale: Medium

French Caribbean Ratatouille

If you eat ratatouille at a restaurant in the French Caribbean for several nights running, chances are it'll taste slightly different every night. It varies, depending on what vegetables are available. This particular recipe is delicious and easy to prepare (especially ahead of time), despite the long list of ingredients. Serve it hot or chilled with spicy grilled fish or meat, add a salad, and some crusty bread to sop up all those good juices.

¼   pound bacon, diced

2   to 3 tablespoons vegetable oil (optional)

3   onions, chopped

3   cloves garlic, minced

2   bell peppers, seeded and sliced

½   pound pumpkin, peeled and cut into 1-inch cubes

¼   pound green papaya, peeled and cut into 1-inch cubes

½   pound eggplant, peeled and cut into ½-inch slices

¼   cucumbers, peeled and sliced

2   Scotch bonnet peppers or habaneros, seeds and stems removed, minced

½   pound tomatoes, peeled, seeds removed, chopped

1   teaspoon dried thyme, or 2 sprigs fresh thyme, chopped

½   teaspoon dried rosemary, or 1 sprig fresh rosemary, chopped

2   teaspoons dried basil, or 3 sprigs fresh basil, chopped

2   teaspoons fresh parsley, chopped

   Salt and pepper to taste

Sauté the bacon in a large, heavy skillet; if there isn't enough fat to sauté the vegetables, add some vegetable oil. Or, you could drain off the fat and substitute vegetable oil.

Add the onions, garlic, and bell peppers to the hot oil, reduce the heat, and sauté the mixture for 2 minutes.

Add the remaining ingredients, except the parsley and salt and pepper, cover, and simmer the mixture slowly for 1½ to 2 hours until all the flavors have melded. Add the parsley and salt and pepper to taste.

The sauté can be served hot or chilled.

Serves: 6

Heat Scale: Medium

The Emancipation and Bankruptcy Fruit

"I wonder how many of my readers can recall the interesting circumstances attending the introduction of the bread-fruit into the West Indies more than a hundred years ago? It was brought from the South Sea Islands in a man-of-war, and its introduction was long considered as an unmixed blessing. But note the fact that a thing may be a blessing or a curse, according to the point of view. The bread-fruit flourished and became abundant, almost the entire subsistence of the negroes. When they were slaves, the planters rejoiced that they could supply their laborers with food so cheaply; but when the negroes became free, the bread-fruit still supplied them without cost, and they would not work in the cane-fields. Thus the food supply originally provided by the planters to reduce their expenses became the means of reducing their cane-fields to worthless waste, and brought many of them to poverty."

F. A. Ober, 1888

Caribbean Cabbage and Green Peas

The simple ingredients in this recipe reflect the small garden patches that are seen throughout the Caribbean. Most everyone has a vegetable garden; given the climate and good growing conditions, vegetables flourish without much care or tending. If callaloo is not available, substitute fresh spinach.

1	tablespoon olive oil	1	tablespoon habanero chile, minced
4	cups cabbage, coarsely chopped	1½	cups frozen petit peas, or blanched fresh petit peas
1	clove garlic, minced	2	teaspoons fresh basil, minced, or ½ teaspoon dried basil
1½	cups chopped callaloo, or fresh spinach		Salt and pepper to taste
1	medium tomato, peeled and diced; reserve the juice		

Heat the olive oil in a large nonstick skillet, add the cabbage and the garlic, and sauté over medium heat for 4 minutes, stirring constantly, until the cabbage starts to wilt.

Add the callaloo, tomato, the reserved tomato juice, hot chile, peas, and the basil and sauté for 2 minutes, stirring constantly. Cover the skillet and steam over medium-low heat for 2 minutes more until the peas are tender. Add salt and pepper to taste.

Serves: 4

Heat Scale: Medium

Trinidadian Curried Cauliflower, Potatoes, and Peas

This dish can be served hot for a side dish, or it can be chilled and served as a salad on fresh greens. The fresh ginger adds a nice tang to some otherwise ordinary vegetables. Do not use packaged yellow curry powder; the taste will overpower the vegetables and be too cloying.

1	tablespoon olive oil	1	teaspoon ground cumin
1	large onion, chopped	¼	teaspoon turmeric
4	garlic cloves, minced	¼	cup fresh cilantro, chopped
2	tablespoons fresh ginger root, chopped	1	tablespoon soy sauce
2	teaspoons Congo pepper (or habanero), minced	⅓	cup water
		4	cups potatoes, cut into 1-inch cubes
2	to 3 tablespoons water	2½	cups cauliflower florets, broken into bite-size pieces
⅔	cup tomato purée		
½	cup dates or raisins, chopped	2	cups green peas, fresh or frozen
1	teaspoon ground coriander		

Heat the olive oil in a large nonstick skillet over medium heat and add the onion, garlic, ginger, and Congo pepper. Sauté the mixture, stirring, until the onion begins to stick and turn a light brown. Stir in the water and continue stirring until the onion softens.

Stir in the next nine ingredients and cook, uncovered, for 15 minutes over low heat.

Add the cauliflower, toss the mixture in the pan, and cover and simmer for 15 to 20 minutes or until the potatoes are almost tender. Then add the peas and cook for an additional 5 minutes.

Serves: 5

Heat Scale: Mild

Sizzling Shrimp and Potato Fritters

Different versions of this basic recipe can be found all over the Caribbean; start with this basic one, and add your own taste preferences, as do many cooks in the islands. This side dish is a tasty addition to a grilled fish or chicken dinner. If you want to reduce the egg content, we suggest using Eggbeaters, or another fresh egg substitute. Even though the list may look long, these fritters are very easy to prepare and—except for the frying—they can be made a few hours ahead of time and refrigerated.

2 large potatoes, washed and quartered	½ habanero chile, seeds and stem removed, minced
Water to cover	1 teaspoon salt
½ teaspoon salt	½ teaspoon freshly grated black pepper
1 cup onion, minced	1 egg yolk
3 tablespoons fresh cilantro, minced	3 tablespoons olive oil
2 tablespoons fresh parsley, minced	¾ pound unshelled shrimp
¾ cup cheddar cheese, grated	¾ cup flour
4 tablespoons butter	2 eggs, beaten
	½ cup bread crumbs
	Vegetable oil for frying

Put the potatoes in a pot, cover with cold water, and add the ½ teaspoon salt. Bring the mixture to a boil, reduce the heat to a rolling simmer, and cook for about 15 to 20 minutes. Drain the potatoes, peel them, and mash them in a bowl.

Add the onion, cilantro, parsley, cheese, butter (cut into small pieces), habanero chile, salt, black pepper, and egg yolk to the mashed potatoes; mix thoroughly and set aside.

Heat the olive oil in a large sauté skillet, add the shrimp, and sauté the shrimp for 3 minutes over medium heat. Remove the skillet from the heat. Cool, peel, and devein the shrimp; cut the shrimp into ¼-inch pieces and mix them into the potato mixture.

Flour your hands (to keep the mixture from sticking to them) and scoop up about 2 tablespoons of the potato mixture and shape them into patties.

Dip the patties into the flour and pat off the excess; dip them into the beaten eggs, and then coat them with the bread crumbs. Place the patties on a cookie sheet and refrigerate them from 30 minutes to 3 hours.

To cook the patties, heat the vegetable oil for frying in a deep-fryer or a large, heavy pot. The oil is ready when a drop of water sizzles in the oil. Add the patties to the oil, but do not crowd them; do two or three batches, if necessary. Fry the patties until they are golden, about 4 minutes, and drain them on paper towels.

Serves: 4 (about 16 patties)

Heat Scale: Medium

The Downside of Bammy

"Bammies are a strange food indeed. They are thick pancakes made of pressed cassava. The grated cassava has the consistency of grated potatoes, but it tastes sweeter. The cassava pancakes are compressed in a mold so that they are thick and dense. Hot off the griddle, they are delicious. The outside is toasty, crisp, and the dense cassava is steaming and moist. But more often than not a bammy is served cold. And when it gets stale, a bammy can have all the culinary charm of a hockey puck. And the process of making bammies is downright frightening. The grated cassava must be pressed hard to remove as much liquid as possible. Why? Because the juice that is pressed out of the raw cassava is a deadly poison!"

Robb Walsh and Jay McCarthy

Jammin' Jamaican Sweet Potatoes

Since Jamaicans prefer sweet potatoes (in fact, they love sweet, sweet potatoes!), this recipe is one that incorporates the best of the country. Serve this with jerk pork or chicken and a zesty salad for a real taste combo that will leave your guests asking for "more, mon."

3	large sweet potatoes	⅔	cup fresh orange juice
1	tablespoon vegetable oil	2	tablespoons fresh lime juice
2	tablespoons melted butter	1	tablespoon dark rum
½	teaspoon habanero powder	½	teaspoon freshly ground Jamaican allspice (see Note)
¼	cup dark brown sugar		
3	tablespoons ginger, freshly grated		

Preheat the oven to 350 degrees for 20 minutes. Wrap the sweet potatoes in foil and bake them for 30 minutes. Remove the foil, wait until the potatoes are cool enough to be handled, and then slice them into ½-inch slices.

Use the vegetable oil to coat a 9- by 13-inch ovenproof baking pan (preferably glass). Layer the potato slices in the pan.

Mix the remaining ingredients in a small bowl and drizzle it over the potatoes.

Cover the potatoes with foil and bake them in a 350-degree oven for 15 to 20 minutes, until they are barely tender. Remove the foil and bake the potatoes for an additional 10 to 15 minutes, until the coating starts to crisp up.

Serves: 4

Heat Scale: Mild

Note: To substitute for Jamaican allspice, use equal parts of ground cinnamon and nutmeg, with half as much ground cloves: use ½ teaspoon ground cinnamon, ½ teaspoon ground nutmeg, and ⅛ teaspoon ground cloves. However, be forewarned, nothing is as good as Jamaican allspice!

West Indies Plantains with Cheese

Plantains can be broiled, boiled, mashed, and fried, and the incredible diversity of this fruit is limited only by your imagination. Joe Brown, a chef in Trinidad, even gave us a recipe for Island Lasagne—the pasta was sliced plantains! This recipe, with a continental flair, includes a light cream sauce laced with cheese to pour over the fried plantains. Another simpler island variation would be to grate some Parmesan cheese over the lightly frying plantains. Try this rich recipe with grilled meat or fish.

2	tablespoons vegetable oil	2	cups milk
3	tablespoon butter	⅛	teaspoon nutmeg, freshly grated
3	ripe plantains, peeled and sliced lengthwise into uniform slices	½	teaspoon salt
1	tablespoon fresh Scotch bonnet chiles, minced (or habaneros), or ½ teaspoon dried habanero powder	⅛	teaspoon ground white pepper
		¾	cup sharp cheddar cheese, grated
2	tablespoons flour	1	tablespoon Parmesan or Romano cheese, grated

Heat the oil and 1 tablespoon of the butter in a large heavy skillet, and, when it is hot, add the sliced plantains in several batches, and sauté them until they are golden brown, 1 to 1½ minutes. Do not crowd the plantains in the skillet.

Place the sautéed plantains on paper towels to drain.

Melt the remaining 2 tablespoons of butter in a small saucepan and add the chiles; sprinkle in the flour and stir the mixture for 30 seconds. Pour in the milk all at once, and stir constantly with a wire whisk until the mixture starts to thicken, about 1 or 2 minutes. The whisk will help to make a smooth, creamy sauce.

Whisk the nutmeg, salt, white pepper, and the cheeses into the sauce and simmer for 30 seconds, or until the cheeses blend into the mixture. Remove the mixture from the heat.

Place the sautéed plantains in an 8- by 8-inch shallow ovenproof dish and pour the sauce evenly over the top of the plantains.

Bake, uncovered, in a preheated 325-degree oven for 20 to 25 minutes and serve hot.

Serves: 4

Heat Scale: Medium

Falernum "Facts"

"If you're served a fruit salad in Barbados, you're likely to encounter falernum as well. It's made, apparently only on this island, from a secret recipe that blends rum, sugar syrup, and lime juice. Falernum, it is said, not only improves the flavor of cut-up fruit but prevents it from discoloring. As for the odd name: A very old story tells of a plantation owner who had his favorite slave toss together a libation for some friends. When one of the guests asked for the recipe, the slave replied, 'It's fuh me to know and you got fa lern um.'"

John DeMers

Aloo Curry (Curried Potatoes)

This curry is found all over Trinidad, with the usual variations from cook to cook. Some of the best we ever had was at an out-of-the-way East Indian restaurant that served this as one of their many *roti* fillings. The curry shows the great melding of East Indian flavors with the other flavors of Trinidad. Serve this potato curry as a side dish or use it as a filling for *roti*.

1 tablespoon West Indian Massala (see recipe, p. 20)	3 tablespoons celery leaves, chopped
3 tablespoons water	1 Congo pepper (or habanero), seeds and stem removed, minced
2 tablespoons olive oil	
¼ teaspoon cumin seed	4 potatoes, peeled and cut into 1-inch cubes
3 cloves garlic, minced	
½ cup onion, minced	2 cups hot water
2 scallions, chopped	

Mix the curry powder and the 3 tablespoons of water in a small bowl and set aside.

Heat the olive oil in a heavy, medium-size skillet. Add the cumin seed and stir-fry for 30 seconds. Then add the garlic, onion, scallions, celery leaves, and the Congo pepper and sauté for 1 minute.

Add the reserved curry paste to the skillet and sauté over low heat for 2 minutes. Add the potatoes and toss them with the sautéed mixture. Then add the hot water, stir gently, and cook over medium heat for 10 minutes, or until the potatoes are tender. Add salt to taste.

Serves: 4

Heat Scale: Medium

Stewed Green Papaya (Papaya Berde)

This is the traditional accompaniment to Curaçao-Style Lamb or Kid Stew (p. 96). Here, green papaya is treated as a vegetable. If you wish to serve this dish as a side dish for another recipe, we suggest you add some hot peppers and some island spices, such as allspice.

1 very green medium-size papaya, peeled and sliced Boiling salted water	1 tablespoon butter ¼ teaspoon nutmeg, freshly grated

Add the papaya slices to the boiling salted water and simmer for 30 minutes, or until the fruit is tender. Drain the mixture in a colander and place the papaya in a small, warmed bowl. Add the butter and nutmeg, toss, and serve hot.

Serves: 4

Heat Scale: Mild

Meet the Calabaza

"At a street market in Philipsburg, Saint Maarten, I spotted them. Unlike the humble and often neglected American pumpkins, these mega-gourds occupied center stage, dwarfing the mangoes, papayas, and bananas. Too large and heavy to be sold whole, the West Indian squash were cut into crescent-shaped wedges, exposing a vibrant orange flesh. A single specimen can weigh more than 100 pounds. By itself, the West Indian pumpkin tastes like a cross between a sweet potato and a butternut squash. It stands up well to many of the Caribbean's herbs and spices: nutmeg, cloves, and allspice coax out the squash's shy, mild flavor, while thyme and parsley lend an earthy nuance. And when island-grown hot peppers are added, the mild turns wild, as the pumpkin flavors are jolted out of bed."

Jay Solomon

Kill Devil: Cooling Drinks and Desserts

Our final chapter is our cool-down chapter, so we've eliminated the chiles and concentrated on finding the drinks and desserts that best complement the hot and spicy dishes in the rest of the book. Fortunately, the region is blessed with an abundance and variety of cool-downs to kill those devilish hot peppers.

The Caribbean depends almost entirely on three major types of drinks: beers, rum drinks, and fruit-based beverages. We've repeatedly sampled most of the popular Caribbean beers, and our favorites are Jamaica's Red Stripe and Dragon Stout, Trinidad's Carib, and Belize's Belikan. Of course, imports are popular too, including Heineken's "greenies," Beck's, and Guinness Stout. On his first trip to Jamaica in 1972, Dave was taught how to make the best beer blend in the region: Mix Red Stripe and Dragon Stout half and half to create an island "black and tan."

Rum is ubiquitous on the islands as well. Charles Schumann, author of the *Tropical Bar Book*, listed eighty-seven different brands of rum being manufactured in the Caribbean basin. Rum, of course, is made by distilling various fermented cane sugar products such as molasses and water or sugar and water. Dark rums are created by adding a small amount of caramel or by aging the product in special wooden casks. In the early days of the Caribbean, it was known as "kill devil" and "rumbullion." These days, most rum for export is manufactured in Barbados, Trinidad, Jamaica, Guyana, Cuba, and Puerto Rico. Rum forms the basis of most of the mixed drinks in the region—and appears in an amazing number of desserts.

Tropical fruit juices form the third drink group, and they appear individually and as mixed juices in addition to their combination with rum. The most popular fruits for juice include limes, oranges, mangoes, papayas, passion fruits, and guavas. It's rough work, but the only way you can find the perfect combination of tropical fruits is to experiment. And then there are so many rums to try as well.

We begin our survey of beverages with a holiday favorite, Flower of Jamaica Drink (p. 260). It is made from Jamaican sorrel, a member of the hibiscus family and native to tropical Asia. Jams, drinks, wine, and a jelly not unlike cranberry are made from its red, slightly acid flower. Martinique Christmas Shrub (p. 261) is another holiday drink and another unusual Caribbean food-and-drink term.

The word "punch" doesn't seem unusual, but when we examined dozens and dozens of recipes using that descriptor, the only common denominators seemed to be fruit. Classic Lime Rum Punch (p. 262), for example, depends only on limes for its fruitiness, while Festive Limbo Party Punch (p. 263) contains three fruit juices and no rum! Cuban Mojito (p. 264), not a punch, is a classic rum drink that has no fruit at all—substituting mint instead. The rum and fruit festival continues with ABC Mango Cocktail (p. 265) from the Netherlands Antilles, the festively named Goombay Smash (p. 266) from the Bahamas, and Calabash Pineapple Cocktail (p. 267) from Grenada.

We would be remiss without a mention of daiquiris, the classic rum drink that some sources say was invented in 1806 and others in 1896. The basis was a rum punch similar to Classic Lime Rum Punch, with but three ingredients: lime juice, rum, and sugar. As with the margarita (invented later), the daiquiri metamorphosed into many, many variations combining different fruits and liqueurs. Resort-Style Tropical Fruit Daiquiri (p. 268), featuring bananas but susceptible to substitutions, is our favorite daiquiri.

How easily bananas can be transformed from a drink to a dessert! Bahamian Banana Fritters (p. 269) illustrate how easily a fritter can be served last in the meal rather than first. Curry powder in a dessert? Why not just a little, as in Tobago Curried Dessert Bananas (p. 270), especially considering that the curry is sweet and served with ice cream? Rum-Drenched Bananas Martinique Style (p. 272) complete our banana-dominated desserts and show how insidiously rum can be included in these Caribbean treats.

Coconut is a favorite ingredient and flavoring, too. In Bajan Coconut Milk Sorbet (p. 273) it is utilized both toasted and in milk form. It forms the topping for a quick dessert, Soon Come Pineapple (p. 274), and is the basis for the small Barbadian cakes known as Coconut Totoes (p. 275). A favorite dessert in Jamaica is Pineapple Fool (p. 276).

Cakes are quite popular in the West Indies, and our survey continues with Antigua Orange Cake (p. 278), one of dozens of versions of that favorite. Nutmeg Cake with Mango Mace Sauce (p. 280) captures the flavor of Grenada's major spice exports, nutmeg and mace, while Key Lime Cake (p. 279) is a typically humorous Caribbean twist on the Florida Keys' famous Key lime pie. Pitch Lake Cake (p. 282) seeks to capture the color (well, kinda) of Trinidad's asphalt-filled Pitch Lake. Sir Henry's Lime Cheesecake with Papaya-Rum Sauce (p. 284) is perhaps our most elegant cake, while Bridgetown Conkies (p. 287) are a traditional steamed dessert from Barbados.

We conclude our Kill Devil desserts with another traditional favorite, Jamaica Christmas Pudding (p. 288), and with a popular island pie, Windward Banana-Lime Pie (p. 290).

Flower of Jamaica Drink

The Jamaican sorrel, which is a member of the hibiscus family, is known as *roselle* in the eastern Caribbean. In Mexico it is called *flor de jamaica*, and the dried sepals of the flowers are used to make drinks, jams, jellies, and even wine. This is a favorite drink at Christmas and New Year's in Jamaica. Dried sorrel is available in Latin markets.

8	cups fresh sorrel or 2 cups dried sorrel	3	quarts boiling water
¼	cup ginger, grated		Rum (optional)
			Sugar

Put the sorrel and ginger in a large glass jar and pour the boiling water over them. Cover and allow to sit overnight. Strain through a sieve. Add rum taste if desired and a little sugar to taste if the drink seems too bitter. Transfer to smaller bottles and refrigerate.

Variations: Add cinnamon sticks or allspice berries for more flavor.

Yield: About 2½ quarts

Note: This recipe requires advance preparation.

The Invention of the Daiquiri

"As with many famous drinks, there is a legend about the origin of the daiquiri. Tradition has it that it was invented near the end of the nineteenth century by two engineers, Pagliuchi and Cox, working at a copper mine in the Cuban province of Oriente. They wanted to serve something to their guests, but had nothing in their canteen but limes, rum, sugar, and ice. The resultant cocktail proved highly satisfactory, and Pagliuchi is supposed to have exclaimed: 'Let's call it a daiquiri!'— a logical suggestion, for that was the name of the closest village."

Charles Schumann

Martinique Christmas Shrub

This oddly named drink is traditional at Christmastime in the French West Indies. In the islands, it takes almost a month to make and is presented to guests on Christmas Eve, when it is served in cordial glasses as an after-dinner drink. Remove the zest from the citrus with a vegetable peeler.

	Zest of 2 lemons or Key limes	1	vanilla bean, split
	Zest of 2 oranges	3	cups sugar
	Zest of 2 tangerines	2½	cups water
2	cinnamon sticks	1	750-ml bottle white rum, plus 1 cup
10	cloves		
10	Jamaican pimento (allspice) berries		

Combine the citrus zests, cinnamon, cloves, pimento, vanilla bean, 2 cups sugar, and 2 cups water in a saucepan. Bring these ingredients to a boil, reduce the heat to the lowest possible setting, and let the ingredients simmer for an hour. Strain.

Combine the remaining 1 cup sugar and ½ cup water in a large saucepan. Bring the mixture to a boil and cook over high heat until the sugar caramelizes, becoming golden brown. Remove the pan from the heat and carefully add 1 cup rum, which will cause the mixture to sputter. Stir the mixture over low heat until the caramel has dissolved in the rum.

Combine the citrus syrup, caramel mixture, and remaining rum in a large bowl and mix well. Using a funnel, pour the mixture into clean wine bottles. The shrub is ready to drink but will be better if allowed to sit for a couple of days in the refrigerator.

Yield: About 1 quart

Classic Lime Rum Punch

There are hundreds of versions of rum punches throughout the Caribbean, and this is one of the simplest, using limes as the only fruit. Angostura bitters are now manufactured in Trinidad.

1	cup sugar	Angostura bitters
1	cup cold water	Granted nutmeg or allspice
½	cup fresh Key lime juice	for garnish
1½	cups white rum	Lime slices for garnish
1	cup crushed ice	

In a small saucepan, combine the sugar and water. Stir well and bring to a boil. Reduce the heat to low and, stirring constantly, continue to cook for about 5 minutes, or until all the sugar has dissolved. Remove the pan from the heat and set aside until the sugar syrup has cooled.

After the syrup is cold, combine it and the lime juice, rum, and ice in a pitcher. Stir well, pour into four tumblers, add a dash of bitters to each, and sprinkle the nutmeg or allspice over them. Add lime slices for garnish.

Variation: Use dark instead of light rum.

Serves: 4

Festive Limbo Party Punch

Here is a rarity: a Caribbean punch that doesn't have rum in it. But you won't miss it because of all the other alcohol. This is an extremely strong punch that we tried in Negril, Jamaica. Take care.

2	cups fresh lemon juice	1	8-ounce jar maraschino cherries, drained
2	cups passion fruit juice		
2	cups fresh orange juice	1	750-ml bottle brandy
1	cup white Curaçao	2	750-ml bottles champagne, chilled
3	cups sugar		
			Pineapple slices for garnish

In a large bowl, combine the juices, Curaçao, sugar, and cherries. Stir well, cover, and allow to stand overnight in the refrigerator. On party day, stir in the brandy and champagne, stir well, garnish with the pineapple slices, and serve.

Serves: About 15

Note: This recipe requires advance preparation.

And Spicy Food at Least Gets You Back up on Your Knees

"To indulge in such reverie is to succumb to one of the northerner's more seductive myths, the myth of a tropical paradise. Tropical drinks are but a delightful accompaniment to the age-old dream. A Jamaican saying puts things in somewhat clearer perspective: 'God caused men to raise themselves up onto their feet; rum sees to it that they fall over again.'"

Charles Schumann

Cuban Mojito

Mojito means "little sauce" in Cuba, where this drink is very popular. The Cubans use *herba buena*, or spearmint in it, but any variety of mint will work.

1	stalk mint, washed	4	ice cubes
	Juice of ½ lime	¼	cup white rum
1	tablespoon superfine sugar (castor)		Chilled club soda

Slightly crush the mint stalk between the fingers and put it in a tall glass. In a small bowl, combine the lime juice and sugar, stirring until the sugar is dissolved. Place the ice cubes in a glass, add the lime mixture, then the rum. Top off with club soda.

Serves: 1

Kill Devil Drinks

"The first documentary mention of West Indian rum dates from the mid-seventeenth century. In a description of Barbados from 1651 we read, 'The chief alcohol produced on this island is rumbullion alias kill devil.' It may be that the word 'rum' does indeed derive from rumbullion, meaning riot or uprising, but it is equally likely that it comes from the Malay *brum*, designating the liquor made from sugar (it was in East Asia that sugar cane was first cultivated). Or it may simply be an abbreviation of the Latin term for sugar *Saccharum officinarum.*"

Charles Schumann

ABC Mango Cocktail

In the Dutch Antilles, or "ABC" islands of Aruba, Bonaire, and Curaçao, this is a favorite before-dinner drink that features mango and blue Curaçao. Superfine, or *castor*, sugar dissolves more easily than table sugar.

½	cup mango flesh, cubed	1½	teaspoons superfine sugar
¾	cup water	3	tablespoons grenadine
¼	cup rum		Crushed ice
¼	cup blue Caraçao		Mango thinly sliced with
1	tablespoon lime juice		the skin on, for garnish

Blend the mango with ½ cup water until smooth, then stir in the remaining water. Strain the juice into a large glass. Add the rum, Curaçao, lime juice, and 1½ teaspoons sugar, cover, and shake vigorously until the sugar has dissolved. Garnish with the mango slices and serve.

Serves: 1

Rumbullion Slang

"Other slang phrases which grew up about the same time included 'Sippers'—just a small sip from a mate's rum issue; 'Gulpers'—one, but only one, big swallow from another's tot; 'Sandy bottoms'—to drain off what was left in the mug offered by a mate; 'See-it-offers!'—emptying the pot; 'The Framework of Hospitality'—where three Sippers equalled one Gulp, and three Gulps one tot. In Nelson's day 'Bob's-a-dying' meant a stupendous, drunken bash."

Hugh Barty-King and Anton Massel

Goombay Smash

Chel Beeson collected this recipe during a trip to the Bahamas. He reported that this drink caught him by surprise and that he learned one important lesson: "Do not drink and dive."

⅛	cup light rum	¼	cup pineapple juice
1	tablespoon coconut rum	2	tablespoons lemon juice

Pour all ingredients into a cocktail shaker and shake well with crushed ice.

Serves: 1

I'll Have a Jayne Mansfield— Make That a Double

"In the twenties, Cuba became the cocktail capital of the world, and certain of its bars are famous as the birthplace of a specific drink. The September Morn, for example, originated in the Hotel Inglaterra, the Mary Pickford at the bar in the Hotel Sevilla. Visitors from the United States were delighted to find drinks named after their stars; they could choose between a Gloria Swanson, a Greta Garbo, a Douglas Fairbanks, or a Caruso. Other names were simply English translations of Cuban place names, such as the Isle of Pines (from Isla de Pinos—also known as Isla de la Juventud), an island south of Havana where the juiciest grapefruit were grown."

                                                        Charles Schumann

Calabash Pineapple Cocktail

From the Calabash Hotel in Grenada comes an unusual cocktail combining the flavors of coconut, grenadine, a liqueur, rum, and pineapple. It's a perfect accompaniment to a Caribbean sunset.

⅛   cup Malibu or other   ⅛   cup Cointreau
     coconut-flavored rum   ½   cup dark rum
⅛   cup grenadine   1   cup pineapple juice

Combine the ingredients in a pitcher and stir well. Fill two tall glasses with ice cubes and fill with the cocktail. Garnish with the pineapple slices.

Serves: 2

Resort-Style Tropical Fruit Daiquiri

As served in resorts all over the Caribbean, here is our favorite daiquiri, with bananas. Other tropical fruit such as pineapple, mango, papaya, or orange can be substituted—or combined with—the banana. For a coconut daiquiri, substitute 3 tablespoons Coconut Cream (see recipe, p. 14) for the bananas.

½   cup white rum
1   tablespoon sugar
¼   cup fresh lime juice
2   bananas, peeled and sliced

Crushed ice
Banana slices and ground Jamaican pimento (allspice) (optional) for garnish

Combine the rum, sugar, lime juice, and bananas in a blender and purée until smooth. Add the crushed ice to two glasses and pour the banana mixture over it. Stir gently. Garnish with the banana slices and pimento, if desired.

Variations: By blending the ice with the banana mixture, the daiquiri is more "frozen." Add ⅛ cup Jamaican orange liqueur before blending.

Serves: 2

Bahamian Banana Fritters

Fritters can appear at nearly any course in a Caribbean feast, and dessert is no exception. This dessert is a snap to make and the fritters combine perfectly with Bajan Coconut Milk Sorbet (p. 273) for a double dessert.

3	ripe bananas, peeled and chopped	2	tablespoons sugar
½	cup rum	1	tablespoon butter
1	tablespoon sugar	½	cup milk
1	teaspoon lime juice	1	teaspoon baking powder
2	cups flour	1	egg

Toss the chopped bananas with the rum and sugar and allow to marinate for 1 hour.

Combine the remaining ingredients, except the oil, to make a batter. Heat the oil in a skillet. Using a perforated spoon, dip the banana chunks into the batter and drop in the hot oil. Fry the fritters, turning occasionally, until they are light brown. Remove, drain, and cool slightly before serving.

Serves: 4

Tobago Curried Dessert Bananas

West Indian Massala (p. 20) is so popular on Tobago (Trinidad's sister island) that a small amount of it shows up in desserts like this one. Serve the bananas with vanilla ice cream.

¼	cup water		⅛	teaspoon ground ginger
1½	tablespoons fresh lime juice		¼	cup sugar
1	tablespoon Neufchatel cheese (or substitute cream cheese)		2	tablespoons currants
2	teaspoons melted butter		4	small, ripe bananas, peeled and cut into quarters crosswise and lengthwise
¼	teaspoon West Indian Massala (p. 20)			Currants for garnish

Combine the water, lime juice, cheese, butter, massala, and ginger in a blender and blend at high speed for 20 seconds.

Transfer this mixture to a skillet and add the sugar and currants. Over medium heat cook until the sugar melts, stirring constantly. Add the bananas and cook for 30 seconds, stirring slowly.

Place four banana slices on four small plates and spoon the sauce over them. Sprinkle with currants.

Serves: 4

Sweet Divali

"Food plays a key role in the celebration Divali, the Hindu New Year which honors Lakshmi, the goddess of wealth. 'During all Divali celebrations, I prepare very elaborate dishes that are strictly vegetarian,' said Savitri Mohammed, whose Hindu grandparents were among the first Indians to arrive in Trinidad. Mohammed runs a lovely bed and breakfast inn in elegant St. Augustine, and she often invites her guests to share in her celebration of Divali. The highlight of her celebration of Divali is her feast of spicy *chana* (chickpeas) braised pumpkin, *kari* (dumplings in sauce), curried mango, the elaborate *dhalpourri*, a rice pudding called kheer, and a selection of sweets. 'Sweets are a must on Divali because they symbolize success,' explained Mohammed, who works for days to prepare a mesmerizing array of the traditional treats using milk and nuts. But unlike East Indian sweets, which are laced with exotic cardamom and rose water, West Indian sweets are typically flavored with cinnamon, nutmeg, and vanilla. She also prepares candy made with *bene* (sesame), coconut, and tamarind mixed with raw cane sugar."

Julie Sahni

Rum-Drenched Bananas Martinique Style

Have you noticed that it's impossible to get away from rum in the Caribbean? This dessert is daring because the alcohol is not burned off but is infused—warmly—onto the bananas.

1	cup sugar	½	teaspoon fresh lemon juice
½	cup water	¼	teaspoon ground cinnamon
2	3-inch strips lemon peel, ½ inch wide	4	firm, ripe bananas, peeled and sliced in half lengthwise
2	tablespoons orange liqueur	½	cup dark rum
½	teaspoon vanilla extract		French vanilla ice cream

Preheat the oven to 375 degrees.

Combine the sugar, water, and lemon peel in a saucepan and heat over low heat until the sugar dissolves. Turn up the heat and boil until the syrup turns an amber color, about 10 minutes. Scrape down the sides of the pan occasionally if sugar crystals form. Remove from the heat and remove the lemon peel. Stir in the liqueur, vanilla, lemon juice, and cinnamon.

Arrange the bananas in a single layer in a shallow baking dish. Pour the caramel mixture over the bananas and bake for 10 minutes.

In a small saucepan, heat the rum over very low heat until hot.

Transfer the bananas and caramel sauce to four serving plates. Place a scoop of ice cream between the two banana halves on each plate and drizzle the rum over all.

Serves: 4

Bajan Coconut Milk Sorbet

Here's a simple and refreshing ice dessert from Barbados that features coconut in two forms—toasted and milk. Remove the sorbet from the freezer at least 30 minutes before serving so it will be soft enough to scoop out of the freezing trays.

2	cups coconut meat, freshly grated	2	drops vanilla essence
3	tablespoons water	2	cups thick Coconut Milk (p. 14)
1	cup sugar		Fresh mint leaves for garnish

Preheat the oven to 350 degrees.

Sprinkle the coconut in a roasting pan and roast it for 15 minutes or until it has lightly browned. Remove and reserve.

Bring the water and sugar to a boil in a saucepan and heat it until the sugar has dissolved, then let it cool. Add the vanilla essence, coconut milk, and toasted coconut to the syrup, stir well, and pour the mixture into two metal ice cube trays from which the dividers have been removed.

Freeze the sorbet for 3 hours, stirring it occasionally to break up the ice crystals. Serve in small bowls garnished with mint leaves.

Serves: 4

Pineapple Fool

This is one of the most popular desserts in Jamaica, and it's easy to see why, considering the ease of preparation. You'll often find it made with mango or papaya as well. We assume that the Jamaican sense of humor created a recipe title that implies that we are fools for desserts such as this one.

2	cups pineapple, finely chopped	3	tablespoons powdered sugar
1¼	cups heavy cream		Chocolate, slivered for garnish (optional)
1½	teaspoons vanilla essence		

Drain the pineapple in a colander until it stops dripping.

Whip the cream together with the vanilla essence and 1 tablespoon of the powdered sugar until peaks form.

Chill the cream and fruit separately for 1 hour.

Just before serving, fold the cream into the fruit, sprinkle with the remaining powdered sugar, and serve in four dessert dishes at once. Garnish with a few chocolate slivers for contrast, if desired.

Serves: 4

In a Fog Over Grog

"From 21 August 1740 onwards, watered-down rum became known as 'grog' after the admiral who had instituted it.

> A mightly bowl on deck he drew
> And filled it to the brink;
> Such drank the Burford's gallant crew
> And such the Gods shall drink;
> The sacred robe which Vernon wore
> Was drenched within the same;
> And hence its virtues guard our shore
> And Grog derives its name.

(Verse written by one of the crew of HMS *Berwick*, another ship in Admiral Vernon's squadron.)"

Hugh Barty-King and Anton Massel

Soon Come Pineapple

Our friend Jim O'Malley collected this recipe for us in one of the Montego Bay Rios resorts, but he lost the name of it, and blames that on the rum in this dessert, which collided with the greenies (Heinekens) he had with the main course, leaving him obliterated. He did remember that the name results from the speediness of the preparation after the initial marination. Serve this coconutted pineapple with a Jamaican coffee liqueur such as Tia Maria.

4	pineapple slices, freshly peeled, ½ inch thick	2	tablespoons brown sugar
¼	cup dark rum	2½	tablespoons shredded coconut
1½	tablespoons unsalted butter, melted		

Marinate the pineapple slices in the rum for ½ hour.

Preheat the broiler.

Brush some of the butter over the bottom of an 8- by 8-inch–broiler-proof baking dish. Arrange the pineapple slices in the dish and sprinkle with the brown sugar. Drizzle the remaining butter over the slices and place the dish approximately 4 inches below the broiler and cook until the tops are golden brown and bubbling (approximately 2 minutes).

Sprinkle the coconut evenly over the pineapple slices and leave them under the broiler until the coconut is toasted, about 30 seconds.

Serves: 4

Coconut Totoes

We've taken coconut and added it to a traditional Jamaican cake, totoes, so named, we think, because the cakes are sliced roughly in the shape of big toes. Serve them at tea or after dinner with coffee.

¼	pound butter		Pinch of ground allspice
1	cup granulated sugar	2	cups grated dry coconut
2	cups flour	2	teaspoons vanilla
2	teaspoons baking powder	1	egg, beaten
1	teaspoon ground cinnamon		About ½ cup milk
¼	teaspoon ground nutmeg		

Preheat the oven to 400 degrees.

Cream the butter and sugar together in a bowl.

Sieve together the flour, baking powder, cinnamon, nutmeg, and all-spice. Add the coconut and mix well. Combine the dry ingredients with the butter-and-sugar mixture.

Add the vanilla, beaten egg, and just enough milk to make a stiff dough.

Grease a shallow glass baking dish with butter and spread the mixture in the pan. Bake for approximately 30 minutes. After it has cooled cut it into 12 squares, roughly in the shape of big toes.

Serves: 12

Antigua Orange Cake

Served at tea, during receptions, and after dinner with liqueurs and coffee, this cake has a persuasive citrus flavor. Substitute lime juice mixed with sugar for another citrus-based cake.

¾ cup unsalted butter	2 cups all-purpose flour
⅔ cup sugar	1 teaspoon baking powder
3 eggs, beaten	About ½ cup fresh orange juice
2 teaspoons finely grated orange peel	

Preheat the oven to 350 degrees.

Grease a 9- by 5-inch loaf pan with butter.

In a bowl, cream the butter and sugar until fluffy. Beat in the eggs one at a time until smooth. Mix in the orange peel. Sift in the flour and baking powder. Add the orange juice and beat until smooth. Spread the batter in the prepared pan. Bake until a toothpick inserted in the middle comes out clean, approximately 45 to 60 minutes. Turn out on a rack to cool. Top with a favorite frosting, if desired.

Serves: 6

Key Lime Cake

Here's a twist on Key lime pie, as baked in Trinidad and Tobago. As the mixture bakes, the cake forms a light sponge layer with a delicious, rich sauce below it. It can be served warm or chilled with ice cream or whipped cream on top.

3	tablespoons butter or margarine	2	teaspoons lime zest
1	cup sugar	¼	cup Key lime juice (or substitute regular lime juice)
¼	cup flour	1½	cups milk
3	eggs, separated	¼	teaspoon salt

Preheat the oven to 325 degrees.

Cream the butter, ½ cup of the sugar, and the flour together. Add the egg yolks (reserve the whites) and beat well. Stir in the lime zest, lime juice, and milk. Set this mixture aside.

Add the salt to the egg whites and beat until stiff. Gradually beat in the remaining ½ cup sugar. Fold this mixture into the first mixture.

Pour the batter into a 1½-quart buttered baking dish and set the dish in a large, shallow pan containing boiling water 1 inch deep. Bake in a 325-degree oven for 1 hour. Cool and serve.

Serves: 6

Nutmeg Cake with Mango Mace Sauce

Here's a tribute to Grenada, the isle of spice that grows most of the world's nutmeg—and mace, since the latter is the lacy red covering over the nutmeg seed. This is a very rich, fruity, and spicy cake.

Cake

2	cups flour	4	large eggs
1	tablespoon freshly ground nutmeg	1¼	cups sugar
1½	teaspoons freshly ground cinnamon	1	cup golden brown sugar
		¾	cup vegetable oil
1½	teaspoons baking powder	1	tablespoon fresh lemon juice
1	teaspoon baking soda	2	cups mango pulp, drained
¾	teaspoon salt	¾	cup cashews, toasted and coarsely chopped
¼	teaspoon ground cloves		

Sauce

1	cup mango nectar	¼	cup unsalted butter
1	cup whipping cream	½	teaspoon ground mace
1	cup packed golden brown sugar	¼	teaspoon cider vinegar

Vanilla ice cream (optional)

Preheat the oven at 350 degrees.

Butter and flour a 9- by 13-inch cake pan with 2-inch sides. Combine the flour, nutmeg, cinnamon, baking powder, baking soda, salt, and cloves in a medium bowl and mix well.

Using an electric mixer, beat the eggs, sugar, brown sugar, oil, and lemon juice in a large bowl until very thick, approximately 4 minutes. Stir in the flour mixture, mango pulp, and cashews, and transfer the batter to the prepared cake pan. Bake until a toothpick comes out clean from the center of the cake, about 65 minutes.

To make the sauce, combine the mango nectar, cream, golden brown sugar, butter, and mace in a saucepan and bring to a boil, stirring occasionally to dissolve the sugar. Boil until the sauce thickens and coats the spoon thickly, stirring occasionally, about 20 minutes. Add the vinegar. Rewarm before using.

Remove the cake from the oven, turn it out of the pan, and cut it into 12 pieces. Divide the warm sauce among the 12 pieces, spreading evenly.

Variation: Top each square with vanilla ice cream and pour the sauce over all.

Serves: 12

Pitch Lake Cake

This dark dessert gets its name from Trinidad's Pitch Lake, an unusual geological formation that is a lake composed entirely of natural asphalt. Interestingly enough, Trinidadians are not familiar with this recipe, since it's from Barbados. This version was supplied by our friend Ann-Marie Whitaker.

8	ounces baking chocolate	¼	cup milk
1	tablespoon instant coffee	1	sponge cake, cut into slices and then into 1½-inch squares
1	tablespoon water		
5	eggs, separated	2	cups whipped cream
	Pinch of salt		Tropical fruit slices, such as mango, banana, orange
⅔	cup coffee liqueur		

To make the filling, place the chocolate, instant coffee, and water in a double boiler and cook for about 5 minutes, or until the chocolate is melted. Remove from the heat and let the mixture cool slightly. In a mixing bowl, beat in the egg yolks one at a time. Add the salt to the egg whites and beat them until they form peaks. Fold the whites into the chocolate mixture and set aside.

Combine the liqueur and milk in a bowl. Line the base of an 8-inch springform cake pan with wax paper, then cover it with a layer of cake slices. Cut the pieces to fit in a patchwork pattern. Sprinkle one-third of the liqueur mixture over it, then cover with one-half of the chocolate mixture. Make two more layers this way, ending with a layer of cake and liqueur. Cover with plastic wrap and place in the refrigerator overnight.

Loosen the sides with a knife and unmold the cake. Place a serving platter on top of the cake and invert. Cover the top and sides of the cake with the whipped cream, garnish with tropical fruit slices, and serve.

Serves: 6

Note: This recipe requires advance preparation.

Rum and Coca-Cola

"Though World War II killed the British market, West Indian Rum received gratuitous promotion in the United States. As part of an exchange arrangement, the British Government obtained the use of twenty-two US warships, and the US Government the use of a string of bases in the West Indies to protect their eastern seaboard. The largest was in the British colony of Trinidad. In the Gulf of Paria, the land-locked strait between the island and Venezuela, the convoys were marshalled for the North Africa landings. Trinidad, and in particular Chaguaramas, played host to some 50,000 American wartime sailors, soldiers and airmen who manned the naval base, the convoy marshalling point, the jungle training centre and the inland airstrip. This introduced them to good quality Trinidad Rum made for local consumption—very different from the low grade spirit being exported to their families on the American continent. They promptly mixed it with the American soft drink 'Coca-Cola' which they could buy in their canteens. When they went back to Ohio and Minnesota on leave, and were finally demobbed in 1946, they sang the praises of Rum and Coke made with 'real' rum. Further promoted for free by the calypso 'Rum and Coca-Cola' plugged by the Andrew Sisters, whose million-selling Decca gramophone record was played relentlessly on the radio, it became the American national drink—and proved vastly popular too in Britain and all over the world."

Hugh Barty-King and Anton Massel

Sir Henry's Lime Cheesecake with Papaya-Rum Sauce

Named for Sir Henry Morgan, the buccaneer who eventually became lieutenant-governor of Jamaica, this cheesecake (served with yet more rum) comes, appropriately enough, from Morgan's Harbour Hotel in Port Royal, near Kingston.

Crust

1¼	cups graham cracker crumbs		6	tablespoons (¼ stick) butter, melted
2	tablespoons sugar			
½	teaspoon grated lime zest			

Filling

5	8-ounce packages cream cheese, at room temperature		2	large egg yolks
1½	cups sugar		3	tablespoons fresh lime juice
3	large eggs		1	tablespoon grated lime zest (about 2 limes)

Sauce

1	small ripe papaya, peeled, seeded, and chopped		3	tablespoons fresh lime juice
3	tablespoons honey		3	tablespoons dark rum

Mint sprigs for garnish

To make the crust, first preheat the oven to 375 degrees.

Combine the graham cracker crumbs, sugar, and zest in a bowl. Stir in the butter and mix well. Press the mixture onto the bottom of a 9-inch springform pan. Bake for 10 minutes. Remove and cool slightly. Reduce the oven temperature to 325 degrees.

To make the filling, beat the cream cheese until fluffy with an electric mixer. Add the sugar and beat until well combined. Add the whole eggs, yolks, lime juice, and lime zest and beat until smooth.

Pour the filling into the prepared crust. Bake until the center is just set, about 1 hour. Transfer the cheesecake to a rack and cool. Cover and refrigerate overnight.

To make the sauce, combine the papaya, honey, lime juice, and rum in a saucepan and bring to a boil. Reduce the heat and simmer until slightly thickened, about 15 minutes. Break the papaya down with a wooden spoon as it cooks to make a smoother sauce. Cover the papaya-rum sauce and refrigerate.

Release the pan sides from the cake. Cut the cake into wedges and transfer to plates. Spoon the sauce over the cake wedges and garnish with mint.

Serves: 8

Note: This recipe requires advance preparation.

And You Can Get Punch Drunk with This Poem

"Punch is generally said to be of Oriental origin. The word *punch* being derived from the Hindustani panch, meaning five, since this drink consists of five ingredients—spirits, lemon juice, spice, sugar, and water. The old rhyming recipe for rum punch still holds good.

> One of sour (lime)
> Two of sweet (sugar or syrup)
> Three of strong (rum)
> And four of weak (ice)"

John A. Lake

In Spanish, It's *Sangria.*

"Father J.-M. Labat during his sojourn in the French Antilles visited many of the British islands including Barbados in 1700. Under the date of 1694, he writes: 'The English have invented two or three sorts of drinks whose use and abuse are attributed to the French, who are ardent imitators of the worst habits of their neighbors. Sangaree is made of Madeira wine, which is placed in a bowl of glass or earthenware with sugar, lime (or lemon) juice, a little cinnamon and powdered clove, plenty of nutmeg, and a slice of toasted bread—even slightly burnt. When you think that the liquid has absorbed the flavor of all the ingredients, it is strained through a fine cloth. Nothing is more delicious, the taste of lime gives refreshing flavor its inventors claim for it, but it is easy to see from its components that it is very strong and goes easily to one's head.'"

John A. Lake

Bridgetown Conkies

The origin of the name *conkies* for these West Indian tamales is a matter of speculation. Because they can be shaped vaguely like small conch shells? Anyway, we encountered both entree versions (with bonney peppers) and desserts like this one. Corn husks or aluminum foil may be substituted for the banana leaves.

½ cup cornmeal

¾ cup fresh coconut, grated

¾ cup sugar

½ cup fresh pumpkin, grated

¼ cup raisins

½ teaspoon ground nutmeg

½ teaspoon ground cinnamon

¼ teaspoon vanilla essence

1 tablespoon butter

1 egg, beaten

About 1 cup milk

4 banana leaves, about 6 by 6 inches

Mix all the ingredients except the banana leaves in a large bowl, adding enough milk to make a firm batter. Let the mixture stand for 15 minutes. Form the mixture into patties of your favorite conch-like shape and wrap in banana leaves and steam for 45 minutes.

Variation: Turn the mixture into a greased baking dish and bake for about an hour and 15 minutes at 325 degrees.

Serves: 4

Jamaica Christmas Pudding

The preparation of this traditional holiday dessert begins with the ritual soaking of the fruits—a signal to the family that Christmas is on the way. It is interesting to note that nearly all of the ingredients are imported. One ingredient that is not imported is the native Jamaican rum. Serve the pudding with the Hard Sauce that follows.

Fruits

1 pound raisins	2 cups rum
½ pound currants	4 cups port wine
½ pound prunes, stones removed	
¼ pound mixed lime and orange peel	

Pudding

1⅔ cups brown sugar	6 eggs
2 tablespoons water	½ teaspoon nutmeg
1½ cups flour	½ teaspoon cinnamon
1 cup bread crumbs	1 tablespoon vanilla
1 teaspoon baking powder	Zest of 1 lime, grated
½ teaspoon salt	1 cup cashews or other nuts, chopped (optional)
1 cup butter	

Combine the raisins, currants, prunes, lime and orange peel, rum, and port wine in a large jar. Seal the jar and refrigerate the mixture for 2 weeks.

Strain the soaked fruits and reserve the liquid. Mince the fruit, place it in a pan, and add 2 cups of the soaking liquid. Simmer for 25 minutes, stirring constantly, then set aside to cool.

In a small saucepan, heat ⅓ cup of the brown sugar with the water until it turns a very dark brown color and set aside.

In a bowl, combine the flour, bread crumbs, baking powder, and salt, mix well, and set aside.

Cream the butter, gradually adding the rest of the brown sugar and the eggs, one at a time. Mix well after each addition. Add the cooled fruit, melted brown sugar, nutmeg, cinnamon, vanilla, lime zest, and chopped nuts, then stir in the flour mixture.

Ideally, you should use two 1-quart pudding basins or tins with tight-fitting covers and line them with wax paper, then pour the mixture into the tins to within approximately 1 inch of the top. Place some greased paper on top of each pudding to cover. However, you may substitute any containers with a lid—the shape won't be traditional, but the taste will.

Use a large pan such as a turkey roasting pan for steaming the puddings. Place an upturned pie tin in the pan, add the pudding containers, and enough water to reach halfway up the sides. Bring the water to a boil, then simmer, adding hot water as necessary to keep the water level at its original height, until the pudding shrinks from the sides of the basin or tin, about 3 hours.

The Jamaica Christmas Pudding can be served hot or cold with the hard sauce recipe that follows.

Serves: 12 to 16

Hard Sauce

½   cup butter
2   cups sifted confectioner's sugar
3   tablespoons brandy

Cream the butter until it is light and fluffy, then add the sifted sugar, mixing with a fork. Add the brandy and mix again. Cover and refrigerate before using.

Yield: About 1½ quarts

Windward Banana-Lime Pie

From the Netherlands Antilles comes a Dutch pie with a favorite island filling made with bananas and lime juice. Note that the pastry does not need rolling out—it is simply patted into place.

Pie Crust

4	cups flour, sifted	¾	cup sugar
1	teaspoon baking powder, sifted	1	egg
½	teaspoon salt	3	tablespoons cold water
¾	cup butter		

Banana and Lime Filling

5	or 6 large ripe bananas, peeled and sliced into rounds	1	teaspoon cinnamon
	Juice of 1 lime	1	egg, well beaten
¼	cup sugar		

Preheat the oven to 350 degrees.

Combine the flour, baking powder, and salt in a bowl and mix well. In another bowl, blend the butter and sugar together until creamy. Add the egg and water and mix well. Stir in the dry ingredients and knead the dough on a lightly floured surface. It should remain soft and spongy. If the dough seems heavy, sprinkle it lightly with water and knead it a second time. Pat the pastry into place in a pie pan, leaving a generous folding of dough over the rim. (This is later folded over the filling to make a wide bank of top crust around the edge of the pie.)

For pastry swirls to top the filling, roll strips of dough about 5 inches long. Coil them, then flatten each with the palm of the hand. Place the coils close together to form an open crust.

To make the filling, place the bananas in a large bowl and squeeze the lime juice over them. Dust the banana rounds with the sugar and cinnamon, tossing lightly so they are evenly coated. Fill the prepared pie shell and arrange the top crust and pastry swirls.

Cover the pie tightly with aluminum foil and place it in the oven. Remove the foil 15 minutes later, but continue baking for an additional ½ hour or until the crust is golden brown.

Serves: 12

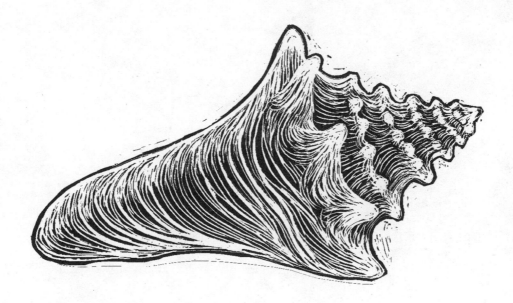

Mail-Order Sources and Retail Shops

Many of the ingredients mentioned in the recipes are carried by the companies listed below.

Mail-Order Catalogs

These are the main mail-order suppliers of chile-related products and Caribbean imports.

Blazing Chile Bros.
(800) 473-9040

Chile Pepper Magazine
P.O. Box 80780
Albuquerque, NM 87198
(800) 359-1483

Chile Today–Hot Tamale
919 Highway 33, Suite 47
Freehold, NJ 07728
(908) 308-1151

Colorado Spice Company
5030 Nome St., Unit A
Denver, CO 80239
(303) 373-0141

Coyote Cocina
1364 Rufina Circle #1
Santa Fe, NM 87501
(800) 866-HOWL

Dean and DeLuca
Mail Order Department
560 Broadway
New York, NY 10012
(212) 431-1691

Don Alfonso Foods
P.O. Box 201988
Austin, TX 78720
(800) 456-6100

Enchanted Seeds
P.O. Box 6087
Las Cruces, NM 88006
(505) 233-3033

Flamingo Flats
P.O. Box 441
St. Michael's, MD 21663
(800) 468-8841

Frieda's, Inc.
P.O. Box 584888
Los Angeles, CA 90058
(800) 421-9477

GMB Specialty Foods, Inc.
P.O. Box 962
San Juan Capistrano, CA
92693-0962
(714) 240-3053

Hot Sauce Club of America
P.O. Box 687
Indian Rocks Beach, FL
34635-0687
(800) Sauce-2-U

Hot Sauce Harry's
The Dallas Farmer's Market
3422 Flair Dr.
Dallas, TX 75229
(214) 902-8552

Le Saucier
Faneuil Hall Marketplace
Boston, MA 02109
(617) 227-9649

Lotta Hotta
7895 Mastin
Overland Park, KS 66204
(800) LOTT-HOT

Melissa's World Variety Produce
P.O. Box 21127
Los Angeles, CA 90021
(800) 468-7111

Mo Hotta, Mo Betta
P.O. Box 4136
San Luis Obispo, CA 93403
(800) 462-3220

Nancy's Specialty Market
P.O. Box 327
Wye Mills, MD 21679
(800) 462-6291

Old Southwest Trading Co.
P.O. Box 7545
Albuquerque, NM 87194
(505) 836-0168

Pendery's
304 East Belknap
Fort Worth, TX 76102
(800) 533-1879

Pepper Gal
P.O. Box 23006
Ft. Lauderdale, FL 33307
(305) 537-5540

Pepper Joe's, Inc.
7 Tyburn Ct.
Timonium, MD 21093
(410) 561-8158

Santa Fe School of Cooking
116 W. San Francisco Street
Santa Fe, NM 87501
(505) 983-4511

Shepherd Garden Seeds
6116 Highway 9
Felton, CA 95018
(408) 335-6910

South Side Pepper Co.
320 N. Walnut St.
Mechanicsburg, PA 17055

Retail Shops

Here are the retail shops or markets that specialize in hot and spicy products. Some of them have mail-order catalogs. It has been difficult to keep up with the explosion in hot shop retailers, so we apologize in advance if we have missed any. For shops listed with post office boxes, call first for directions to their location.

Calido Chile Traders
5360 Merriam Dr.
Merrian, KS 66203
(800) 568-8468

Caribbean Spice Company
2 S. Church St.
Fairhope, AL 36532
(800) 990-6088

Central Market
4001 N. Lamar
Austin, TX 78756
(512) 206-1000

Chile Hill Emporium
P.O. Box 9100
Bernalillo, NM 87004
(505) 867-3294

The Chile Shop
109 East Water Street
Santa Fe, NM 87501
(505) 983-6080

Chili Patch U.S.A.
204 San Felipe NW
Albuquerque, NM 87104
(505) 242-4454; (800) 458-0646

Chili Pepper Emporium
328 San Felipe NW
Albuquerque, NM 87104
(505) 242-7538

Chile Pepper Mania
P.O. Box 232
1709-F Airline Hwy.
Hollister, CA 95023
(408) 636-8259

Chutneys
143 Delaware St.
Lexington, OH 44904
(419) 884-2853

Colorado Spice Company
5030 Nome St. Unit A
Denver, CO 80239
(800) 67-SPICE

Coyote Cafe General Store
132 West Water Street
Santa Fe, NM 87501
(505) 982-2454; (800) 866-HOWL

Dat'l Do-It Hot Shop
P.O. Box 4019
St. Augustine, FL 32085
(904) 824-5303; (800) HOT-DATL

Dat'l Do-It Hot Shop
Dadeland Mall
7535 North Kendall Drive
Miami, FL 37211
(305) 253-0248

Down Island Ventures
P.O. Box 37
Cruz Bay, St. John, U.S. Virgin Islands
(809) 693-7000

Eagle Mountain Gifts
634 S. China Lake Boulevard
Ridgecrest, CA 93555
(619) 375-3071

Fiery Foods
909 20th Avenue South
Nashville, TN 37212
(615) 320-5475

Free Spirit
420 S. Mill Avenue
Tempe, AZ 85281
(602) 966-4339

Garden Gate Gift Shop
Tucson Botanical Gardens
2150 North Alvernon Way
Tucson, AZ 85712
(602) 326-9686

GMB Specialty Foods, Inc.
P.O. Box 962
San Juan Capistrano, CA
   92693-0962
(714) 240-3053

Gourmet Gallery
320 N. Hwy 89A
Singua Plaza
Sedona, AZ 86336

Hatch Chile Express
P.O. Box 350
Hatch NM 87937
(505) 267-3226

Hell's Kitchen
216 Lipincott Avenue
Riverside, NJ 08075
(609) 764-1487

Hell's Kitchen
Pennsasken Mart-Store #328
Rt. #130
Pennasken, NJ 08019
(609) 764-1330

Hot Hot Hot
56 South Delacey Ave.
Pasadena, CA 91105
(818) 564-1090

Hot Kicks
4349 Raymir Place
Wauwatosa, WI 53222
(414) 536-7808

Hot Licks
P.O. Box 7854
Hollywood, FL 33081
(305) 987-7105

Hot Lovers Fiery Foods
1282 Wolseley Avenue
Winnipeg, Manitoba R3G IH4
(204) 772-6418

Hot Papa's Fiery Flavors
11121 Weeden Road
Randolph, NY 14772
(716) 358-4302

The Hot Spot
5777 South Lakeshore Dr.
Shreveport, LA 71119
(318) 635-3581

The Hot Spot
1 Riverfront Plaza #300
Lawrence, KS 66044
(913) 841-7200

Hot Stuff
227 Sullivan Street
New York, NY 10012
(212) 254-6120;
(800) 466-8206

Hot Stuff
288 Argonne Avenue
Long Beach, CA 90803
(310) 438-1118

Hots for You–Chile Pepper
   Emporium
8843 Shady Meadow Drive
Sandy, UT 84093
(801) 255-7800

Jones an Bones
621 Capitola Avenue
Capitola, CA 95010
(408) 462-0521

Le Saucier
Faneuil Hall Marketplace
Boston, MA 02109
(617) 227-9649

Lotta Hotta
3150 Mercier, Ste. 516
Kansas City, MO 64111
1-800-Lott-Hot

New Orleans School of Cooking
620 Decatur St.
New Orleans, LA 70130
(504) 482-3632

The Original Hot Sauce Company
Avenue of Shops
1421-C Larimer St.
Denver, CO 80202
(303) 615-5812

Pampered Pirate
4 Norre Gade
St. Thomas, U.S. Virgin Islands 00802
(809) 775-5450

Peppers
2009 Highway 1
Dewey Beach, DE 19971
(302) 227-1958; (800) 998-3473

Pepperhead Hot Shoppe
7036 Kristi Court
Garner, NC 27529
(919) 553-4576

Pepper Joe's, Inc.
7 Tyburn Court
Timonium, MD 21093
(410) 561-8158

Potpourri
303 Romero NW
Plaza Don Luis, Old Town
Albuquerque, NM 87104
(505) 243-4087

Pungent Pod
25 Haviland Road
Queensbury, NY 12804
(518) 793-3180

Rivera's Chile Shop
109$\frac{1}{2}$ Concho Street
San Antonio, TX 78207
(210) 226-9106

Salsas, Etc.!
3683 Tunis Avenue
San Jose, CA 95132
(408) 263-6392

Salsas, Etc.!
374 Eastridge Mall
San Jose, CA 95122
(408) 223-9020

Sambet's Cajun Store
8644 Spicewood Springs Road, Ste. F
Austin, TX 78759
(800) 472-6238

Santa Fe Emporium
104 W. San Francisco
Santa Fe, NM 87501
(505) 984-1966

Santa Fe School of Cooking
116 West San Francisco Street
Santa Fe, NM 87501
(505) 983-4511

Santa Fe Trading Company
7 Main St.
Tarrytown, NY 10591
(914) 332-1730

Señor Chile's at Rawhide
23020 North Scottsdale Road
Scottsdale, AZ 85255
(602) 563-5600

Sherwood's Lotsa Hotsa
P.O. Box 2106
Lakeside, CA 92040
(619) 443-7982

Some Like It Hot
3208 Scott St.
San Francisco, CA 94123
(415) 441-7HOT

Some Like It Hot
301 S. Light Street
Harbor Place
Baltimore, MD 21202
(410) 547-2HOT

The Stonewall Chili Pepper
    Company
P.O. Box 241
Stonewall, TX 78671
(210) 644-2667;
(800) 232-2995

Tabasco Country Store
Avery Island, LA 70513
(318) 365-8173

Tabasco Country Store
Riverwalk Marketplace
1 Poydras Street
New Orleans, LA 70130
(504) 523-1711

Uncle Bill's House of Hot Sauce
311 N. Higgins Avenue
Missoula, MT 59801
(406) 543-5627

The Whole Earth Grainery
111 Ivinson Avenue
Laramie, WY 82070
(307) 745-4268

Glossary of Caribbean Foods and Cooking Terms

Note: Many of the ingredients in the following list are available in Caribbean, Latin, and Asian markets.

Accra: A fritter usually made with salt-cod and highly seasoned.

Ackee *(Blighia sapida):* The national fruit of Jamaica; it is eaten as a vegetable. Unripe, it contains hypoglycin, a poison, so the fruit must be eaten ripe and the black seeds avoided. For that reason it cannot be imported into the United States. Saltfish and ackee are a traditional breakfast.

Agouti: An edible, rabbit-like rodent.

Aloo: Hindi for potato.

Allspice *(Pimenta dioica):* The words "pimenta" or "pimento" apply to this nutmeg-tasting island spice, not to the olive-stuffing Capsicum pepper, which is a "pimiento."

Amchar: Mango. Also a type of massala used to season cooked green mangoes.

Anchaar: A hot East Indian curried pickle, often made with sun-dried mangoes. Also spelled "amchar" and "anchar."

Annatto: Orange-colored seeds of a small shrub (Bixa orellana); they add a bright red color to foods. Known as achiote in Spanish-speaking countries.

Bacalao: Salt cod.

Bajan: From Barbados or of Barbados origin; Barbadian.

Bake: In the eastern Caribbean, a native bread prepared with dough that can be either fried or baked.

Balangen: Melongene, eggplant.

Bammy: In Jamaica, a pancake made from grated cassava; it is often served with fried fish.

Beigun: Eggplant.

Bellyfull: Any filling food. Also, a type of dessert.

Black pudding: A blood sausage.

Blaff: A fish dish from the French Caribbean; said to be the sound the fish makes while cooking.

Bodi: In Trinidad, string beans more than a foot long. They are called boonchi on other islands, such as Aruba.

Boucanee: Smoking with fire and wet leaves.

Breadfruit *(Artocarpus communis):* A round, green, fruit that is available fresh and canned in the United States. The weight of the fresh fruit varies from two to five pounds per fruit.

Buljol: In the eastern Caribbean, a dish made with salted fish and seasoned with lime, chiles, tomatoes, and onions.

Bullas: Jamaican hard cookies made with ginger and brown sugar.

Bun: A Jamaican dark fruitcake.

Bun-bun: The burned layer on the bottom of a pelau pan.

Bush: Anything green and leafy.

Bush meat: Game such as iguana, agouti, opossum, or armadillo.

Buss-up-shut: A flaky bread served with curries. The name derives from "burst-up-shirt," a reference to the torn, clothlike appearance of the bread.

Calabaza: The giant West Indian pumpkin *(Curcurbita moschata)* that is more like a squash.

Callaloo: This word has two different meanings. It is the green leaves of the aroid Colocasia esculenta, or taro, and the name of a soup or stew made with those leaves.

Cascadura: A primitive, oily, armored catfish that is a Trinidad delicacy.

Cashew *(Anacardium occidentale):* This tree produces a sour "fruit" (a modified stalk) as well as a nut. The nut is poisonous until roasted.

Cassareep: Boiled-down cassava juice used in pepperpot soups.

Cassava *(Manihot esculenta):* An edible root also called manioc, yuca, and tapioca that must be cooked before being eaten. It is available fresh, frozen, and canned in the United States. All the peel, both ends, and the stringy fiber in the center must be removed before eating.

Chadon Ben: See Shadow Bennie.

Channa: Chick peas or garbanzo beans. Also chana.

Chayote: Sechium edule, a type of squash.

Chip-Chip: An edible mollusk found at low tide on the beach in Trinidad. Also, a Trinidadian coconut candy. Also, a dance step.

Cho-Cho: See Chayote.

Christophene: An alternative name for chayote.

Chutney: East Indian hot and spicy sweet pickle that is popular in the Caribbean. The Hindi word is chatni, sometimes "chutni."

Cilantro: Coriander leaves.

Coco: See Eddoe.

Colombo: A type of hot curry introduced into the French Caribbean in the 1800s by migrant Indian workers mostly from Bengal.

Congo: Local name for the Trinidad pod type of Capsicum chinense, a hot pepper species called habanero in Mexico and Scotch bonnet in Jamaica.

Conkies: In Barbados, entrees or desserts made from cornmeal or cornflour and steamed in banana leaves.

Coo-Coo: Okra and cornmeal "bread."

Crapaud: Large frogs of Dominica and Montserrat.

Culantro: See Shadow Bennie.

Cush-Cush: Yam.

Dhal (or Dal): Split peas.

Dasheen: The leaves of the taro plant.

Doubles: Curried channa served between two pieces of fried bara bread and garnished with kucheela; popular in Trinidad.

Dunkanoo: A Jamaican dessert of grated corn, sugar, cinnamon, ginger, and coconut milk.

Eddoe (*Colocasia antiquorum*): Closely related to the taro plant, the eddoe is a small tuber with white or purplish flesh. Also called coco; substitute potatoes.

Figs: Small bananas.

Floats: A fried yeast bread.

Foo Foo: A plantain dumpling. Also, a dish soup containing pounded plantains, yams, and cassavas. Also spelled fufu.

Funity: A bundle of soup ingredients such as turnips, carrots, celery, and thyme.

Ganja: Marijuana, *Cannabis sativa*.

Granadilla: Passion fruit.

Ground provisions: Root crops such as taro, carrots, and potatoes.

Hops bread: A baked yeast bread.

I-tal: Rastafarian natural vegetarian meals.

Jelly nut: The soft, unformed flesh of an immature coconut; considered to be a delicacy.

Jeera: Cumin. Also spelled jira.

Jerk: A Jamaican spice and barbecue method.

Jonga: Freshwater crayfish in Jamaica.

Jug-Jug: A complicated West Indian pudding made with pigeon peas; a national dish of Barbados.

Kitchen pepper: A variety of *Capsicum annuum* that grows outside kitchen windows in Jamaica.

Kucheela: A hot and spicy East Indian mango relish. Also spelled "kuchela" and "kuchila."

Kurma: An East Indian candy made from deep-fried flour and then coated with sugar.

Lambie: Conch.

Lappe: Rabbit.

Lechón: Suckling pig.

Manicou: Opossum.

Mannish water: A Jamaican soup with goat meat, Scotch bonnets, and white rum.

Maroons: Descendants of escaped slaves who live in Jamaica's Cockpit Country.

Massalas: Spice blends used in curry dishes.

Matrimony: A Jamaican dessert with star apples and oranges.

Mauby *(Colubrina reclinata):* The bark of this Caribbean carob tree is used to make a drink by the same name. The dried bark is often sold in the United States in Latin markets.

Melongene: Eggplant.

Ochro: Okra.

Oil-Down: To cook absorbent fruits and vegetables in coconut milk until it is absorbed, leaving only a film of coconut oil in the pan. This is the term in the eastern Caribbean; in the western part of the region, it is called "run-down."

Ortanique: A cross between an orange and tangerine, grown in Jamaica.

Pachro: Sea urchin.

Passion fruit *(Passiflora edulis):* The very tasty fruit of a tropical vine.

Pawpaw: Papaya.

Pelau: A rice dish with meat, peas, and coconut milk, popular in the eastern Caribbean.

Pholouri: A fried split pea appetizer.

Pigeon peas *(Cajanus cajun):* A pea similar to black-eyed peas. Also called gandule or gungo.

Piri Piri: A spicy hot Portuguese pepper oil.

Plantain *(Musa paradisica):* These long, banana relatives are used both green and ripe. When green, they are fried, added to stews, and made into dumplings. When ripe, they are fried, eaten as a vegetable, added to breads, and made into desserts.

Poncha crema: A Trinidadian egg nog.

Pumpkin *(Cucurbita moschata):* Technically, this is a winter squash, rather than what is known as a pumpkin in the United States. The hard skin is normally orange. Substitute Hubbard, acorn, or butternut squash.

Quenk: Wild pig; peccary in Trinidad and Tobago.

Roocoo: Achiote; annatto seeds.

Roti: A curried filling wrapped in chapatti bread. Also, the various breads used to make roti.

Ruku: Annatto oil.

Run-Down: See Oil-Down.

Saffron (or Indian saffron): Turmeric.

Saheena: A fritter made with ground channa and dasheen leaves. Also spelled "sahina."

Salt cod: Salted fish that must be soaked in water and rinsed several times before using. Any cooked, flaky white fish is an acceptable substitute.

Sancoche: A filling stew in Trinidad and Tobago.

Seamoss: A gelatinous drink made from dried kelp.

Sewain: A vermicelli dessert popular at Muslim festivals. Also spelled "sawine."

Shaddock *(Citrus grandis):* A grapefruit-like fruit, also called pomelo.

Shadow Bennie: Nickname for chadon ben, an aromatic herb *(Eryngium foetidum)* used in sauces and stews, especially in Trinidad and Tobago. The Spanish name is culantro; the Hindi name is bandhania.

Shrub: In Martinique, a citrus Christmas drink.

Sofrito: A Puerto Rican sauce with salt pork, annatto, and peppers.

Solomon Gundy: In Jamaica, a pickled herring spread. It is the corruption of the Old French word for an elaborate salad, salmagundy.

Sorrel: The sepals of a species of hibiscus *(Hibiscus sabdariffa)*, used to make a drink. It is called roselle in the eastern Caribbean and flor de jamaica in Mexico.

Souse: A popular Sunday breakfast dish in Trinidad and Barbados that is made from pickled pork parts. Also, other foods treated with acidic liquids such as lime or vinegar.

Stamp and Go: Codfish cakes or fritters in Jamaica.

Stoba: Stew in the Netherlands Antilles.

Talkaree: In Trinidad, vegetables cooked down as an accompaniment to rice or roti. Also spelled "talkari."

Tamarind *(Tanarindus indicus):* A bean-bearing tree that was brought to the West Indies from India. The pods are used fresh and dried. The fresh pulp surrounding the seeds is extracted and sold as fruit nectar and pulp in Latin and Asian markets. The seeds, sur- rounded with dried pulp, can be scraped out of the dried pods and rehydrated.

Tannia *(Xanthosoma sagittifolium):* This root vegetable is called a number of names, including yellow malanga. It is commonly served in soups and stews.

Taro *(Colocasia esculenta):* An edible tuber rich in starch. A related variety is called Eddoe.

Tatoo: Armadillo.

Tawa: A large, flat griddle for cooking roti breads.

Taza sale: Salted kingfish.

Toolum: Also spelled "tulum." A sticky candy made from molasses and grated coconut.

Totoes: Jamaican cakes that are similar to cakes in the eastern Caribbean.

Tum-Tum: Mashed green plantain.

Ugli fruit: A cross between and orange and a grapefruit.

Yam *(Dioscorea batatas):* A favorite West Indian tuber. Sweet potatoes may be substituted.

Zaboca: Avocado.

Yuca: Cassava.

Bibliography

Alvarez, Josefina. *All About Cuban Cooking.* Los Angeles: AACC Publisher, 1991.

Baim, Michael. "Jammin' for the Best Jerk in Jamaica." *Chile Pepper,* Sept./Oct., 1994, 24.

Barnes, Peggy. "Caribbean Kitchens." *Chile Pepper,* Jan./Feb., 1993, 24.

Barrett, Leonard. *The Rastafarians.* Boston: Beacon Press, 1977.

Barrow, Errol W. and Kendal A. Lee. *Privilege: Cooking in the Caribbean.* London: Macmillan Caribbean, 1988.

Barty-King, Hugh and Anton Massel. *Rum Yesterday and Today.* London: Heinemann, 1983.

Bastyra, Judy. *Caribbean Cooking.* Kingston, Jamaica: Heinemann Publishers (Caribbean), 1989.

Beal, Doone. "Nevis." *Gourmet,* Oct., 1976, 50.

Beal, Doone. "Martinique." *Gourmet,* Sept., 1984, 48.

Beal, Doone. "Saint Martin." *Gourmet,* Mar., 1989, 60.

Beckett-Young, Kathleen. "Jamaican Jerk: Barbecue Comes Hot, Hotter, Hottest." *San Antonio Express-News,* Feb. 18, 1990, 2-L.

Beeson, Chel. "Goat Peppers and Grouper Fingers." *Chile Pepper,* April, 1991, 27.

Bell, Patricia. "A Taste of Puerto Rico." *Gourmet,* Nov., 1991.

Belleville, Bill. "Conch Cooking." *Caribbean Travel and Life,* July–Aug., 1989, 70.

Benghiat, Norma. *Traditional Jamaican Cookery.* London: Penguin, 1985.

Blue, Anthony Dias. "Legends of Rum." *Bon Appétit,* July, 1991, 30.

Bourne, M.J., G.W. Lennox, and S.A. Seddon. *Fruits and Vegetables of the Caribbean.* London: Macmillan Education, 1988.

Brown, Ellen. "A Delicious Time in the Bahamas." *Bon Appétit,* July, 1987, 93.

Cannon, Poppy. "The Cooking in Paradise." In *Ian Fleming Introduces Jamaica,* ed. by Morris Cargill. New York: Hawthorne Books, 1965.

Clark, E. Phyllis. *West Indian Cookery.* Walton-on-Thames, England: Nelson Caribbean, 1976.

Davila, Vivian. *Puerto Rican Cooking*. Secaucus, NJ: Castle Books, 1988.

DeBoissiere, Jean. *Cooking Creole* (1948). Port of Spain, Trinidad: Paria Publishing, 1992.

DeGaray, Rodolfo and Thomas Brown. "Cuban Foods That Bite Back." *Chile Pepper,* Jan.–Feb. 1992, 29.

DeMers, John. *Caribbean Desserts*. Freedom, CA: The Crossing Press, 1992.

DeWitt, Dave and Nancy Gerlach. *The Habanero Cookbook*. Berkeley, CA: Ten Speed Press, 1995.

DeWitt, Dave and Arthur Pais. *A World of Curries*. Boston: Little, Brown, 1994.

DeWitt, Dave and Mary Jane Wilan. *Callaloo, Calypso & Carnival: The Cuisines of Trinidad and Tobago*. Freedom, CA: The Crossing Press, 1993.

Facey, Valerie (ed.). *Busha Browne's Indispensable Compendium of Traditional Jamaican Cookery*. Kingston, Jamaica: The Mill Press, 1993.

Fenzi, Jewell. *This Is the Way We Cook: Recipes from Outstanding Cooks of the Netherland Antilles*. Curaçao: Thayer-Sargent Publications, 1971.

Ferguson, Basset. *Cooking Caribbean, A Way of Life: A Nevis Cookbook*. Harper's Ferry, WV: Green Heron Press, 1979.

Gerlach, Nancy. "Do the Jerk!" *Chile Pepper,* Jan.–Feb. 1993, 14.

Gerlach, Nancy. "The Blistering Bahamas." *Chile Pepper,* Mar.–April, 1995, 28.

Gilmore, John. "Guadeloupe—A Different Caribbean." *Caribbean Week*, June 10–24, 1994, 22.

Gonzales, Michael. "Jerk Pork Jamaica Style." *Caribbean Week*, June 13–26, 1992, 12.

Gosse, Henry. *A Naturalist's Sojourn in Jamaica*. London: Longman, Brown, Green & Longmans, 1851.

Hanle, Zack. "Tropical Feast for Friends." *Bon Appétit,* Jan., 1983, 78.

Harris, Jessica B. *Iron Pots and Wooden Spoons*. New York: Ballantine, 1989.

Harris, Jessica B. "Hot Times." *Eating Well,* Jan.–Feb., 1991, 56.

Harris, Jessica B. "Jamaica: A Cook's Tour." *Caribbean Travel and Life,* July–Aug., 1994, 99.

Hawkes, Alex. D. "Tropical American Soups." *Gourmet,* Feb., 1977, 35.

Hunt, Sylvia. *Sylvia Hunt's Cooking*. Port of Spain, Trinidad: Scrip-J Printers, 1985.

Hunt, Sylvia. *Sylvia Hunt's Sweets*. Port of Spain, Trinidad: Scrip-J Printers, 1985.

Hurston, Zora Neale. *Voodoo Gods—An Inquiry into Native Myths and Magic in Jamaica and Haiti*. London: J.M. Dent & Sons, 1939.

Indar, Polly B., et al. (Eds.). *Naparima Girls' High School Diamond Jubilee (1912–1987) Recipe Book*. San Fernando, Trinidad: Naparima Girls' High School, 1988.

Jordan, Shirley. "Savoring the Isle of Spice." *Chile Pepper,* Sept./Oct., 1994, 16.

Krochmal, Connie and Arnold. *The West Indies Cookbook*. Albuquerque: Border Books, 1992.

Kopytoff, Barbara Klamon. "Maroon Jerk Pork and Other Jamaican Cooking." In *The Anthropologist's Cookbook,* ed. by Jessica Kuper. New York: Universal Books, 1977, 141.

Lake, John A. *The Culinary Heritage of Barbados*. St. Michael, Barbados: Barbados Hilton, 1976.

Lalbachan, Pamela. *The Complete Caribbean Cookbook*. Boston: Charles E. Tuttle Co., 1994.

Lewis, Matthew. *Journal of a West Indian Proprietor, 1834*. London: Greenwood Press, 1929.

MacDonald, R. Bruce. "A Cuban Food Odyssey." *Chile Pepper,* Sept./Oct., 1994, 20.

Mackie, Cristine. *Life and Food in the Caribbean*. New York: New Amsterdam Books, 1992.

McCarthy, Jay B. "Jamaican-Style Barbecue." *Fine Cooking,* June/July, 1994, 42.

Miller, Elsa and Leonard Henry. *Creative Bahamian Cooking & Menus*. Kingston, Jamaica: Kingston Publishers Ltd., 1982.

Mills, Therese. "The Food." In: *David Frost Introduces Trinidad and Tobago,* ed. by Michael Anthony and Andrew Carr. London: André Deutsch, 1975.

Morgan, Jefferson. "A Virgin Islands 'Pub Crawl'." *Bon Appétit,* Aug., 1987, 67.

Morgan, Jinx and Jennifer. "Guadeloupe: Island with a French Accent." *Bon Appétit,* July, 1990, 30.

Morgan, Jinx and Jennifer. "A Taste of Paradise: Jamaica." *Bon Appétit,* Mar., 1991, 119.

Moses, Knolly. "Roti on the Run." In: *Insight Guide to Trinidad & Tobago,* ed. by Elizabeth Saft. Singapore: APA Productions, 1987.

Negré, Dr. Andre. *Caribbean Cooking*. Papeete, Tahiti: Les Editions du Pacifique, 1978.

Nicholas, Tracy. *Rastafari: A Way of Life*. Garden City, NY: Anchor Books, 1979.

Ober, F.A. *The Knockabout Club in the Antilles*. Boston: Estes & Lauriat, 1888.

Ortiz, Elisabeth Lambert. *The Complete Book of Caribbean Cooking*. New York: M. Evans, 1973.

Outerbridge, Alexis. *Outerbridge's Original Sherry Peppers Sauce Cookbook*. Bermuda: Outerbridge & Outerbridge, 1991.

Nelson, Kay Shaw. "Barbados's Flyingfish." *Caribbean Travel & Life,* July/Aug., 1992, 76.

Payne, Bob. "Martinique: Romance, Rum and Red Peppers in the French Caribbean." *Bon Appétit,* Feb., 1994.

Pitt, Yvonne and Vilma Bier. *Our Own Cookbook of Trinidad and Tobago and Brazil*. Port of Spain, Trinidad: The College Press, 1985.

Pringle, John Kenneth McKenzie. *A Collection of 19th Century Jamaican Cookery and Herbal Recipes* (1893). Kingston, Jamaica: The Mill Press, 1990.

Purcell, Carl and Ann. "Conched Out." *Caribbean Travel & Life,* Sept./Oct., 1992.

Raichlen, Steve. "Scotch Bonnet Chili Packs Fiery Wallop." *The Washington Times,* July 11, 1990, F2.

Raichlen, Steve. "The Ubiquitous Fritter." *Caribbean Travel and Life,* Mar./Apr., 1992, 102.

Raichlen, Steve. "Herbs and Spices: A Cornucopia of Caribbean Seasonings." *Caribbean Travel and Life,* Nov./Dec., 1993, 90.

Roberts, Jill. *A Hamper of Recipes from Jamaica*. Kingston, Jamaica: Heinemann Publishers (Caribbean), Ltd., 1987.

Sahni, Julie. "Curry Powder." *Caribbean Travel and Life,* Mar.–Apr., 1991, 72.

Schumann, Charles. *Tropical Bar Book*. New York: Stewart, Tabori & Chang, 1986.

Slater, Shirley. "Good Times in Barbados." *Bon Appétit,* Feb., 1987, 92.

Smith, Paul G. and Charles B. Heiser, Jr. "Taxonomy of *Capsicum sinense Jacq.* and the Geographic Distribution of the Cultivated Capsicum Species." *Bulletin of the Torrey Botanical Club,* Vol. 84, No. 6 (Dec., 1975), 413.

Sokolov, Raymond. "Back to the Roots." *Natural History,* Oct., 1988, 27.

Sokolov, Raymond. "In the Pan-Caribbean Kitchen." *Natural History,* Nov., 1988, 84.

Sokolov, Raymond. "A Portable Feast." *Natural History,* May, 1991, 84.

Sokolov, Raymond. *Why We Eat What We Eat*. New York: Touchstone, 1991.

Solomon, Jay. "Pepper Power." *Caribbean Travel and Life,* Mar.–Apr., 1993, 108.

Solomon, Jay. "Caribbean Pumpkin." *Caribbean Travel and Life,* Sept./Oct., 1993, 98.

Sombke, Laurence. "Caribbean Cooking Goes North." *Cook's Magazine,* Oct., 1987, 32.

Sookia, Devinia. *Caribbean Cooking*. Secaucus, NJ: Chartwell Books, 1994.

Spence, Wenton O. *Jamaican Cookery: Recipes from Old Jamaican Grandmothers*. Kingston, Jamaica: Heritage Publishers, 1981.

Subramanian, Aruna. *Aruna's Vegetarian Recipes*. Trinidad & Tobago: Indian Women's Group of Trinidad & Tobago, 1988.

Super, John C. *Food, Conquest, and Colonization in Sixteenth-Century Spanish America*. Albuquerque: University of New Mexico Press, 1988.

Trotta, Geri. "Grenada." *Gourmet*, Jan., 1990, 70.

Valldejuli, Carmen Aboy. *The Art of Caribbean Cookery*. Garden City, NY: Doubleday & Co., 1963.

Valldejuli, Carmen Aboy. *Puerto Rican Cookery*. Gretna, LA: Pelican Publishing Co., 1994.

Vink, Graham. "Caribbean Dreamin'." *Spokane Spokesman-Review*, July 13, 1994.

Walsh, Robb. "Do the Jamaica Jerk." *The Austin Chronicle*, April 15, 1994, 32.

Walsh, Robb and Jay McCarthy. *Traveling Jamaica with Knife, Fork & Spoon*. Freedom, CA: The Crossing Press, 1995.

Willinksy, Helen. *Jerk: Barbecue from Jamaica*. Freedom, CA: The Crossing Press, 1990.

Wolfe, Linda. *The Cooking of the Caribbean Islands*. London: Macmillan Publishers, 1985.

Wolff, Amy. *Mountain Made, Best Made Cookbook: A Complete Guide to Haitian Cooking*. Port-au-Prince, Haiti: Mountain Maid Self-Help Project, n.d.

Index